D0821170

Basic Elements of Music

Basic Elements of Music

A Primer for Musicians, Music Teachers, and Students

Michael J. Pagliaro

ROWMAN & LITTLEFIELD
Lanham • Boulder • New York • London

Published by Rowman & Littlefield
A wholly owned subsidiary of The Rowman & Littlefield Publishing Group, Inc.
4501 Forbes Boulevard, Suite 200, Lanham, Maryland 20706
www.rowman.com

Unit A, Whitacre Mews, 26-34 Stannary Street, London SE11 4AB

Copyright © 2016 by Michael J. Pagliaro

All rights reserved. No part of this book may be reproduced in any form or by any electronic or mechanical means, including information storage and retrieval systems, without written permission from the publisher, except by a reviewer who may quote passages in a review.

British Library Cataloguing in Publication Information Available

Library of Congress Cataloging-in-Publication Data

Names: Pagliaro, Michael J.
Title: Basic elements of music : a primer for musicians, music teachers, and
   students / Michael J. Pagliaro.
Description: Lanham, Maryland : Rowman & Littlefield, [2016] | Includes index.
Identifiers: LCCN 2015040380 (print) | LCCN 2015040962 (ebook) | ISBN
   9781442257788 (cloth : alk. paper) | ISBN 9781442257795 (pbk. : alk.
   paper) | ISBN 9781442257801 (electronic)
Subjects: LCSH: Musical instruments. | Music—History and criticism.
Classification: LCC ML460 .P3115 2016 (print) | LCC ML460 (ebook) | DDC
   780—dc23
LC record available at http://lccn.loc.gov/2015040380

∞™ The paper used in this publication meets the minimum requirements of American National Standard for Information Sciences—Permanence of Paper for Printed Library Materials, ANSI/NISO Z39.48-1992.

Printed in the United States of America

Contents

Acknowledgments

I would like to express my appreciation to the following for their contribution to this book:

Michael J. Pagliaro, III—my grandson, for his drawings, digital concepts, and artistic work.

Robert Raciti, Jr.—who demonstrated extraordinary ability in helping to digitize many of the figures used throughout the book. I must mention, he did so on a computer he built himself. What a generation!

Thank you both for being you.

Introduction

Music is organized sound. To appreciate how it is organized and what is involved in the organization process, one must have knowledge of the basic elements of music. The *Merriam-Webster Dictionary* offers the following definitions for music:

> Music 1 a: the science or art of ordering tones or sounds in succession, in combination, and in temporal relationships to produce a composition having unity and continuity. b: vocal, instrumental, or mechanical sounds having rhythm, melody, or harmony.

At first read that sounds comfortably feasible and seems to explain the term *music* in a very understandable style. If, however, one dissects that definition, one discovers a deeper, more complex concept of this marvelous subject.

Webster's definition uses these words and phrases: science, art, sounds in succession, in combination, in temporal relationships, unity, continuity, rhythm, melody, harmony, vocal, instrumental, and mechanical. In fact, music is comprised of all of those elements interwoven in a manner so complex as to be incomprehensible to the average person not reasonably informed in the subject. Like the human body, we all know how it looks and a bit about how it works but, under that surface, all we can easily understand is that there are numerous elements working in concert to permit the total being to function.

Basic Elements of Music is a starting point from which one can proceed to more advanced study in an area or areas of particular interest. The contents of this book can serve as an introduction to music for the novice or the college music major, or as a means of expanding an instrumentalist's knowledge in topics that have been missed because of the all-consuming challenge of instrumental music study.

The reader is introduced to information essential for a basic understanding of music in its broadest sense. The material is covered in survey form and includes the history of music and the composers who made that history; the history of the instruments and how they function; an introduction to the science of sound; sound production; the various types of ensembles; the fundamentals of music theory; form in music; music notation; and music nomenclature. The chapters are written on an introductory level but with erudition worthy of serious study. This work does not fall into the "Books for Dummies" category.

In most cases, an individual's first experience with music study is instruction on an instrument or voice. If taken seriously, the nature of such study can be very demanding and all-consuming. One will tend to focus on "practicing the clarinet" with little or no exposure to the other components of the subject. The many topics presented in this book will introduce the reader to the world of music outside his or her limited experience. This new exposure can then serve to redirect study in music or to augment one's present study.

This book can also function as a reference for general music teachers who seek topics for lesson planning. A chapter can be used as a core from which lessons can be planned and expanded. Instrumental music teachers can use the material as a source from which to gather information to expand the scope of their lessons. In doing so those teachers will provide supplementary material relevant to the study of the subject instrument, an expansion of instrumental music curricula seldom employed.

When reading through the chapters, keep in mind that this is only an introduction to each topic, and that an almost incomprehensible amount of additional information exists beyond this content. At some point in the reading, pick a topic word, google it, and be amazed at what will come up. There is more to music study than meets the ear.

Note: The text includes cross references to related chapters in the book and occasionally repeats information as needed to facilitate understanding without having to read the entire book in sequence.

1

An Overview of the History of Music

The amount of information available on the history of music is infinite. That being the case, a single chapter on the subject can serve only as an indicator of what
happened and who was involved in making it happen. Early music history is mostly
anecdotal, with a significant portion of that being conjecture and deduction. As time
passed, more accurately documented source material appeared, providing a clearer
understanding of the evolution of music in the various cultures and time periods.
As a result, the quantity of published material is so vast that to undertake an all-
inclusive presentation on this subject would be impractical, unwise, and probably
impossible. For that reason this chapter's coverage will begin with the Middle Ages
and proceed through the Renaissance, Baroque, Classical, Romantic, and Contemporary periods. At the end of each topic I have listed one website that offers a free
example of the music under discussion. Some of these sites will subject the viewer to
a commercial minute, but it is worth the inconvenience to get what follows.

I chose to limit the time frame and cover the material with a narrative approach
rather than burden the reader with details of the lives and times under discussion.
This is not a doctoral thesis; it is an introduction to things that happened in music
over a period of several hundred years. Relax and enjoy the story.

PRIMITIVE MUSIC

As stated in the introduction, the *Merriam-Webster Dictionary* defines music as "the
science or art of ordering tones or sounds in succession, in combination, and in temporal relationships to produce a composition having unity and continuity." Simply
stated, music is organized sound. With that in mind, one can go back 43,000 years
to where it is believed the first flute-like instruments appeared. It is logical to assume

that if an instrument was present, some sort of music was also present. However, going back to the very beginning may not be a good starting point. The Middle Ages, when music began to take a form more closely related to that which we know today, may be the better way to start.

Note: Throughout this chapter there will be one website listening reference at the end of each topic; however, numerous others do exist.

THE MIDDLE AGES

During the period in European history from approximately A.D. 400 to 1400, a style of music developed as part of the growth of the Christian church. Pope Gregory I is credited with introducing, by dictum, liturgical music now referred to as Gregorian chant, plainchant, or plainsong. A text, derived from the Bible or other liturgical sources, was set to a style of music called a chant. The words were set to a series of repeated notes which started and ended a note or two below the repeated series. The notes did not have a particular meter or rhythm. The chants were based on the eight "church modes" (see chapter 16 for more on modes) which were performed in unison (everyone singing the same note) and a capella (without instrumental accompaniment).

http://tunein.com/radio/Calm-Radio---Gregorian-Chant-s142218/

Notation—Up to the tenth century, music notation consisted of an assortment of symbols called neumes, which provided an implied direction for the pitches to go up or down. Neumes, when used in combination with other figures, gave directions for tempo and rhythm. Thus a form of notation evolved and gradually expanded to indicate more precisely the performance details of the chant and, to some degree, the interpretation or performance style. Words could be set to the chants with one note for each syllable, called syllabic; several notes for one syllable, called neumatic; or numerous notes per syllable, called melismatic.

In the early part of the eleventh century, Guido d'Arrezo, an Italian monk, devised a system of notation that eventually became the diatonic scale we know today. He created a four-line staff in combination with syllables to represent the pitches C through A. The notes C, D, E, F, G, A were named *ut* (later to become *do*), *re*, *mi*, *fa*, *sol*, and *la*. Later, the syllable *ti* (B) was added as a leading tone to complete the octave at *do*. Guido's work in theory laid the groundwork for composers to notate their compositions in greater detail, relieving performers of the task of improvising or having to learn the music by rote.

Polyphony—In the tenth century, singing in unison was expanded by adding to the chant a melody line singing in parallel fourths or fifths, four or five notes apart from the original chant. In some cases a continuously sounded bass note, called a drone, was added. Eventually, the second voice began to deviate from the strict pattern of parallel fourths or fifths by adding melodic and rhythmic interest. By the twelfth century, the process was expanded to include three and four voices.

Counterpoint—Among the various forms used to combine musical lines was a practice called counterpoint. This is a technique of composition combining two or more independent voices which, in the strictest contrapuntal sense, must be harmonically compatible while melodically independent. The primary focus was on melodic design and interaction, with less concern regarding the harmonic structure. To that end an intricate series of rules developed and was ultimately accepted as being the standard for true counterpoint.

Guillaume de Machaut—Machaut (ca. 1300–1377), a poet and composer, played a significant role in the *ars nova*, or new art, soon to follow. In addition to being a renowned poet, Machaut made a substantial contribution to the development of sacred and secular choral music. He is also credited with setting to music the first complete arrangement of the ordinary (unchanging) part of the Mass. His career centered on composing for royalty, aristocrats, and those in high social positions.

It was at this point that the restrictions of thirteenth-century music started to relax and the polyphony of the sacred music from the previous century began to be applied to secular music.

http://www.last.fm/music/Guillaume+de+Machaut/+tracks

THE RENAISSANCE (REBIRTH)

From about 1400 to 1600, the Renaissance was a period during which the arts and sciences flourished exponentially. Composers no longer abided by restrictions imposed on them by the Roman Catholic Church, and polyphony was set free.

Josquin des Prez—des Prez (1450–1521), a most prolific Flemish composer, demonstrated his versatility in polyphonic vocal music by composing French secular songs (chansons), Italian love songs in the lighter vane (frottole), as well as Masses and other sacred polyphonic a capella music. As a theorist he was without equal, a fact that is manifest in the technical perfection of his some 760 works. Of equal distinction were his melodies, which when combined with his other musical attributes, ranged from simple well-designed compositions to those that were a challenge to the virtuosity of the highest ranking performers of the day. What a guy!

http://www.jango.com/music/Josquin+Desprez?l=0

Minstrels—During the Renaissance, entertainment for the masses was provided by itinerate performers who survived by exhibiting a variety of skills. Minstrels traveled about singing, dancing, juggling, and providing assorted sleight-of-hand and animal acts. In addition to providing entertainment for the general population, these no-mads served as purveyors of news, gossip, and probably some misinformation in the absence of newspapers and other sources of news dissemination.

Other Itinerant Musicians—On a higher social level were musicians and poets who performed for the aristocracy. Some were themselves royalty and members of this group. These entertainers were accepted in the courts and by the upper classes in general. They demonstrated a greater level of sophistication in their presentations than did the minstrels. In southern France these more sophisticated performers were known as troubadours; in northern France, trouveres, and in Germany, minnesing-ers. They provided entertainment for grand banquets and various refined social, municipal, and military events. The themes for these performances centered on matters of the heart, passion, civil strife, war, honor, and any other topic that would engender a high level of emotion. It was also during this period that documenting the events of the time began to occur.

Other composers who made significant contributions to Renaissance music include Guillaume Dufay (ca. 1397–1474) and Giovanni Pierluigi da Palestrina (1525–1594).

Guillaume Dufay—Dufay, a priest, focused on church music in the form of Masses, sacred short polyphonic pieces sung a capella, called motets, and secular pieces called chansons. He was lauded for the manner in which he was able to incorporate his gift for melody with expert execution of form. His music was performed in every venue of the time, making him the most prominent composer of the period. Dufay composed in every secular and liturgical form.

http://www.last.fm/music/Guillaume+Dufay

Giovanni Pierluigi da Palestrina—Palestrina was noted for his work with liturgical music. He is considered by many to have created the quintessential Roman Catholic Church music paradigm for polyphony in the style of the Renaissance period. During his tenure as organist at St. Agapitos Church and then as music director of the Julian Chapel at St. Peters, Palestrina composed over 500 pieces using all forms of liturgical music, in addition to 104 Masses. Throughout his career he established and adhered to a composition form that controlled melodic line, consonance, and dissonance. In so doing the results were splendid examples of harmonic balance and voicing. Palestrina's strict set of principles defined rules for the direction of melodic lines, intervals, and dissonance.

http://classical-music-online.net/en/composer/Palestrina/1634

Claudio Monteverdi—Monteverdi (1567–1643) is considered by music scholars to be the pivotal music personality between the Renaissance and Baroque periods. There is some question as to crediting him for writing the first opera. Jacopo Peri wrote the opera *Dafne* in 1597 and *Euridice* in 1600, the former score lost but the latter still in existence. It is, however, *L'Orfeo* by Monteverdi, composed in 1607, that is the earliest opera still being performed.

Monteverdi studied in the cathedral in Cremona and, at age twenty-four, began his career as a composer and performer in the court of Duke Vincenzo Gonzaga of Mantua. In 1612 Monteverdi was employed as maestro di cappella at the Basilica of St. Mark, where he completed his career in 1643. Concurrent with fulfilling his job requirement to compose sacred music, he was also able to compose secular music with distinctive form and melodic design that encompassed the polyphonic style of the Renaissance with the homophony of the evolving Baroque period.

http://www.last.fm/listen/artist/Claudio%2BMonteverdi/similarartists

THE BAROQUE PERIOD

It was during the period from 1600 through 1750 that the art of counterpoint was brought to its peak. The rules of composition were expanded to allow greater use of dissonance with expanded vocal and instrumental participation. Compositions were written in the figured bass form, in which the bass line was written with numerical figures indicating the required harmonies. The performer was left to improvise the accompanying parts above that bass line.

The concerto form was adopted, in which a soloist or small ensemble performed with an orchestral accompaniment. The practice of antiphonal performance was introduced, with two or more individual performing groups responding to each other musically. The opera and oratorio were evolving concurrently, implementing the new forms and techniques into those greater settings. A freedom of musical form and the augmentation of instrumentation and vocal participation resulted in ensembles of all varieties and sizes.

The Baroque period was one of enormous expansion in music style, form, instrumentation, and the manner in which performances were staged. Some of the names associated with this evolution were Arcangelo Corelli, Antonio Vivaldi, Johann Sebastian Bach, and Domenico Scarlatti.

Arcangelo Corelli—Corelli (1653–1713) was a trifecta of musical talent in the Baroque era. Teacher, concert violinist, and composer, he was renowned for his work in each of those areas. As a teacher and violinist he was acclaimed for establishing a violin playing technique. The violin, as a new instrument of the time, owed much of its introduction to the music world to Corelli's teaching, performance, and writings. Corelli is also credited with expanding the concerto grosso form (combining a small solo ensemble with a full orchestra), to the point where his work became a model for future composers.

http://www.last.fm/music/Arcangelo+Corelli

Antonio Lucio Vivaldi—Vivaldi (1678–1741), as an ordained priest with a one-year tenure, had a deep-seated musicianship that soon altered his career goals, the result being the world of music he created. Employed as teacher of the violin by the Ospidale della Pieta in Venice, Italy, an orphanage for the illegitimate children of royalty, Vivaldi spent the major portion of his professional career teaching, as well as composing both instrumental music and opera. It is estimated that he wrote twenty-two operas, more than five hundred concertos, and forty cantatas. Those numbers are estimates since it was not uncommon to discard a score after it had fulfilled its role in a performance.

http://www.last.fm/music/Antonio+Vivaldi/_/The+Four+Seasons

Johann Sebastian Bach—Bach (1685–1750) was born in Germany to a family of musicians, but was orphaned at the age of ten. That unfortunate beginning did not hinder his music education, since he lived with his musician brother who taught him to repair and play the organ, and introduced Johann to music composition. At age fourteen he studied the harpsichord, organ, and vocal music along with the liberal arts at St. Michael's school in Luneburg. Throughout his productive years, Bach had exposure to Corelli and Vivaldi, from whom he gleaned music-writing techniques in form, rhythm, and theory that would serve him throughout his entire career.

Bach was a prolific composer, leaving a legacy of more than 1,100 compositions for organ, voice, harpsichord, and other instruments in all the forms of the time. To this day his works have influenced the education of every serious music student, as well as numerous renowned composers.

https://www.youtube.com/watch?v=6JQm5aSjX6g

Domenico Scarlatti—Scarlatti (1685–1757) was born in Naples, Italy. His father Alessandro, a composer and mentor to his son, influenced Domenico's early life as a composer and organist. Between 1701 and 1729 Scarlatti traveled throughout Europe, beginning in Naples and then to Venice during which time he became a celebrated harpsichordist. In Rome Domenico was judged to be superior in harpsichord skills to George Frideric Handel. From Rome as maestro di cappella in St. Peter's Basilica, Scarlatti moved to London. From there it was Lisbon, back to Naples, and finally ending in Madrid where he spent the remainder of his life teaching and composing some 500 pieces for the keyboard.

http://www.last.fm/music/Domenico+Scarlatti

THE CLASSICAL PERIOD

The word *classical* has multiple meanings, all implying that which has taken place over a long period of time, and as such, has become traditional. When applied to the music that was created between 1735 and 1825, one might reconsider the term *classical* to mean a refined, sophisticated style of musical form. This Classical period in music was a reaction to the complex, ornate flamboyance of the polyphony of the Baroque period. Music of the Classical period consists of clean, unencumbered melodic lines supported by primarily pure diatonic harmonies. The overall effect is one of elegance and simplicity of line, harmony, and form.

Francesco Durante, Giovanni Pergolesi, Franz Joseph Haydn, Wolfgang Amadeus Mozart, and Ludwig van Beethoven can be considered the big five in this musical movement. Each made a significant contribution to the progression of music from the previous Baroque period through the Classical period to the Romantic period that followed. One additional composer of this period who was not considered a classical composer in the traditional sense, but significantly affected the evolution of music, was Jacques Offenbach. More on his contribution later.

Francesco Durante—Durante (1684–1755) was a student of Alessandro Scarlatti, father of Domenico Scarlatti. Durante was prominent among the first composers to begin the transition from the complex rococo style of Baroque composition to the simpler form of the classical approach. As a composer and teacher, Durante was able to influence the direction of music composition to the more simplified "classical" art form. Among his more successful students was Giovanni Pergolesi, whose works reflected the simplification of melodic lines and how they were harmonized. Durante focused on sacred music, using that venue to advance a strict code of rules of composition that centered on principles of refined clarity of form and balance.

https://www.youtube.com/watch?v=35ui00XekxQ

Giovanni Pergolesi—Pergolesi (1710–1736) lived a mere twenty-six years, and that short life was rife with illness. He was born in Jesi, Italy, where he spent his early years studying composition, the violin, and the organ. In 1725 Giovanni traveled to Naples where he advanced his studies and matured into a position of renown in the world of music for the aristocracy. He composed sacred, instrumental, and operatic music; his work in the opera led to Pergolesi being considered the father of opera buffa.

Opera in its early stages was composed in two genres, opera seria or serious opera and opera buffa or comic opera. Opera seria, as the name implies, dealt with serious issues of the time. It was directed toward an audience of royalty, nobility, and the intelligentsia. The first appearance of opera buffa took the form of short one-act comic relief interludes performed between the acts of an opera seria. Pergolesi was a master of opera buffa to the degree that his works prompted squabbles among the prominent composers of the time as to the validity of French opera seria as opposed to Italian opera buffa. Added to the misfortunes of Pergolesi's life was the fact that most of his comic and serious operas, along with his sacred music, were not published until after his death. He died in poverty and was buried in a common grave.

http://www.52composers.com/pergolesi.html

Jacques Offenbach—On a less sophisticated level, and concurrent with the work of Pergolesi, a lesser form of opera which resembled opera buffa was evolving in France. This type of music was referred to as low comedy and high comedy opera. Low comedy opera appropriated existing melodic themes, often from the repertoire of the masters, and applied those melodies to the libretti of the moment. These were often disreputable tales of a satirical nature dealing with the lowest elements of society, both social and political. High comedy opera tended toward a more urbane musical product featuring original music centered on romantic escapades of the aristocracy.

An interesting sequence of events with unintended consequences of significance in the music world took place in Paris, France, during the middle of the nineteenth century. In an effort to ensure there not be any substantial challenge to the grand opera that was sponsored by the French government, legislation was enacted restricting impresarios to one-act productions with a maximum of three performers. Jacques Offenbach (1819–1880), a German immigrant, cellist, and to that point unsuccessful composer of opera comique, raised enough financial backing to produce a series of musical performances that fit the restrictions of the time, and so, the operetta was born with renowned success. Eventually, the absurd restrictions were lifted and Offenbach went on to enjoy a worldwide career as composer of more than one hundred operettas.

In general, operettas focus on humorous, lighthearted libretti accompanied by light music. The music alternated with actual spoken words compared with the recitativo (sung speech) and aria sequences found in operas. Operettas are shorter than operas and are generally intended to entertain the audience in a lighter vein as would a contemporary Broadway musical. The primary difference between the operetta and a musical is in the performer's singing ability and the ratio of spoken words to singing. In the simplest terms, operettas consist primarily of singing interrupted with some spoken parts. Musicals are the opposite, centered on the spoken word interrupted with song. Operettas are performed by opera singers who possess those singing qualities and training associated with traditional opera. Musicals are staffed with actors who can sing. They each hold a solid and greatly appreciated position in the world of music.

https://www.youtube.com/watch?v=g34ivbIWmLE&feature=player_embedded

Franz Joseph Haydn—Haydn (1732–1809) lived in Austria for most of his life. Haydn's parents were not trained in music but were active as musical amateurs and recognized their son's musical abilities at a very early age. They arranged for his music education through the local schoolmaster and choirmaster, with whom Haydn spent his early years. Life was not pleasant for the boy but he was able to sing boy soprano parts and quickly learned to play the harpsichord and violin.

At age eight Haydn was sent to St. Stephen's Cathedral in Vienna where he spent the next nine years studying voice and the harpsichord along with Latin and other academic subjects while he worked as a chorus member. His living conditions were less than desirable during those years, so that at times, Haydn literally had to sing for his supper.

As Haydn matured his voice changed, resulting in his no longer being able to maintain a boy soprano position in the choir. He was dismissed and relegated to work as a freelance musician, doing whatever was necessary to survive. During that period he was able to glean from his experiences the fundamentals of composition and counterpoint. It was with this knowledge that he was able to compose an opera and numerous other compositions. Those achievements, along with his work as a freelance musician, allowed him to expand his professional horizons and ultimately acquire patronage from the aristocracy.

After a series of less-than-stellar positions in service along with an unsuccessful marriage in 1761, Haydn was offered and accepted the position of vice-kapellmeister for the extraordinarily wealthy and powerful Esterhazy family. Upon the demise of the kapellmeister, Haydn was put in charge of the entire music output of the Ester-hazy Empire, where he spent the years 1761 to 1780.

Haydn's work as a composer and musician resulted in being credited by musicologists for having significantly influenced the expansion of chamber music and the musical form used in his 108 symphonies. Haydn composed a total of 750 works.

Perhaps Haydn's most significant contribution to the music world was his development of the sonata allegro form (see chapter 15). This form involves structuring a composition, usually the first movement of a symphony, into four parts. It begins with an exposition in which the main themes are stated. That is followed by a development where, as the name implies, the themes are developed; a recapitulation restates the themes, and finally, a coda or finale completes the form. In addition to developing the sonata allegro form, Haydn established a structure for an entire symphony with four movements, those being fast; slow; playful (scherzo), often a dance rhythm such as a minuet; and a fast, often rondo dynamic finale.

http://www.jango.com/music/Franz﹢Joseph+Haydn?l=0

Wolfgang Amadeus Mozart—Mozart (1756–1791) was born in Salzburg, Austria. His father, Leopold, was assistant concert master at the Salzburg court, a violinist, and a composer of some note. Leopold, recognizing his son's extraordinary musical gift, encouraged his early start of music study so that by age six Wolfgang was performing publicly. To the advantage of musicians of that time, a rivalry was taking place among the aristocracy of the various city-states. Included in the "possessions" one needed as evidence of wealth and power were musicians as part of the court cadre. Leopold and his protégé son capitalized on this social phenomenon by attaining various positions as musicians for the nobility. So began the career of one of history's most prolific composers and musicians.

Leopold toured Europe with his son and daughter, who was also a child prodigy. This experience exposed the young Wolfgang to numerous professional musicians, one of whom was Johann Christian Bach, son of Johann Sebastian Bach. With each new friend came new musical experiences, all influencing Wolfgang's already fertile musical mind.

There are several anecdotes associated with Wolfgang's extraordinary memory. It is said that he was able to compose an entire symphony in his mind and then sit down and write out a perfect score. Another narrative tells of a time when in Rome he heard a liturgical selection once and was able to write out the entire score from memory. True?

Mozart's short life was replete with exhilarating successes combined with distressing episodes. He began performing at age six, wrote his first symphony at eight, first opera at twelve, and beginning in 1770 worked for ten years as court musician for the archbishop of Salzburg. Although Mozart was not happy in that position, he did enjoy several successful premiers in Milan, Munich, Vienna, and Prague.

In 1773, after a lengthy performance tour during which time he composed numerous pieces, Wolfgang returned to Salzburg where he accepted a position as court musician. There he enjoyed great popularity and composed in every genre. In spite of this success, the young composer's need to attain greater heights and more income prompted him to venture on two tours, neither of which was particularly successful. By age twenty-one Wolfgang had composed symphonies, sonatas, string quartets, violin and piano concerti, along with an assortment of serenades. This phenomenal achievement would certainly more than satisfy others as lifetime goals, but it was not enough for the young genius. In 1777 Mozart left his post in Salzburg to seek a more challenging experience. Unfortunately, his voyage was not successful and he returned to Salzburg where he continued to compose liturgical works, among them the Coronation Mass.

In 1782 Wolfgang married Constanze Weber, with whom he had six children, four of whom did not survive. During the 1780s the Mozarts lived a splendid lifestyle, which ultimately drove them into debt. In 1791 he died at the age of thirty-five, having lived a short, whirlwind life of enormous creativity, leaving a legacy of a variety of music, up to that time never equaled.

Mozart is considered to have made the greatest historical contribution to the music repertoire. His development of the structure and form of the symphony, concerto, opera, and instrumental ensembles laid a foundation upon which future composers would build their works. During his lifetime Wolfgang composed over 600 pieces, including string quartets, operas, masses, symphonies, and concerti, all warmly received then and now.

http://www.last.fm/music/Wolfgang+Amadeus+Mozart

Note: It is at this point in history that the dearth of source material on composers and the music world in general began to be rectified, as music historians and the subject of musicology came into being. Extended biographical information on the composers is now available, with great detail on their personal and professional lives. Should a particular individual be of interest or more detailed study be desired by the reader, the information is available both in libraries and on the Internet. A word of warning: the Internet is not always a reliable source for accurate reporting.

THE ROMANTIC PERIOD

Romanticism is a state of being in which a participant's philosophy and creativity are focused on the preeminence of the individual. In the late eighteenth century the creative community became less concerned with the established "rules of engagement" from the past Classical era, trending instead toward an artistic creativity centered on emotion, a response to one's innate creativity, and a reaction to the inner self.

The art forms, music among them, turned toward nationalism, as well as highly charged emotional issues of the heart, mind, and soul, expressed through a less restricted form for the various media. Among these was the opera, which offered a plot through which composers were able to express their nationalism. Instrumental music was expanded both in its orchestration and in the themes taken from music indigenous to the local culture. There was an enrichment of the harmonic and melodic structures, with fuller, bolder harmonies accompanying extended lyrical melodies.

Added to this enrichment were the advances in musical instrument technology, which refined instruments already in use while expanding the existing instrument inventory with new designs and equipment. Better instruments, producing better sounds, provided composers the opportunity to write with more elaborate instrumentation and a broader range of timbre and richness of sound. This multifaceted expansion of music performance broadened the audience beyond the elite to include the general population.

Ludwig van Beethoven—Beethoven (1770–1827) was born in Bonn, Germany. He may best be remembered for expanding the structure and instrumentation of many musical forms. His symphonies were grander, sonatas bolder and more dynamic, concertos more forceful, and his vocal works, when combined with an orchestra, became one homogenous musical experience.

Beethoven idolized his grandfather, who was a highly regarded kapellmeister and musician. His father on the other hand was a cruel taskmaster who taught his son music, resulting in the boy manifesting his prodigious ability in a public performance at age seven. Academically, Ludwig was not a particularly good student, but his musical ability was such that at age ten he was able to transfer his efforts to full-time music study. Within two years he published his first work and by age fourteen he took the position of assistant court organist.

At age seventeen Ludwig was sent to Vienna where he was to study with Mozart. That episode was short-lived due to Ludwig's mother's illness, forcing him to return to Bonn. For the next five years he honed his musical skill working as a musician in Bonn. He then moved back to Vienna where he was able to study with such celebrated musicians as Franz Joseph Haydn and Antonio Salieri.

Beethoven's reputation as a pianist and improvisationist firmly established his position, both with the general public and with the music community of Vienna, as a musician of extraordinary talent. This reputation provided him the opportunity to develop associations with the aristocracy, who were pleased to become his benefactors. From that point on he began public performances, and composed and published numerous selections for the piano, yielding both critical acclaim and monetary success.

Beneath all these wonderful accomplishments was looming a tragedy of monumental proportions, for this great producer of sounds that would please the music world for centuries to come was losing his hearing. In his mid-twenties he began to suffer from tinnitus, ringing in the ears, and from that time on his hearing gradually diminished to the point where he became profoundly deaf. Perhaps most remarkable was the fact that he composed and conducted his Ninth Symphony while totally unable to hear a sound.

To compensate for this condition, Beethoven conducted many of his conversations in writing. He maintained a book in which he would write his statement, and his partner of the time would respond in writing. The result was a series of about four hundred of these books, half of which have survived, acting as diaries relating his conversations and revealing in some detail his thoughts on matters musical and philosophical.

Beethoven composed more than 650 pieces of music, including symphonies, concertos, sacred music, a Mass, chamber music, piano sonatas, an opera, and hundreds of assorted pieces for instruments and voice. He may well be considered the threshold to the Romantic era in music.

http://www.jango.com/music/Ludwig+van+Beethoven?l=0

Frédéric Chopin—Chopin (1810–1849) was born in Zelazowa Wola, Poland. As is the case with many prodigies, he began his career in music with his first published composition at age seven and gave his first public performance at age eight. After studying at the Warsaw Conservatory for three years, he moved to Vienna where in 1829 he astounded audiences with his ability to combine his technical prowess with sensitivity beyond that of most performers.

For a period of about three years Chopin toured Europe, finally settling in Paris where he soon affiliated himself with other great or soon-to-be great composers. It was there that, by the age of twenty-two, he had established a reputation among the literati and the upper social class as a piano teacher and a composer of piano music extraordinaire.

On a personal level, Frédéric experienced several light romances until he met a female novelist who wrote under the pen name George Sand. In 1839 Chopin, accompanied by Sand, began a seven-year period of coexistence and musical productivity that would yield a major portion of his piano works, which live on today. During the next nine years leading up to 1848, Chopin's deteriorating health affected his behavior, and his relationship with Sand ended, never to be reconciled.

Chopin's last tour was of the British Isles, resulted in his health declining further. Returning to Paris in a frail physical and depressed emotional state over his shattered relationship with Sand, Chopin died at the age of thirty-eight.

http://www.last.fm/music/Fr%C3%A9d%C3%A9ric+Chopin

Robert Schumann—Schumann (1810–1856), the son of a publisher, was born in Germany and began music study at age six. With a traditional early education, at age eighteen he entered law school only to find that music, not law, was his passion. One year later, with his penchant for music dominating his focus, he left law studies and moved to Heidelberg where he devoted his entire effort to music, composition, and performance. There he studied piano with Friedrich Wieck, a renowned teacher whose daughter Clara, at nine years old, was well on her way to a career as a concert pianist. It was Clara who would someday become Robert's wife.

Schumann would have become a virtuoso pianist but for an accident to his right hand which ended that aspiration. It was this misfortune that redirected his energies toward composition, resulting in a period of great creativity combined with a failed love affair and ultimately his marriage to Clara Wieck. During those years Schumann began to be recognized as a composer of piano music in various forms, and of numerous song cycles based on the works of poets as well as individual songs dealing with the emotions of love and life.

Schumann broadened his musical output to include the symphony and concerto, along with orchestral music in assorted lesser forms, chamber music, and an oratorio. In the years to follow he filled the roles of conductor and professor of piano in the Leipzig Conservatory. In 1850 he enjoyed a resurgence, during which time he accepted a position of music director at Dusseldorf, was able to compose a cello concerto and another symphony, took on the role of conductor which was unsuccessful, and ultimately lost his position in Dusseldorf. From that point on his life and work experienced a gradual decline both mentally and physically, culminating in Schumann being committed to an asylum, where he died in 1856.

http://www.last.fm/music/Robert+Schumann

Giuseppe Verdi—Verdi (1813–1901) was born in La Roncole, in Parma, Italy. There is little documentation on his early life, except to say that his father was an innkeeper who appreciated his son's musical proclivity and encouraged him to study music. Between the ages of twelve and twenty, Giuseppe was actively engaged in music study and conducting. He then moved to Milan where, for the next three years, he continued his studies and had the opportunity to be exposed to opera. It was that music form that captured Verdi's musical mind, and so began the career of the musician often described as the greatest composer of opera in history.

From Milan, Giuseppe moved to the position of town music master in Busetto. It was there that he met and married Margherita Barezzi and composed his first successful opera, *Oberto*. Shortly thereafter Verdi's infant son and daughter died, followed by the passing of his wife. The despair of those tragic events was further exacerbated by the lack of success of his second opera, *Un Giorno*. In a state of depression, Verdi decided to end his career. Fortunately for the world, a friend convinced him to try one more opera. He did and produced *Nabucco*, which was widely lauded. And so Verdi's career was launched.

The following years were filled with a prolific output of operas along with a love affair that ultimately ended in his marriage to Giuseppina Strepponi. In addition to writing the many operas that are still the highlights of opera seasons worldwide today, Verdi had grown to be a symbol of nationalism. His performances were concluded with ovations intertwined with chants of "Viva Verdi," wishing Verdi a long life but also exclaiming the double entendre V.E.R.D.I., for **V**ictor **E**manuele **Re** (king) **D'** (of) **I**talia. Verdi considered his greatest contribution to the music world to be the Casa di Riposo per Musicisti, a retirement home in Milan he established for elderly musicians. Giuseppe Verdi and his wife are buried there.

http://www.jango.com/music/Giuseppe+Verdi?l=0

Johannes Brahms—Brahms (1833–1897), a key figure in the Romantic era, was born in Hamburg, Germany. His father, a professional double bassist, began Johannes's music study at age seven, and by his teens Johannes was earning his way as a performer in the local community. A serendipitous meeting with Robert Schumann, the celebrated music critic and composer, resulted in Schumann extolling the virtues of the young Johannes's extraordinary ability as a composer and performer. And so his professional career began. The two men became close friends, remaining so until Schumann's death in 1856.

Brahms spent his career as music director of various vocal groups in Hamburg and then in Vienna. During those years he composed music in all forms. These included concertos, both double and single, a requiem Mass, many theme and variations, chamber music, piano selections, and hundreds of art songs, called lieder, for solo voice and piano.

On a personal level Brahms enjoyed a very close friendship with Robert Schumann and his wife Clara, with whom he remained a platonic but much-loved friend after Schumann's death.

http://www.jango.com/music/Johannes+Brahms?*l=0*

Peter Ilyich Tchaikovsky—Tchaikovsky (1840–1893) had an early life that differed from that of many comparable composers because, although he began piano lessons at the age of five, he did not begin to study music on a significant level until he was twenty-one years old. After a brief stay at the Russian Musical Society, he entered the St. Petersburg Conservatory where he studied composition and taught piano. Three years later he took the position of professor of harmony at the Moscow Conservatory.

Tchaikovsky's gift for melody was the vehicle that led to him being considered by many to be Russia's most widely celebrated composer. That gift, combined with his proclivity for dramatic instrumentation combined with colorful orchestration, resulted in composing in a style that had great appeal to wide audiences. Although he did make several attempts to compose operas (which were not well received), his greater strength was in the composition of orchestral music.

In 1878, through the generosity of the widow Nadezhda von Meck, Tchaikovsky was given financial backing that would allow him to concentrate all his time on composing music. Interesting is the fact that his arrangement with von Meck included an agreement that they should never meet. Throughout his life he composed 169 pieces in many instrumental forms. Some of the most famous to this day are *The Nutcracker* and *The Sleeping Beauty* ballets, Piano Concerto No. 1, and Symphony No. 6, also known as the *Pathétique*. Tchaikovsky's life-long struggle with his homosexuality, which at the time was condemned by society and the church, caused him to engage in a short-lived marriage and then spend the remainder of his life suffering from periods of great humiliation and despair. There is some question as to the cause of his death, some suggesting that he committed suicide because of his homosexuality.

http://www.jango.com/music/Pyotr+Ilyich+Tchaikovsky?l=0

THE TWENTIETH CENTURY

With the arrival of the twentieth century a new style of music composition, without restrictions, came on the scene. Impressionism, expressionism, and neoclassicism, along with a new technology in sound production, were the themes of the day. These, combined with a segment of the music-producing world that chose to hold on to the traditional forms from the past, appeared simultaneously to create a wonderful, complex, diverse world of music for the public to enjoy. The arts community was seeking a new approach to creativity.

Impressionism was one of the three important music composition philosophies. It was the intention of the composer to relate through music his or her impressions of a particular concept, item, or situation. Form was no longer a mainstay of a piece, nor was it necessary to adhere to a particular tonality. The diatonic scale was often replaced with modes and the pentatonic (five-tone) and whole-tone scale. Parallel chords were used in series with added sevenths, ninths, elevenths, and thirteenths.

Claude Debussy—Debussy (1862–1918) is considered to be the forefather of the Impressionist movement. A gifted pianist, his studies began at the Paris Conservatory when he was eleven years old, and continued in Rome after winning the Prix de Rome. It was during that period that he began to reveal his unique style of composition. Claude had the good fortune of becoming associated with Madame Nadezhda von Meck, Tchaikovsky's benefactor, teaching her children and traveling with them throughout Europe. This experience gave Debussy the opportunity to broaden his musical horizons.

One might define Debussy's music as being a transition from the structured, sonorous, melodic sounds of the Romantic era to an atmosphere of ethereal, dreamlike sensitivity where sounds were an entity unto themselves rather than required to be only part of the whole. Rhythm, melody, and harmony, when used to create music, no longer needed to follow the traditional rules of a predetermined structure. Instead, they were ingredients in a formula which, when properly combined, became the entity.

Debussy developed the whole-tone scale which, as the name implies, is a scale consisting of intervals of whole steps, as compared to a diatonic scale which is composed of a combination of whole and half steps (see chapter 16). His harmonic structure was also unconventional, in that chords were built on his whole-tone scale, the modes of the Medieval period, and other unconventional sources. An equal degree of creativity can be found in his innovative use of combined rhythms. The effect was the desired end product, with little regard for how it was achieved.

Debussy's personal life was fraught with numerous passionate love affairs. He finally married in 1899. That marriage ended in 1904, as Claude found his wife was intellectually and musically unsophisticated. From that point on he had several other affairs and fathered one child. Debussy died of cancer at age fifty-five.

http://www.jango.com/music/Claude+Debussy?l=0

Expressionism—Expressionism is an approach to composition that occurred during the second quarter of the twentieth century. It was intended to express in sound the intense unrest that was manifest in society. The traditional practices used in music composition were replaced with a general intensification and distortion of melody, harmony, and rhythm. Tonality was replaced with atonality, consonance with dissonance, simplicity with complexity, and discernible melody with the abstract. The objective was to create music that would be compelling while establishing a new concept for musical sound. Consonant harmony, rhythmic clarity, and instrumental balance were to be replaced with what one might consider to be organized cacophony. Tradition was out; countertradition became the order of the day.

Arnold Schoenberg—Schoenberg (1874–1951) was born in Vienna to a family of moderate means with no music training but with a love for the subject. At age eight Arnold began studying the violin, composing for his instrument and eventually studying traditional harmony and counterpoint. His most significant contribution to music composition was advancing the theory that music need not have a tonal center, nor be written in a specific key. Music could be atonal, that is, without a tonal center of gravity.

Unlike many of his predecessors, Arnold's career in music had a comparatively slow start. At age sixteen he became involved with an orchestra, and at twenty offered his first significant piece for public performance. He spent two years teaching in a Berlin music academy, moved to Vienna to start his own school, and it was there that he met Alan Berg and Anton Webern, both of whom later became disciples of Schoenberg's concept of atonality. A performance of Schoenberg's atonal music in 1908, often referred to as the "Scandal Concert," stunned the audience accustomed to hearing traditional tonal music. This point may be considered to be crossing the threshold from traditional harmonies and orchestration to the birth of "modern" music.

Schoenberg devised the twelve-tone system of composition, also called dodecaphony or serialism. The object of the process was to ensure that all twelve notes of the chromatic scale were given equal emphasis, thereby avoiding a tonality with a tonic point of reference. The composer would create a unique series of twelve tones chosen from the chromatic scale using any pattern of inversions, transpositions, or reversal. The melodies were then derived from that unique series of tones. Arnold became a naturalized U.S. citizen in 1941. He died in July 1951.

An interesting development arose from this series of changes in composition style. There was a general lack of enthusiasm for the atonal music sound, leaving in place a segment of the classical music listening public that preferred the architecture of tonality and form. To their delight, some composers of the Schoenberg period continued to hold on to traditions with a slight evidence of modernity. Perhaps the most familiar of these "traditional" composers was Sergei Rachmaninoff.

http://classical-music-online.net/en/production/12118

Sergei Vasilievich Rachmaninoff—Rachmaninoff (1873–1943) was born to an aristocratic but financially unstable family. As a result, he had to rely on his paternal grandfather to arrange for a music education. In 1883, at age ten, Sergei was sent to study at the Saint Petersburg Conservatory. Concurrently, his maternal grandmother exposed him to Russian Orthodox services, which provided him the opportunity to experience liturgical music, further enhancing his early musical exposure. In spite of these opportunities, and the extraordinary innate musical talent Rachmaninoff was harboring, his general accomplishments were less than stellar. It was not until he attended the Moscow Conservatory that he began to manifest his musical genius. In 1891 he graduated from the conservatory with honors and began serious composition. His work at the conservatory consisted of a symphonic piece, a symphonic poem, and a fantasia for orchestra.

From that point on Rachmaninoff's career in composition and performance as a pianist and conductor flourished. His compositions were clearly representative of Russian Romanticism in their lush orchestration and in the composer's impassioned use of the piano. He was lauded as one of the outstanding pianists of his time, an attribute that is evident in his astute use of the piano as a medium for communicating the concept of Romanticism through music.

http://www.pianoparadise.com/downloadmp3/rachmaninov.html

THE PRESENT

The advent of a new technology in the electronic production of sound, coupled with advances in recording, modifying, and broadcasting sound, motivated composers to expand their horizons to use this technology and create a new style of music performance. Consequently, amplified instruments, recordings from the gramophone's rotating cylinder to the CD, broadcasting via radio and television, along with whatever else will appear by the time this book is published, have opened a vast array of opportunities for the creative mind to explore and exploit. Music performance is no longer limited to a particular location or building. Music can be broadcast worldwide, and live performances can take place in stadiums for audiences of a hundred thousand or more. There are no bounds to the possibilities for the expansion of music in every form and through every medium.

GLOSSARY OF TERMS RELATED TO MUSIC HISTORY

This glossary will help the reader define terms that are related to the history of music. See the discussion above for more in-depth information on these items.

Baroque The period in music history circa 1600 to 1750, during which developed an enormous expansion in music style, form, instrumentation, and the manner in which performances were staged.

Camera Italian word meaning "room" used to identify the secular Baroque chamber sonata or sonata da camera.

Chanson A French secular song.

Classical The period in music history circa 1750 to 1830, where music form took on a refined, sophisticated style.

Cornetto A wind instrument dating from the Medieval period (ca. 1500 through the eighteenth century). It was made of wood, played with a cup mouthpiece similar to those used on contemporary brass instruments, and had tone holes for the player to alter the pitches.

Frottole An Italian love song.

Gregorian chant Unaccompanied single-note church music with an undefined rhythm, named after Pope Gregory, whose papacy spanned 590 to 604.

Impressionism A period during the late nineteenth and early twentieth centuries when composers abandoned the structure and form of the previous years in lieu of a more sensual approach to expressing mood and emotion through sound.

Kapellmeister German word for director of music.

Leitmotif German for a melodic or rhythmic theme associated with a particular individual, idea, or action.

Lied German word for song.

Lute A pear-shaped, ancient string instrument with structural attributes similar to those of a violin. (See chapter 4 for more about the lute.)

Lyre The term *lyre* is applied to a wide spectrum of instruments with strings, ranging from a U-shaped instrument with strings that are plucked to a category of early Medieval bowed instruments. (See chapter 4 for more about the lyre.)

Madrigal A fourteenth-century unaccompanied secular Italian part-song. Usually four to six voices in contrapuntal form, the madrigal spread throughout Europe and remained popular through the next three centuries.

Mass The Roman Catholic worship service to celebrate the transformation of bread and wine into the body and blood of Jesus Christ. The ordinary of the Mass, which consists of the parts of the mass that reoccur, has been set to music throughout the ages. The Bach B Minor Mass may be considered the quintessential work in this category.

Melisma Words using numerous notes per syllable in Gregorian chant were referred to as melismatic.

Missa Latin for Mass.

Neoclassical A term used to describe the period during the twentieth century when composers reverted to the musical forms and techniques from the previous "classical" music periods.

Opera Theater set to music. (See chapter 18 for more on the opera.)

Operetta A short, light opera.

Polyphony The practice of writing music in two or more melody parts as opposed to a single line.

Program music Music composed to represent a story line in sound. The form, melody, and harmonic structure tell a story in sound rather than follow a particular musical architecture.

Rococo A reaction to the strict Baroque structure in Paris during the eighteenth century as composers created a lighter, more sanguine approach to their work.

Romanticism The period from the nineteenth to the twentieth centuries, characterized by a departure from the strict musical structure of the past to a greater interest in philosophy and creativity, focused on the preeminence of the individual.

Serialism A system of composition developed in the early twentieth century by Arnold Schoenberg, characterized by a pattern of the twelve tones of an octave, which were restated in different transpositions, inversions, and other creative formats.

Symphony An extensive orchestral composition usually containing four movements in various forms that are structured to follow a predetermined format.

2

Sound Production

THE ANATOMY OF A MUSICAL INSTRUMENT

Musical instruments are devices that have been developed to produce and manipulate sounds. These instruments achieve such a high degree of accuracy that they enable a player to produce an almost infinite variety of musical sounds. Although musical instruments are far from perfect, their inventors, developers, and manufacturers have refined their products to the point where the most gifted performer is able to demonstrate his or her virtuosity.

Musical instruments use three basic operating systems to produce sound. These are: a sound generating system, a sound amplification system, and a sound manipulating or mechanical system.

Sound Generation—Sound-generating systems are different for each category of instrument. Woodwind instruments use three types; brass instruments, one; non-fretted string instruments, one; and percussion instruments, four.

Woodwind instruments generate sound by using a single reed in conjunction with a mouthpiece, as in a clarinet or saxophone; a double reed, as in an oboe or bassoon; or a flat shelf-like surface positioned to allow a stream of air to undulate over and under the edge of the shelf, as in a flute or recorder.

Brass instruments generate sound by having the player's lips buzz within the confines of a cup-shaped mouthpiece. This process is common to all brass instruments. It should be noted that there are variations in embouchure (the shape of one's lips, facial muscles, and mouth) and buzzing techniques that apply to the different brass instruments. The basic principle, however, is the same in all cases.

Non-fretted string instruments (violins, etc.) generate sound by setting a string into motion (vibration) by either drawing a bow across the string's surface or by plucking the string with the fingers. There are some alternative methods of generating sound from strings, but these are specific to producing special effects and are not relevant to this text.

Percussion instruments produce sound by reacting to any type of agitation such as being struck, scraped, or, in the case of something with sound-producing particles in an enclosed vessel, shaken. There are also instruments considered to be percussion that produce sound by a player blowing into them. Although not percussive in nature, these produce special effects and so are not usually considered to be members of either of the wind instrument sections.

Amplifying Sound—Sounds produced by an instrument's sound generator alone cannot provide sufficient volume or the timbre necessary to satisfy the musical and esthetic requirements of a listener. Therefore, a sound amplification system is needed to complement the sound-generating processes. Sounds require a support system to supply the amplitude (volume) necessary for basic tones, called fundamentals, and their ancillary tones, called overtones, to attain a desired timbre. (See the science of sound below for more on this topic.) The support system is, in fact, the body of the instrument. It is the design and construction of the body in conjunction with the sound-generating system that ultimately produce the characteristic sound or timbre of an instrument.

Thus far, a device comprised of a sound-producing mechanism (mouthpiece or reed) coupled with a support system (the instrument's body) to provide the amplitude and timbre desired for a specific sound effect has been described. This coupled acoustic system, that is, the sound source and the associated structure or body of the instrument, still cannot provide a musician with the equipment necessary to produce and manipulate sounds with sufficient variety and versatility to perform music. The coupled device is limited to producing only those sounds that are fundamental to the physical characteristics of the design. Consequently, a brass instrument construction would be capable of producing only those pitches that are the product of the player adjusting his or her lip tension or embouchure; a woodwind design would only produce the fundamental of that instrument, and a string instrument would only produce those pitches to which the strings are tuned.

It is at this point in the design of an instrument that an additional system is necessary. That system must alter the length of the sound-producing vibrating column so the pitches that exist between the fundamentals can be added to those basic open tones.

Controlling Sound—Sound is controlled through mechanical systems such as valves and slides for brass instruments; tone holes, ring keys, and padded keys for woodwind instruments; and the shortening of strings through the use of fingers of the left hand on non-fretted string instruments. These systems, added to the basic design of the instrument's body, and joined to a sound source, permit the player to lengthen or shorten the vibrating column of air or string by small degrees. In so doing, the player can produce the pitches that lie between the fundamental tones in wind instruments, and the tones that exist between the pitches to which the open strings are tuned in non-fretted string instruments.

As the vibrating column of air or the vibrating string is shortened, the pitch is raised. Conversely, as the vibrating column of air or the vibrating string is lengthened, the pitch is lowered.

Woodwind instruments alter their basic tones through holes in the body of the instrument. Some holes are open and some have padded cup-shaped keys covering them. If the holes are open, the effective sound-producing length of the instrument is as long as the distance between the sound generator and the first open hole (see chapter 11, figure 11.2). As the holes are covered, the sound-producing column of air within the instrument becomes longer and the pitches lower.

Brass instruments have valves or slides that open sections of tubing to lengthen or shorten the vibrating column of air (see chapter 8, figure 8.2). The same principle of shorter to higher and longer to lower applies with these instruments.

String instruments change notes when the player uses the fingers of the left hand to lengthen or shorten the strings by pressing (stopping) the string to the fingerboard at any given point. Again, shorter vibrating strings produce higher notes and longer strings, lower notes. (See chapter 5 on different notes.)

It is the combination of the sound generator, the body of the instrument, and the devices used to alter the length of the vibrating column of air or string that make a wind or string instrument capable of producing all of the notes that are within a particular instrument's range.

Transposition—Some instruments are labeled transposing instruments, and are referred to as being in a certain key. One will see a B-flat clarinet, an E-flat saxophone, or an F horn. These key names refer to the actual note one will hear when the written note C is played on the instrument. This begs the question: why are not all instruments made in the same key? The answer is somewhat complicated.

Each instrument has a specific limited range. In order to expand that range, other versions of the same instrument are made in different sizes. Smaller sizes produce notes in higher ranges and larger sizes produce notes in lower ranges. An example would be the clarinet family, which consists of clarinets called an E-flat sopranino, B-flat soprano, E-flat alto, E-flat contra-alto, B-flat bass, and BB-flat contrabass. All these instruments share the same fingerings so that a clarinetist can go from one instrument to any other by simply adjusting to the different instrument size and embouchure.

A change in the size of an instrument results in a corresponding change in the key in which it plays. If that change in key is an octave, the new instrument will be in the same key as its parent. An instrument in C recreated to sound an octave higher will also sound in the key of C. If the change is other than an octave, the new instrument will be in whatever key represents the new interval. As an example, an instrument in C recreated so that it sounds a fifth higher will be in the key of G, which is five notes or a fifth higher than the original instrument in C.

If related instruments were all made in the same key, they would each need different fingerings. To avoid this, the key that results from an instrument's design is used and all instruments in the family then have the same fingering. This helps a player switching from one instrument to another within the same family. To accommodate for the difference in key tonality, the written notes for each instrument are transposed into whatever key is necessary to make the sound compatible with that of the other members in the ensemble.

Summary—The combination of the sound generator, coupled with the body of the instrument and the devices used to alter the length of the vibrating air column or string, makes a wind or string instrument capable of producing all of the notes that are within that particular instrument's range. Brass instruments have valves or slides that open sections of tubing to lengthen or shorten the vibrating column of air. Woodwind instruments have a series of holes in the body of the instrument, which the player can open or close to lengthen or shorten the vibrating column of air in the instrument. String instrument players lengthen or shorten the strings by pressing (stopping) the string to the fingerboard at any given point with the fingers of the left hand.

THE SCIENCE OF SOUND

Sound occurs when a force excites vibrations in the atmosphere. These vibrations are projected by a series of compressed and released waves of air pressure. Molecules of air are pushed against each other, acting as a train would when the last car is pushed and each car preceding the last one responds in turn, creating a chain reaction. Since one single molecule of air cannot travel very far on its own, many molecules must push against each other in order to permit the sound to travel.

When this action and reaction takes place in the air, a wavelike motion produces groupings of molecules positioned in alternating sequences. The first grouping of compressed molecules is called compression. The grouping created by the void left behind the compression is in a more open spatial relationship, and is called rarefaction. It is the combined action of compression and rarefaction that results in one complete cycle (figure 2.1).

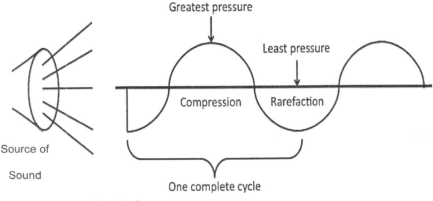

Figure 2.1. Complete Cycle

When vibration is initiated on a string, movement begins at the point of rest or origin. The movement proceeds to the farthest distance it can travel from the beginning point of rest. The movement then begins a return trip, traveling back past the original point of rest and on to the farthest distance it can travel on the opposite end. The movement then travels back again, returning past the point of origin to repeat the cycle (figure 2.2).

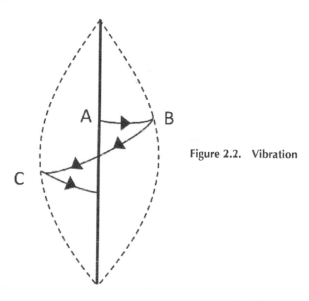

Figure 2.2.   Vibration

This entire voyage completes one cycle. Similarly, one cycle in sound consists of a vibration passing by means of compression and rarefaction through every position which encompasses its starting point. This type of pure tone is called sinusoidal, and its image is called a sine wave (figure 2.3).

Figure 2.3.   Sine Wave

When sound is generated on a musical instrument, the sound presents itself in a symmetrical pattern of vibrations. These vibrations include a fundamental note along with a number of other related notes sounding in lesser degrees of amplitude or volume.

The fundamental note alone is a pure tone and can be visualized as a simple wave, free from any accompanying vibrations or tones. Pure tones are best produced electronically and are generally considered to be musically uninteresting. When a tone is generated on a musical instrument, it is almost always accompanied by a series of related sounds or tones called harmonics, overtones, or upper partials. These three terms can be used interchangeably.

Harmonics—Harmonics (overtones, upper partials) are secondary vibrations occurring concurrently with the fundamental tone and consist of successive multiples of the whole vibrating body. The segments occur as one-half, one-third, one-quarter, and so on of the original vibrating column and sound, with less amplitude than the fundamental.

Harmonics are embellishments of the fundamental tone. They are not distinguishable by the listener as entities in themselves but rather serve as ornamentations to the fundamental. As such, harmonics give a distinctive character to a pitch, allowing the listener to distinguish among the different instruments or voices. As an example of a fundamental tone and its harmonics using the note C, when C is played, the sound one hears is that fundamental C with the addition of the note C an octave above, and then in ascending intervals G, C, E, G, B-flat, and C. All of these are in decreasing amplitude depending on the instrument producing the note (figure 2.4). Unless a tone is deliberately produced electronically without these upper partials, every tone heard is a combination of many tones with emphasis on the fundamental or tone name.

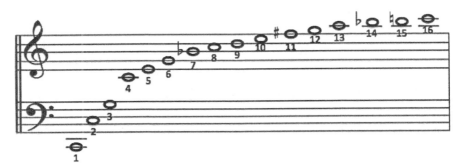

Figure 2.4.   Harmonic Series

Vibrations per second are commonly referred to as cycles per second (cps) or Hertz (Hz), named after the physicist Heinrich Hertz. The number of Hz refers to a number of complete cycles per second, and so 30 Hz means 30 cycles per second. Any given tone is the product of the number of vibrations or cycles which occur per second, e.g., A 440 is that tone which is produced by a sound generator producing 440 vibrations or cycles per second.

Pitch versus Tone versus Noise—Although noise is occasionally used in musical performance, pitch and tone are used most frequently. It is, therefore, necessary to understand those attributes of sound production which modify noise, converting it into pitch and tone.

Pitch refers to the highness or lowness of a tone. The notes of an ascending scale (do, re, mi, fa, sol, la, ti, do) go up in pitch. The pitches are successively higher. Conversely, in a descending scale (do, ti, la, sol, fa, mi, re, do) the notes go down in pitch and are successively lower. Any series of notes can take one of only three possible directions in pitch: they can ascend, descend, or remain the same.

Tone refers to the quality of the sound. Tone is a word that can be used in place of timbre, as both refer to the overall nature of a sound. The tone quality or timbre of an oboe differs significantly from that of a flute. An oboe, because of the multitude and strength of upper partials it produces, has a nasal penetrating sound. A flute tone with weaker upper partials is more pure and less aggressive.

Timbre is the product of the addition of harmonics to a fundamental sound. These additional sounds, called harmonics (see above), result from the inherent acoustical characteristics of the sound-producing mechanism, that is, the instrument producing the sound.

The difference in timbre that is sensed by the listener is the result of the strength (volume/amplitude) of the additional sounds (harmonics) and how they relate in volume to the fundamental. The greater the strength of the additional sounds, the more intense the timbre of the sound of the instrument. The less strong the additional sounds, the less intense the timbre.

Noise is sound that does not have a particularly audible pitch. One cannot sing a noise. It is a disorganized combination of frequencies.

Amplitude is a form of energy that refers to the volume or loudness of a sound. Greater amplitude produces louder sounds, whereas less amplitude produces softer sounds. Amplitude is one of the several physical components that goes into the total character of a musical tone. Amplitude is the force with which the sound is being produced. The more forceful the vibrations per second, the louder the sound. Conversely, the weaker the vibrations per second, the softer the sound.

Amplitude does not affect pitch. Any pitch can be produced at any amplitude and, therefore, can sound at any volume. As is the case with any force, there is a gradual decrease of the energy as it is confronted with resistance such as friction, absorption, or dispersion. With this gradual decline in energy, the tone will dissipate or fade away.

Summary—Sound occurs when a force excites vibrations in the atmosphere. When a tone is generated on a musical instrument, it is almost always accompanied by a series of related sounds or tones called harmonics, overtones, or upper partials. These secondary vibrations embellish the fundamental tone, giving it a distinctive sound quality or timbre.

The meaning of the following terms can sometimes be confused:

Amplitude refers to the volume of sound. Any sound can be produced at any volume without changing the nature of the sound.

Pitch denotes the highness or lowness of a sound.

Timbre or tone refers to the quality of a sound.

Noise is sound that does not have a particularly audible pitch. One cannot sing a noise. It is a disorganized combination of frequencies.

GLOSSARY OF TERMS RELATED TO SOUND PRODUCTION

The following glossary will help the reader define terms that are related to sound production. See the discussion above for more in-depth information on these items.

Amplitude A measure of the force of a vibration producing sound. Greater force (amplitude) produces louder sound, and less force (amplitude) produces softer sound.

Bow A curved stick fitted with horsehair or a substitute that is used to produce sound on instruments of the violin family.

Brass instrument A wind instrument (labrosone or lip reed) made of brass, which produces sound by the player blowing air and vibrating his or her lips into a cup-shaped mouthpiece.

Cup-shaped The concave shape of the mouthpiece used to produce sound on a brass instrument.

Cycle Vibrations per second that produce sound. One vibration is one cycle, and 440 cycles per second produces the note A4.

Double reed A combination of two reeds bound together to serve as a mouthpiece and sound generator on an oboe, bassoon, and other instruments in the woodwind family.

Embouchure The shape of one's lips, teeth, mouth, and facial muscles when combined to play a brass or woodwind instrument.

Fingerboard The upper surface of the neck on a string instrument. The player presses a string against the fingerboard at specific points to produce a particular note.

Fingerings The term used in music to address the pattern of fingers used to produce a given note on an instrument.

Flat shelf The shelf-like part of a woodwind instrument's mouthpiece, against which the player's breath strikes to produce a sound.

Frequency A measure of how often an event is repeated during a specific period of time. In music, frequency refers to the number of wave cycles per second.

Fret A thin strip of metal or other substance inserted into the fingerboard of a string instrument, dividing the fingerboard into half-tone segments.

Harmonics (overtones, upper partials) Embellishments of a fundamental tone. They are secondary vibrations occurring concurrently with a fundamental tone, and consist of successive multiples of the whole vibrating body. The segments occur as ½, ⅓, ¼, and so on of the original vibrating column and sound with less amplitude than the fundamental.

Hertz (Hz) A term named after physicist Heinrich Hertz, used interchangeably with cycles per second (cps).

Key The tonal center of gravity of a piece of music. That center is the product of the relationship of the notes to each other and the scale on which the piece is based.

Mechanical systems The keys and/or valves on a musical instrument that are used to change the instrument's fundamental pitch. On a string instrument, the mechanical system is the player's fingers.

Mouthpiece The part of a wind instrument that, in conjunction with the player's mouth, is used to produce the initial sound.

Noise Sound that does not have a particularly audible pitch. One cannot sing a noise. It is a disorganized combination of frequencies.

Non-fretted String instruments, such as those in the violin family, that do not have frets on their fingerboard.

Padded Soft pads on the keys that cover the tone holes in the body of woodwind instruments.

Percussion Instruments that are struck in some manner to produce sound.

Pitch The highness or lowness of a note.

Pluck Picking at a string as opposed to bowing it.

Range An individual's or an instrument's span of notes, from the lowest to the highest.

Ring keys Keys on a woodwind instrument that encircle a body tone hole but do not have a pad. The pad of the player's fingertip covers the ring and in so doing covers the tone hole.

Single reed An oblong, rectangular slice of bamboo attached to an instrument's mouthpiece as part of the sound generator for the instrument.

Valve A mechanical device in a cylindrical or rotary configuration on a brass instrument, used to direct the flow of air through the instrument.

Woodwind instruments Instruments such as a clarinet or saxophone that produce sound using a reed. Exceptions are the flute and recorder which are considered woodwind instruments but produce sound by the player blowing a stream of air across a hole in the head joint, the first section of the instrument (see flat shelf).

3

Non-fretted String Instruments Defined

String instruments are chordophones, instruments whose source of sound is vibrating strings. The four classifications of string instruments that produce sound in this manner are those that are played by plucking strings, by strumming more than one string at a time, by bowing strings, and by striking strings.

Plucked string instruments are played by plucking individual strings with the fingers as one does when playing a harp or with a plectrum (pick) on a guitar. A strumming technique, often used when playing a guitar, requires the player to pass the fingers or plectrum across several strings at once. Both of these techniques are interchangeable. The strings on all string instruments can be plucked or strummed.

Bowing is another method used to play chordophones. The instruments of the violin family, namely, the violin, viola, cello, and double bass, are bowed chordophones. The strings on these instruments are set into motion by the player passing a wooden bow strung with horsehair (there are man-made substitutes for both) across the strings. The plucking and strumming techniques can also be used on these instruments, but the reverse is not possible. The bodies of plucked and strummed instruments, like those of a guitar, do not provide a place for a bow to pass over the strings effectively.

Another type of chordophone is an instrument that produces sound by its strings being struck. An example of this is the piano, where the piano keys activate a mechanism that causes a felt-covered hammer to strike a string.

Since a vibrating string alone does not produce much sound, all string instruments must have some form of amplifier to increase volume. There is a specially fabricated wooden board on the back of upright pianos and the underside of grand pianos called a sounding board. When a string is struck by a hammer and set into motion, it produces a sound that travels to the sounding board where it is amplified and carried out to the listener.

The chordophones in the violin and guitar families have bodies of various shapes and sizes that act as their amplifiers. When a string is set into motion on one of these instruments, the sound travels via a bridge from the string to the instrument's body, which is set into motion, thereby amplifying the sound. More details on this are found in chapter 5.

GLOSSARY OF TERMS RELATED TO STRING INSTRUMENTS

This glossary will help the reader define terms that are related to string instruments. These terms are used for bowing directions. See the descriptions above for more in-depth information on these items. *Note:* The universal language for music is Italian; however, this does not preclude one using any other language to express musical terms. All musical terms to follow are Italian unless otherwise indicated.

Arco Use the bow to play the section.
Au talon (French) Play this passage at the frog end of the bow.
Avec le Bois (French) Use the bow stick in place of the bow hair to bow the string.
Collé (French) Use a light but clearly articulated short bow stroke. Attack the string from above, have a brief contact with the string, and then a clean release upward.
Col legno battuto Strike the string with the wooden bow stick using a bouncing motion.
Col legno tratto Use the bow stick in place of the bow hair to bow the string.
Détaché (French) Bow individually articulated notes smoothly with no pause between them.
Détaché lance (French) Bow individually articulated notes smoothly with a slight pause between them.
Flautando Direct the bowing pattern closer or slightly over the edge of the fingerboard. This will modify the sound to more closely resemble that of a flute. (See sul tasto below.)
Jeté (French) Throw the bow across the string to make it bounce, producing a series of short notes similar to skipping a rock across water.
Legato Use a smooth bowing motion with no articulation between notes except for the change in pitch.
Marcato Use a strongly articulated bold stroke.
Martelé (French) Use an aggressive, accented attack to the note with an immediate release.
Martellato Use an aggressive, accented attack to the note with immediate release.
Pizzicato Pluck the string.
Ponticello Direct the bowing close to the bridge to produce a more aggressive sound. See Sul ponticello below.
Punta d'arco Direct the bowing to the tip of the bow to produce a less aggressive sound.

Ricochet (French) Bounce the bow off the string in a succession of notes.

Sautillé (French) Use a light, resilient bow stroke bouncing across the string.

Spiccato Use a bouncing bow stroke across the string to produce very short separated notes

Staccato Produce a short note using any of the "separated note" techniques listed.

Sul Italian for "on." It is also used to indicate "near," as in sul ponticello. The Italian word for near is actually *vecino*.

Sul ponticello Bow near the bridge to produce a more aggressive sound.

Sul tasto Bow over or near the fingerboard in order to modify the sound.

Tasto The fingerboard.

Tremolo Play the same note repeatedly by moving the bow back and forth rapidly with a wrist motion.

4

The History of Non-fretted String Instruments

THE FIRST STRING INSTRUMENTS

The history of musical instruments has been investigated by some of the greatest minds in musicology and academia with results mired in conflicting opinions, contradictory factoids, and a general disarray and confusion of information. For this reason the subject is presented using a simple survey form based on the various points of view on each topic. In many cases the "experts" themselves qualify their findings with a disclaimer similar to this one.

The survey begins with the history of "non-bowed, plucked or strummed string instruments" and gives an overview of what probably happened to result in the evolution of the violin family instruments we now use.

Plucked Instruments—Musical instruments have been in existence in various forms for millennia. One might speculate that several thousand years B.C., someone set a single taut string in motion and it generated a sound. That action would have been the first step in the evolution of string instruments. The four classifications of string instruments that developed from that fundamental experience are described in the previous chapter. These are played by plucking, strumming, bowing, or striking strings

Evidence of the existence of non-bowed string instruments dates as far back as 2500 B.C. in Mesopotamia (Iraq). Among those instruments were lyres, lutes, zithers, kanteles, and psalteries. These plucked string instruments were primarily used as accompaniment for vocal solos and oral presentations of poetry and prose (figure 4.1).

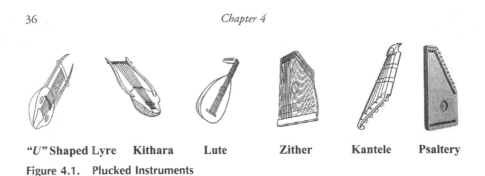

"U" Shaped Lyre   Kithara   Lute   Zither   Kantele   Psaltery

Figure 4.1.   Plucked Instruments

Lyre—The term *lyre* is applied to a wide spectrum of instruments with strings. Dictionary definitions of lyre range from a U-shaped instrument with strings that are plucked, to a category of early medieval bowed instruments. The consistency of inconsistency often rears its ugly head in matters of the music world.

The early instruments that fall into the U-shaped, plucked lyre category had a basic structure consisting of a hollow base at the bottom of the instrument, which acted as a resonating chamber. Two arms, one attached on either side of the chamber to form the "U" shape, were connected at the top by a bar that served as a structural support for the instrument.

The strings, usually gut, were attached to the top connecting bar, extended down over a bridge, and were attached at the bottom resonating chamber. In some instruments the strings were connected directly to the bridge whereas on others the strings went over the bridge, continuing on to a tailpiece.

The different pitches of the strings of the U-shaped lyre were achieved by increased thickness for the lower notes or by adjusting the tension of the strings. This basic lyre structure appeared to be the foundation for the myriad versions of plucked string instruments that appeared in ancient Persia, Greece, and Rome. Some of these instruments eventually became the Spanish guitar.

Illustrations from various art forms show seven-string instruments being held with the left hand and plucked with the right hand. Other later examples show similar instruments with as few as four and as many as ten strings. Since very few actual instruments have survived or have been discovered thus far, conclusions regarding their design and the manner in which they were played continue to be based on speculation and observations of the artwork from the period under study.

Kithara—The kithara is one of the early instruments that meets the requirements for inclusion in the lyre category. The kithara had the basic lyre structure of a resonating chamber, side arms, and strings attached to a crossbar on top. The strings passed over a bridge and were attached to a violin-like tailpiece as opposed to being attached directly to the instrument's base. The player used a plectrum to pluck the strings. The kithara was used as an accompaniment to recitations of prose, poetry, vocal performances, and dancing.

Lute—The lute differs from the U-shaped lyre category of instruments in that its basic structure is similar to that of the violin with some variants and with an entirely different appearance. Starting at the top, the lute has a peg box with tuning pegs to which strings are connected. The peg box in earlier lutes was bent back at a significant angle. The peg box was followed by a nut, a fretted fingerboard, and a bridge to which the gut strings were directly attached. The frets were made by tying gut around the fingerboard. Wooden frets were sometimes strategically located to aid in shifting registers.

The body of the lute was pear-shaped with the back built of wooden strips, as opposed to the violin back which is either one piece or two at most. The top of the lute was made of one piece but with only one tone hole, called a rose, in the center of the top.

Zither—Zither is a label applied to string instruments that share a structure in which all the strings are extended across a sound board. Zithers were designed to be played on a flat surface or on the player's lap; these instruments varied greatly in size and shape but generally took the form of an elongated hollow box. Zithers could range in size from approximately a square foot up to three square feet.

Unlike more contemporary instruments such as the violin or guitar, the variety of shapes and sizes of instruments called zithers, which have evolved throughout the centuries, is so remarkably abundant and racked with conflicting data and opinion that it is not possible to chronicle this instrument's evolution. Some attribute the popularity of these instruments to their acoustic simplicity, since constructing one originally required little more than basic cabinet maker skills and a musical inclination.

Zithers can be found built with three configurations. In one arrangement the instrument does not have a neck or frets so there is no opportunity for the player to adjust the pitch while playing a given string. The strings can be plucked or strummed like those of the guitar, but each string can produce only the pitch to which it is tuned.

In another design there is a fretted fingerboard with about five strings that run parallel to the soundboard, which contains the remaining strings. The five strings are used to play the melody while the remaining strings can be strummed or plucked as accompanying figures.

The bowed zither deviates from the common box-shaped instrument to provide a structure where a bow can pass over strings. This modification was accomplished by changing the shape of the sounding body to either a triangle, violin shape, or some other configuration that would allow a bow to pass over the strings.

Kantele—The kantele is considered to be one of the earliest of the plucked zither family instruments. Its origins date back several thousand years to the Baltic countries, where references to the instrument can be found in Finnish literature of that period. Following the pattern of its cousins, the kantele was not used as a solo instrument but rather as an accompaniment to prose and vocal performances.

By virtue of its design and prescribed playing technique, the kantele falls into the category of the zither family. The instrument had a hollow wooden body which acted as a sound resonator over which five horsehair or gut strings were stretched. They were joined to tuning pins at one end and to a crossbar at the other end. The absence of a bridge or nut resulted in the distinctive bell-like sound associated with that instrument.

The strings were tuned to either a major or minor diatonic scale (see chapter 16). The kantele was placed on a flat surface or on the player's lap, where it could be strummed or plucked with the fingers or a plectrum. When played with the fingers, it was possible to produce both melody and accompaniment by judiciously assigning each finger to a particular string. Most music played on the early kantele was improvised rather than prescribed.

Psaltery—The psaltery is another version of a zither with a series of pre-tuned strings attached at the top and bottom of a soundboard. The pitch for each string was a product of its length; therefore, higher-pitched strings were shorter and lower pitches were longer. To accommodate for this arrangement, the sounding board body of the psaltery had to assume a trapezoidal shape.

At some point it became apparent that a sound produced by rubbing a tacky stick or chord across a string would produce a sustained richer sound than that produced by plucking the string. And so appeared the bowed psaltery. This triangle-shaped instrument was developed with a string pattern that would facilitate the process of a bow being applied to one string at a time.

Summary—Among the early images of non-bowed string instruments is ornamentation on a sarcophagus in Crete dated 1400 B.C. Numerous other examples are to be found in all forms of art throughout the centuries to follow. The wide variety of shapes and iterations seen in these illustrations can be thought-provoking while confusing, since it becomes difficult to separate accuracy and fact from artistic license and imagination. One must wonder how much of what is evidenced in art from the past actually did exist.

The number and variety of plucked and strummed string instruments that preceded the appearance of the first bowed string instruments are as great and diverse as to make documenting their evolution with any degree of accuracy almost impossible. The most dedicated organologists (musicologists who specialize in the study of musical instruments) can, at best, compile a treatise on the instruments from those millennia based mostly on speculation and deduction.

EARLY BOWED INSTRUMENTS

This period also shares the same dearth of specific documentation concerning the history of bowed instruments. The absence of facts continued up to the beginning of the sixteenth century, when the history of musical instruments began to be recorded.

Prior to that, one has to rely on literature and poetry on other subjects that contained references to string instruments, because few actual early instruments have survived. The texts from these writings indicate that instruments with strings that were both bowed and plucked did exist. More graphic examples are found in the paintings and statues from the early centuries showing the instruments being played.

Numerous music-producing devices with a body of some sort, either containing a fingerboard or connected to a type of fingerboard with a peg box and strung with tunable strings, began to appear at about 900 A.D. These instruments functioned in a manner similar to that of modern non-fretted string instruments and so might logically be considered to be their predecessors (figure 4.2). Because the evidence is scattered and lacking in valid source material, it is not possible to trace the "invention" of the instruments of the violin family back to a particular point in time. Among the most likely forerunners of the viola and violin were respectively the rebab, spike fiddle, rebec, vielle, viola da braccio, and viola da gamba. The cello and double bass then followed as an outgrowth of the viola and violin.

Rebab Spike Fiddle   Rebec   Vielle   Viola da Braccio Viola da Gamba

Figure 4.2.   Bowed Instruments

Rebab—The Arabic word rebab refers to a bowed string instrument. The rebab was usually constructed with a pear-shaped body that was hollowed out from a block of wood. A thin sheet of wood or animal hide was then attached to the hollowed-out section to act as a top. Unlike the modern violin, the fingerboard was constructed as part of the body instead of as a separate piece attached to the instrument.

Rebabs are generally thought to have had two strings, though one will find references to some models with three strings. The rebab was played with a bow and was used both as a solo instrument and as accompaniment to dialogue and song. As far back as the eighth century, the rebab was being played in North Africa, the Middle East, and in Europe. Its widespread popularity can be attributed to the simplicity of design, portability, and playability. Rebabs circulated throughout the Islamic trade routes of the time.

Spike Fiddle—Another form of rebab, a spike fiddle, was constructed with a round body. The neck on this instrument supported the strings and consisted of a rounded pole that extended down through the body to form an endpin. The player held the spike fiddle upright, resting it on the ground like a cello or on the player's lap.

Rebec—The rebec, which has a body, fingerboard, and tuning pegs similar to those of the rebab, may be an expansion of that instrument. A significant difference between the two is found in the body of the rebec, which was created from a gourd or fabricated gourd shape instead of being carved from a solid piece of wood as was the rebab.

The body of the rebec was boat-shaped, and the fingerboard with its tuning pegs was a separate entity attached to the body as compared to the rebab fingerboard being part of the body. The rebec originally had two strings, similar to the rebab, with a third string added later on. This instrument enjoyed its popularity in Europe during the fifteenth and sixteenth centuries.

Vielle—The vielle appeared somewhat earlier in France during the Medieval period from the thirteenth to the fifteenth century. This instrument was closer in design to the modern violin. Rather than having a gourd-shaped body, as did the rebab and rebec, the vielle's body was constructed with an upper and lower bout and a narrower mid-section which allowed a player to use a bow more easily.

The body of the vielle was larger than that of the modern violin in both length and depth. The peg box was flat, with the pegs protruding from the top. The vielle had five strings as compared to the two and three strings of the rebab and the rebec. The vielle was most widely used by troubadours who were writers of poetry and music of the period. The instrument eventually found its way into all levels of society, from the intellectual elite to the common man. Currently, attempts to recreate these instruments are under way by luthiers, who are taking their clues from stone carvings and ancient paintings.

THE BEGINNING OF THE VIOLIN FAMILY

Lira da Braccio—*Note:* One will find reference to this instrument as lira da braccio, di braccio, and da braccia. Correct Italian grammar would dictate that the word braccio be preceded by the preposition di, or braccia, by da. This is just one example of the inconsistencies one will come across in researching the history of instruments of the violin family.

Following the vielle in the evolution of bowed string instruments was the lira da braccio (of the arm) which first appeared in Italy. This was a bowed string instrument more closely resembling a violin, but with a wider fingerboard. The lira da braccio could have as many as seven strings. Four over a fingerboard were tuned to E, A, D, and G, as are the strings of a violin. An additional low D string was also placed over the fingerboard, and two other strings ran parallel to the fingerboard. These two strings, tuned in octaves, were played as drones or pedal tones. The tuning pegs on the lira da braccio were installed on the top of a flat leaf-shaped peg box instead of on the sides of a hollowed-out peg box as found on contemporary instruments.

Scholars have deduced that the upper strings of the lira da braccio were used to play the melody while chords using triple and quadruple stops (notes played on different strings simultaneously) were played on the lower strings. The technique needed to play tones simultaneously limited the performer in both versatility and in the use of harmonic inversions. These limitations led performers to migrate eventually toward the Andrea Amati violin for its sweet sound and for all of the versatility that we know is possible when a violin is played by a well-trained musician.

Considering all of the history outlined above, one may conclude that the instruments we know today are more a culmination of a multi-century evolution of plucked and bowed stringed instruments than actual inventions. It is not possible to name an "inventor" of the violin as we know it today; however, the two names that appear as most likely candidates for the title are Andrea Amati and Gasparo da Salo. It was during their productive years that recorded history began to appear. The records documented to some degree the biographies and instruments of prominent luthiers of the time.

The records from that period show a growing number of luthiers from every part of Europe. These artisans advanced the development of the four string instruments of the violin family in many directions. Unfortunately, the problem is no longer one of insufficient documentation, but rather of a tsunami of somewhat loosely connected anecdotal evidence describing the works of all these individuals, their biographies, and their contributions. Supporting that written history are some of the actual instruments still in existence that were made by those luthiers.

The First Violin?—Gasparo di Bertolotti da Salo (Gasparo da Salo) of Brescia (ca.1540–1609) and Andrea Amati of Cremona (ca.1525–1611) were luthiers who are considered to be makers of the first violin. There is some confusion with respect to who holds that title because the records show that Amati was known as a "lute maker" as opposed to a "violin maker." Those on the Amati side justify his position by saying that the term "violin" was still in its infancy, not known to many and, therefore, not applied to Amati. There are recorded documents showing that Amati sold twenty-four violins to King Charles IX of France in 1560. Fourteen of these are still in existence. On the basis of that fact, one could then justifiably conclude that Amati was, indeed, a violin maker. What is generally accepted is that both men made significant contributions to the original design of the violin we use today.

The evolution of musical instrument technology and an increasing demand by contemporary composers for more versatility and tone projection from string instruments has prompted some changes to be made to the neck, fingerboard, sound post, and bass bar of the existing so-called "Baroque" or original instruments of the sixteenth and seventeenth centuries. The higher-tension strings that were developed in later years to increase volume and improve tone production required the instruments to have a longer neck with a slightly elevated angle of projection for the fingerboard. This change also called for a heavier bass bar and sound post to conduct that additional sound throughout the instrument. As a result, almost all surviving instruments from that period have been subjected to those changes.

THE SCHOOLS

The word *school* will most often bring to mind a structure in which groups of children and others receive some form of education. A lesser-known definition refers to a location consisting of a broader geographic area where, over a period of time, a group of individuals with a common interest live and work in close proximity. Their goal would be to develop their skills and broaden their knowledge to advance their cause. Such was the case with luthiers from the mid-1500s to about 1725. During that period the violin, viola, cello, and double bass were developed and refined to the extraordinarily high degree of perfection we enjoy today.

Over a period of some 200 years, a number of such schools appeared throughout Europe. Among them were the Brescian, Cremonese, Neapolitan, Tyrolean, and French schools, each named for its geographic location. Their inhabitants distinguished themselves by making significant contributions to the development of the instruments of the violin family.

Cremonese School—Andrea Amati (1525–1611) was the principal figure in the Cremonese school of violin making. His early works consisted of rebecs and other string instruments that preceded the violin. At this point in time, historians begin to see actual documentation showing the development of the instruments of the string family. Amati and his contemporaries were commissioned by royalty, among them King Charles IX of France, and wealthy aristocrats such as the Medici family to make a variety of instruments for use in the courts and at lavish gatherings. During this period the violin began to take hold as the instrument of choice and, consequently, the art of making string instruments began to flourish.

The Amati family consisted of Andrea, Antonio, Girolamo, Nicolo, and Girolamo II, all of whom carried on the Amati tradition of making extraordinary string instruments up to 1740. Their gift to the music world endures in their instruments that have survived, along with the improvements and innovations they made that are still in use today.

Nicolo, Andrea's grandson, served as teacher to many of the master luthiers of that period. Andrea's sons, Girolamo, Antonio, along with Nicolo and Andrea's nephews, devoted some of their luthier skills to the development of the double bass. Unfortunately, interest in this large instrument waned because of its size and the amount of wood and labor needed to produce one. Other contemporaries of the Amati family were Jacob Stainer, later to join the Tyrolean School, Antonio Stradivari and his two sons, Francesco and Omobono, and the five members of the Guarneri family including Andrea, Pietro, Giuseppe, Giuseppe del Gesu, and Pietro de Venice.

Francesco Ruggieri (1620–1695) is said to have been Nicolo Amati's first pupil. After a shorter than usual apprenticeship, Ruggieri proceeded on his own to make violins in the pattern he learned under the Amati family. Ruggieri is recognized for developing a more refined pattern for the cello. This instrument was very well received for its smaller size and became a model for future cello makers.

Antonio Stradivari (1644–1737) was independently wealthy, allowing him the liberty to experiment and develop his craftsmanship as he wished. Stradivari's productive life, which was, in fact, almost every day of his life, can be divided into three periods. The first was the Amati period from 1668 to 1686, where his instruments manifested the Amati pattern with some modifications. This period was followed by a span of about eight years where Stradivari's longer and narrower instruments took on a more sophisticated elegance. During these years he developed a different, lighter varnish evident on those instruments. It was not until his last period from 1695 on to the end of his life that Stradivari's instruments reached the magnificence of tone production and physical perfection for which he has been lauded for centuries. Some suggest that the instruments he made after 1725, when he was in his eighties, show a decline in workmanship. In his lifetime Antonio Stradivari made upward of 1000 instruments.

Carlo Bergonzi (1683–1747), also from the Cremonese School, ranks in skill as a luthier just a shade below Stradivari. A neighbor and then student of Stradivari, Bergonzi was able to refine his talents as a violin maker to the point where he became Stradivari's repair technician. Bergonzi was so highly regarded in this role that his repair business prevented him from making many violins. His luthier skills are most admired for the extraordinary degree of perfection and the balance of form he was able to achieve in the construction of his instruments. Most notable was the perfectly symmetrical elegance of his scrolls.

Brescian School—Located at the base of the Alps in the Lombardy region of northern Italy, Brescia began to grow as a center for master luthiers with the work of Gasparo da Salo in the mid-1500s. In this luthier's mecca, the violin, viola, cello, and double bass were conceived and developed from their predecessors, the viola da braccia, viola da gamba, and the many other viols that had evolved up to that time. These older instruments served as models from which the luthiers developed the four instruments of the violin family. This is not to say that the process was premeditated or by design. Rather, it was a natural outgrowth of the need to provide musicians with instruments that would cover the soprano, alto, tenor, and bass range of the human voice. One can also find in the documented history of Brescia the first reference to the word violin (violino), the diminutive of viola.

The two best-known names from the Brescian School are Gasparo di Bertolotti, a.k.a. Gasparo da Salo (1542–1609), and Giovanni Maggini (1580–1630). These two master luthiers contributed significantly to the music world with their individualism and experimental creativity. Gasparo di Bertolotti was born in Salo, a town in Italy, and so came the name Gasparo da Salo. During his tenure he developed the longer-shape violin that produced the more strident sound needed to hold a position in the brass-oriented ensembles of that time. This elongated shape was to be the model Stradivari used for his instruments.

Da Salo was prolific in his output, not only in his violin making but also in producing different size violins and violas which were intended to play in the alto and tenor range. These included violas da gamba, cellos, double basses, and other assorted, lesser-known instruments of the string family of that period. The luthiers of the Brescian School were held in highest esteem until the onset of the plague, which decimated that population.

A contemporary of da Salo was Giovanni Paolo Maggini. Born in nearby Botticino, Maggini studied at a young age as an apprentice with da Salo and remained in that position until his early twenties. Contrary to his master's violin designs, Maggini developed a pattern featuring a larger configuration with larger sound holes and a lower arching top. His earlier works are considered by some to lack the finesse of those made by the other masters of that time; however, his proclivity to experiment with sound production ultimately resulted in instruments of outstanding quality in the materials they contain, the high degree of artistry in ornamentation, and in the mellifluous sound they produce. He made about seventy-five instruments, mostly violins and violas, two cellos, and what might possibly be one of the first double basses.

Neapolitan School—The Cremonese School of violin making began to diminish in importance as a result of the decline in the economy, the plague, and many years of war and political strife. Concurrently, in the south of Italy, the area of Naples was growing economically and culturally. That expansion fostered an increasing demand for musical instruments, which resulted in the growth of the Neapolitan School of violin making. It was in that area, from the late 1600s for a period of about 120 years, that a new crop of master luthiers came together geographically and professionally to produce a series of extraordinary instruments.

Alessandro Gagliano (1640–1725) was the head of a family of luthiers that, over a period of almost 300 years, provided a direct line from the Cremonese School, where he studied, up to the twentieth century. The Gagliano family closed shop in 1925. Born to an aristocratic family, Alessandro had little formal training, developing his skills as a luthier independently. As a result, his workmanship lacked the finesse of his contemporaries, but he did distinguish himself with his cellos. These were regarded by many as being distinctive in both design and tone production. He is also lauded for the varnish he developed, which showed new clarity and depth with a distinctive crimson hue. It is generally accepted by the *cognoscenti* that his varnish is equal to if not better than that of the Cremonese masters.

Unlike Alessandro, his sons and brothers chose to follow the elongated pattern for instruments established by Stradivari. This change then became the norm for most instruments made by luthiers of the Neapolitan School. Alessandro's sons, Nicolo and Gennaro, are considered to have produced the best work of the entire Gagliano family.

Tyrolean School—Parallel in time with the above masters was the Tyrolean School, where Jacob Stainer (1620–1683) reigned as primo luthier. Stainer, a student of Nicolo Amati, developed a somewhat different design for his instruments that featured a much higher arch on the top and back than those of the Stradivari models. Stainer was also noted for his unique scrolls, which often featured carved heads in place of the traditional scroll shape.

A contemporary of Stainer was Matthias Klotz (1656–1743). Klotz studied with Stainer and Giovanni Railich in Padua, Italy. The results were instruments that contained the characteristics of both of these masters. Klotz finally settled in Mittenwald, Germany, where he used his entrepreneurial skills to develop a complete violin industry. Like that of the Gagliano family, Klotz's business also became the family business, producing many instruments that are still available today.

French School—Nicolas Lupot (1784–1824), born in Stuttgart, Germany, studied under his father, François, in Orleans, France. Nicholas reached his prime by his mid-twenties and was most noted for copying the Stradivari design as well as designs of other masters. Nicolas did not distinguish himself so much for his originality but rather for the delicate refinement he added to the patterns of others. He was ranked by many as the master luthier of the French School. King Louis XVIII placed an order with Nicolas for an entire orchestra of elaborately decorated string instruments. Unfortunately, Lupot died before the project was completed.

Keeping with the concept of copying the work of others rather than trying to create his own distinct pattern was Jean-Baptiste Vuillaume (1798–1875). He is to this day still recognized as being able to recreate the styles and varnishes of the master luthiers of the past with extraordinary accuracy. His copies of Stradivari violins were so perfect that some of the current appraisers are still unsure when they attempt to identify a Stradivari instrument if, in fact, it may have been one of the copies made by Vuillaume.

Jean-Baptiste was also an entrepreneur. In 1828 he started his own business, where he marketed his reproductions along with other high-quality instruments. He expanded his business by employing other craftsmen to make bows, resulting in the growth of some of the finest French bow makers of that period.

Summary—The "schools" of violin making mentioned above are only some of many that came into being throughout Europe beginning in the sixteenth century. Venice and Absam (Austria), along with other lesser known clusters of luthiers on every level, served as embryos that gave birth to an entire family of musical instruments that have served and will continue to serve humanity for centuries to come.

THE HISTORY OF BOWS

The concept of generating vibrations by rubbing something against a taut string was the exercise that probably resulted in the very earliest bows being created. That "something" could have been some sort of reed or stick with a surface rough enough to generate vibrations. Evidence of chords and hair tied or connected in various ways to bow-shaped sticks appears in drawings dating as far back as the eighth century. That configuration would allow the chords or hairs to have free contact with a string on an instrument and, when rubbed against the string, produce a vibration (sound). Drawings of bows can be found with every conceivable arc shape imaginable. The only recurring theme is that they were all designed with a curved stick that would accommodate some form of chord-like material or hair.

The lack of source information available to document the early history of instruments of the violin family is even greater for the bows used to play those instruments. A study of sculpture and paintings from the past gives some hint as to the size, shape, structure, and playing positions for instruments from a given period, but those same artworks give short shrift to the bow. One might speculate that the artists either did not know the important role bows played in sound production, or that in the totality of the art work, the bow was in their minds not significant enough to warrant detailed attention.

Those who write on this subject will justifiably hedge on the time of the appearance of the first bows, often referring to the tenth century in central Asia as a starting point where bowed string instruments began to appear. That time frame is one of speculation and not necessarily fact. One begins to see a shape closer to that of the modern bow in the drawings that were made in the seventeenth century. Unfortunately, there is no indication of the exact date when these drawings were made, so they cannot be used by musical instrument historians to deduce the sequence of bow development. It is therefore possible that a more sophisticated bow could have preceded the rendering of a less advanced model.

Beginning in the early Baroque period, a variety of bow designs began to appear as a result of the requirements of a changing style of music composition. Before the appearance of the violin, string instruments were primarily used as backgrounds to musical themes. Consequently, their contribution to an ensemble consisted mainly of rhythmic patterns rather than of melody. Producing rhythmic patterns required a less sophisticated bow and as a result the bows were shorter and had a wider arc designed for the player to use with an underhanded grip. There are some contemporary bow makers who specialize in making bows in the patterns used in ancient times. The work of these archetiers is the best source for examples and information on this part of musical instrument history.

In mid-seventeenth century Italy the music began to emphasize a lyrical, bel canto (see chapter 18) style that motivated the Italian musicians to gravitate toward using the more flexible, graceful overhand bow grip. This hand position, in conjunction with a longer, better balanced bow, facilitated greater control by the player. With that control came an expansion of the bowing techniques needed to execute all of the stylistic techniques ranging from a very smooth sensitive tone production to the crisp articulation associated with spiccato bowing. The sticks became straighter, and tended toward the present-day camber. The bows became lighter and better balanced, and the mechanism to control the tension of the hair more refined.

It was during this period that an extensive variety of bows was produced with different designs that provided the tools for experimentation. This process eventually led to the classic model bow now known to the music world. The operative word here is "eventually," for there would be yet another period of bow making during which experimentation driven by musical needs continued to motivate makers to further perfect their product.

Composers were widening their musical horizons to include a broader spectrum of solo and larger ensemble music. Expanding the instrumentation and intensity of the music gave rise to numerous bowing techniques needed to satisfy those musical needs. This, in turn, motivated the bow makers to further refine their products. It was at that time that the metal underslide was added to the space between the frog (the wooden block at the end where the bow is held) and the stick, and the tip and frog began to take on the characteristics that are familiar to us today.

During this period a man considered to be the Stradivari of bow making, François Xavier Tourte (1747–1835), began his training as a luthier with his father, Nicolas Pierre (1700–1765). In addition to carrying out his duties as a luthier, Francois began to improve the bow. After his father's demise, Tourte joined with G. B. Viotti, a violin virtuoso, in a successful effort to improve the design of the bow by restructuring the balance, increasing the weight of the frog and tip, and altering the bow's length. Tourte refined the process for creating the camber in the bow stick by using heat instead of the carving method commonly used at the time. Of profound significance was the invention of the moveable frog through the use of the screw-and-eye mechanism that is currently in use on virtually every bow made today.

In addition to these inventions and improvements was Tourte's innovation to spread the hairs at the frog through the use of a wedge of wood inserted between the hair and a metal band called the ferrule. As currently seen in bows, this small but very important addition resulted in the individual hairs being firmly held parallel to one another rather than clumping.

Tourte's obsession with perfection resulted in his destroying any bow made in his shop that, in his judgment, was not perfect. One might speculate that although this level of perfection resulted in the magnificent bows we all know, this behavior also was responsible for the possible loss of some extraordinary bows that, although in his eyes not perfect enough to enjoy life, would probably serve the music community as splendid tools of the trade. His bow design became the archetype for all the prominent bow makers to follow.

Tourte's redesigning of the balance and structure of the bow stick, along with his mechanical innovations with the frog, not only improved the bow as a tool but also actually changed the sound of the instruments on which these bows are used. For any string instrument the bow is a significant partner in the sound-producing elements, not only in terms of the physics of the sound, but also as the primary tool the performer uses to play the instrument. With the exception of pizzicato (plucked) playing, the player controls every nuance of every note played through the use of the bow. Dynamics, timbre, articulation, volume, phrasing, and all the subtleties of sound production are the result of a partnership among the bow, the player, and the instrument. Due to this confluence, one might safely say that Tourte's contributions to bow design revolutionized the acoustics of all bowed string instruments.

The three most renowned bow makers to follow Tourte were Ludwig Bausch (1805–1871), Francois Voirin (1833–1885), and Eugene Sartory (1871–1946). These names are frequently found on contemporary bows, just as one can find the name Stradivari on labels of violins not made by him. Such labels are more an indication of style than of origin.

Summary—In response to the original question, "Where did the instruments of the violin family come from?" the short answer must be that there were too many people in too many places doing too many things over too many years to allow any kind of definitive comprehensive statement that could be considered valid. The rebab, rebec, vielle, viola da gamba, and viola da braccia, along with all of the secondary experimental instruments that came and went over the centuries, paved the way for luthiers to settle on the violin, viola, cello, and double bass. These four instruments were most suitable for satisfying the musical needs of performers by providing a complete range of pitches with timbres that were both harmonious and complementary to each other. These basic instrument designs also permitted a performer to exercise technique and musicianship with reasonable facility.

A safe assumption would be that the viola came first, was refined into a violin, expanded into a cello, and then grew into a double bass. When did this happen, and who did it? This author has yet to find any specific history that is not modified by some other specific history that tells the story in a slightly different way. The bottom line has to be that many people developed these instruments over a long period of time in different places using original ideas in many different ways. The good news is that we now have all four of these wonderful instruments that will be available to enjoy for centuries to come.

5

How Non-fretted String Instruments Work

THE VIOLIN FAMILY

The four instruments of the violin family (figure 5.1), the violin (1), viola (2), cello (3), and double bass (4), are very similar in their design, acoustics, and construction and share many playing techniques and fingering patterns.

Using the violin in figure 5.2 as an example, these instruments function as follows: The mechanism that supports the strings consists of the scroll (A), peg box (B), pegs (C), neck (D), fingerboard (E), bridge (F), saddle (G), tailpiece (H), tailgut (I), and end button (J). The body of the instrument is made up of a top (belly) (K), f holes

1. Violin   2. Viola   3. Cello   4. Double Bass

Figure 5.1.   Violin Family

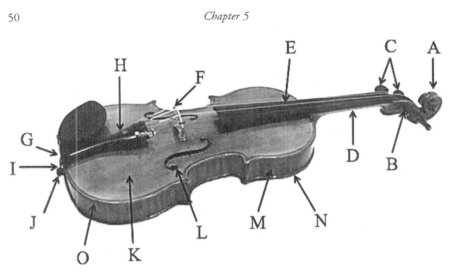

Chapter 5

Figure 5.2. Violin Parts

(L), sides (ribs or bouts) (M), a back (back plate) (N), and purfling (O) surrounding the top and back plates. These parts form the exterior of the body.

Inside the instrument (figure 5.3), supporting the exterior of the instrument are the ribs (A), top and bottom block (B), corner blocks (C), bass bar (D), and sound post (E).

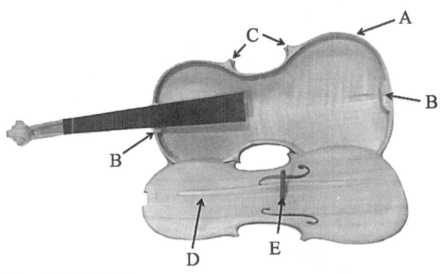

Figure 5.3. Violin Interior

How They Work—Using figure 5.4 as a guide, when a string (1) is set into motion, its vibration is conducted by the bridge (2) to the top of the instrument (3), transferred via the sound post (4) to the back (5), and distributed laterally throughout the

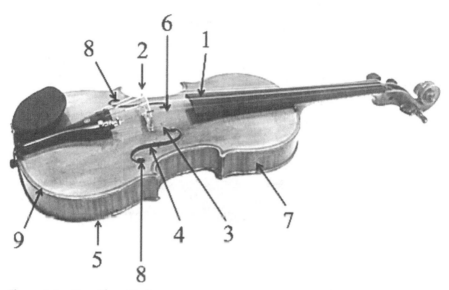

Figure 5.4. How They Work

top by the bass bar (6). The top and back are supported by the sides or bouts (7). The combined motion of these parts sets the air contained within the body of the instrument into a pumping motion that forces the resonating sound out of the instrument through the f holes (8). The purfling (9) controls the vibration of sound throughout the top and back while reinforcing the structure of those two parts of the instrument.

The Bow—Violin, viola, cello, and double bass bows are also very similar in design, construction, and in how they are used (figure 5.5). The differences are in their size and in the shape of their frogs, the end of the bow where it is held.

A violin bow frog is squared off at the back (A). A viola bow is slightly larger in all dimensions and has a rounded edge on the back of its frog (B). A cello bow is still larger than the viola bow in all dimensions, and also has a rounded edge on the back of the frog (C). The double bass uses two different types of bows, called the French style and the German style. The French bass bow (D) has the same design as that of the viola and cello, but is much larger. The German bass bow (E) sports a grip-type frog and is held in the palm of the hand with the fingers on the top, through the middle, and on the bottom of the frog.

A bow whose stick is made of pernambuco wood and strung with horsehair is the bow of choice. Pernambuco is a hardwood native to Brazil and the wood of choice for bows. A more cost-effective and practical choice for beginning students is a bow made with a fiberglass stick and fiberglass hair or horsehair. Fiberglass bows are much less expensive, very durable, and are considered by most teachers of beginning students to be a very adequate substitute for the more expensive wood with horsehair combination.

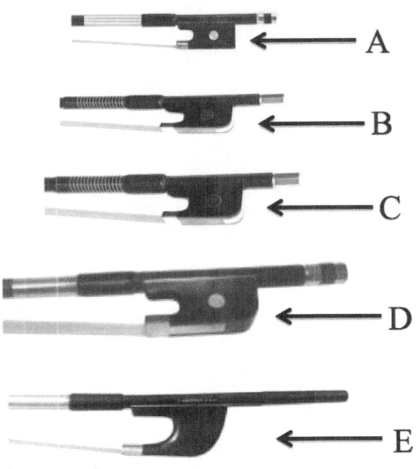

Figure 5.5.　Bow Frogs

About Horsehair—When viewed with the naked eye, horsehair appears to be smooth, but under examination with a microscope, the surface of the hair is quite rough. Particles called follicles project from the hair and form an abrasive surface. Rosin, a tree sap derivative, is applied to bow hair to increase its gripping power.

When a rosined bow hair is drawn across a string on an instrument, the hair grips the string and excites it into motion, causing the vibration that produces a tone. As the bow is drawn across a string, the bow hair appears to be in constant contact with the string; however, this is not the case. Instead, what is occurring is the bow hair gripping and releasing the string in a rapid sequence, replicating a plucking action. This action causes the string to be drawn to a point where its lateral tension is sufficient to overcome the gripping force of the rosined bow hair. When the string reaches that point, it releases itself from the bow and returns to cross its point of origin, proceeds to its opposite lateral extreme, only to be gripped again by the bow hair and then to repeat the process (figure 5.6).

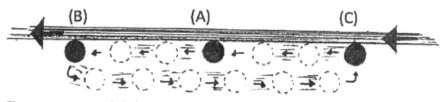

Figure 5.6.   Bow Hair String Contact

The final effect is one of a string gripped (A) by the bow hair, pulled to a point of tension (B), breaking free from that grip and rebounding to a point opposite that from which it was just released (C), and then being caught again by the bow hair to start the process again. All of this occurs in such rapid succession that it is invisible to the naked eye.

Tuning—The violin, viola, and cello all have wedge-shaped wooden pegs that are forced into holes in the peg box (figure 5.2B). These instruments are tuned by turning the peg in the direction needed while simultaneously pushing it in so that it is forced into the holes of the peg box. If the peg is not forced into the peg holes, the peg will not hold the string in tune. Further adjustment can be made in small degrees by tightening or loosening a fine tuning device located on the tailpiece.

Because of the greater thickness of double bass strings, a worm-and-gear system is used on that instrument to tune and maintain accurate intonation. This system merely requires turning the peg in the direction needed, with no pushing action.

Open Strings—In order to facilitate identifying the pitch of a note written with a letter name in a text, a system of numbers is used that establishes middle C as C4 (see scientific pitch notation in chapter 16). All the notes ascending from C4 up to the next octave will have the number 4 after them. The note C one octave above C4 is numbered C5. The note C below C4 is C3. All the notes between the Cs carry the number corresponding to the C below the subject note.

The strings on the violin, viola, and cello are tuned in intervals of a fifth (see chapter 16). The double bass is tuned in fourths. Starting from the lowest string, the instruments are tuned as follows:

The violin—G3, D4, A4, E5
The viola—C3, G3, D4, A4
The cello—C2, G2, D3, A3
The double bass—E1, A1, D2, G2.

The notes on the violin, viola, and cello sound as written. The notes on the double bass sound one octave below the written notes.

Different Notes—String instruments do not have mechanisms to alter the basic notes as do woodwind and brass instruments. String instrument players are able to raise the pitch of each string in half-step increments or in any interval up to seven steps above the open string by depressing the string to the fingerboard with the fingers of the left hand. The distance between each finger can be adjusted to produce either a half step or whole step. Adding fingers adds steps. Adding multiple fingers produces intervals. Although rarely used, there are string instruments that are restructured so that one can finger the instruments with the right hand. This arrangement allows left-handed players to use their stronger hand for bowing.

Producing Sound—There are several ways to produce sounds on violin family instruments. Most common is by drawing a wooden bow strung with horsehair across a string. The player can also pluck the strings with the right or left hand, bounce the stick side of the bow on the string, or draw the stick side of the bow across the strings to produce a special effect. The term used for playing with the wooden part of the stick is con legno, Italian for "with the wood."

Structural Differences—Structural differences among these instruments, aside from their size and playing range, are slight, and the instruments function in much the same way.

The **violin** is the most acoustically perfect of the four. The viola, cello, and double bass are progressively (but not proportionately) larger while still maintaining essentially the same structure and design of the violin. However, their acoustical perfection does wane as their sizes increase.

The **viola** is often described as being a large violin because both instruments share many characteristics of design, physics, construction, and appearance. The instrument is tuned a fifth lower than the violin but is one-seventh larger, making the difference in pitch disproportionate to the difference in size. This ratio of tuning to size results in the darker timbre associated with the viola.

While the body of a full-size violin is almost always the same size, 14 inches (35.5 cm) long, the size of a viola body can vary as much as four inches. Viola body sizes can range from 13½ inches to 17½ inches in length, with the widths ranging proportionate to the length.

Another difference between the violin and viola appears in the size-to-pitch ratio. An instrument that is tuned a perfect fifth below the violin should be considerably larger than the viola if it were to follow the size-to-pitch ratio set by the design of the violin. In fact, the size of the viola should be so great that it would not be manageable as an instrument to be played under the chin. Since the viola is not correctly proportioned to its tuning, viola makers can enjoy a bit of latitude when designing the instrument and can alter the size to produce the tone quality desired.

The **cello**, or **violoncello**, is also disproportionate in size to its difference in tuning. It is tuned a full octave below the viola, but the cello is smaller than its acoustical requirement. The discrepancy is compensated for by a significant increase in the depth or thickness of the body of the instrument. With the increased depth, the lower tones are able to resonate with the characteristic cello timbre.

Because of its relatively large size, the cello is supported by an end pin that extends from the bottom of the instrument. The end pin is adjustable to accommodate different size players. The cello rests with its end pin on the floor while the player balances the instrument between the knees. In this position, the strings are reversed from those on the violin and viola. In playing position the lowest string, the C string, now becomes the first string on the right hand of the player, as opposed to violins and violas in playing position, which have the highest string at the player's right side.

The **double bass** is the lowest-sounding instrument of the violin family. Although it also shares the principles of the string instrument design, the double bass has the greatest structural differences of the family. In addition to its larger size, the double bass differs slightly in shape from the three smaller instruments. While the shoulders of these instruments are at a 90-degree angle from the fingerboard, the size of the double bass requires that the shoulders be sloped in order to allow the player to reach the higher playing positions comfortably.

Another difference is found in the back of some double basses. Rather than being rounded, the back of the larger instrument starts out sloping outward and then levels off to a flat back for the major portion of the instrument. This design allows the maker to use less than half of the wood required for a rounded back without sacrificing any structural integrity.

Some double basses have a fifth string enabling the performer to play down to C, a third below the lowest string on the instrument. An additional way to achieve this extended range is by installing a device that lowers the pitch of the fourth string.

A Review of How They Work—The complete amplifying process on the instruments of the violin family is as follows: The string's vibrations are conducted by the hardwood (usually maple) bridge to the softer wood (usually spruce) instrument top. The vibrations are then transported via the softwood sound post to the hardwood back of the instrument and, via the softwood bass bar, laterally throughout the entire top. The hardwood back and softer wood top are joined by hardwood sides. Combined, the top, sides, and back form an air space in which the sound circulates. The interaction of all of these components forms the amplifier for the sound produced by the strings. The combined motion of these parts sets the volume of air contained within the body of the instrument into a pumping motion that forces the resonating sound out of the instrument through the f holes. In this manner the instruments produce sound.

Summary—In spite of the more than 300-year history of the violin, the exact interaction that takes place among these components is not yet fully understood. The mathematical simplicity and consistency of the design of these instruments becomes evident when one observes that violins hardly vary in their proportions.

The greatest amount of wood is found beneath the bridge. The thickness of the wood decreases to half that amount at the sides of the top while remaining consistent throughout the length of the bass bar. Farther across the top of the instrument, the measurement at the thinnest part of the top becomes equal to one-quarter of the thickest part. The ratios then progress from the whole (thickest) to one-half of the whole (medium) and then to one-quarter of the whole (thinnest).

The amplifier or body of these instruments is deceptive in its simple appearance, and yet it utilizes a most complex system for distributing vibrations. The vibrations are carried throughout the physical structure of the wooden body and travel in every direction. This diversity of movement causes the instrument to vibrate and oscillate horizontally, vertically, and diagonally. Simultaneously, the air contained within the body is set in motion, increasing and decreasing in volume while traveling in and out of the body through the f holes.

The main function of the bodies of woodwind and brass instruments is to contain the columns of air that are set into motion, act as a structure onto which various mechanical devices are incorporated, and to extend or shorten that vibrating air column. In the case of the violin family, the body acts as the amplifier of sound that profoundly affects the quality of tone produced and has no part in changing pitch. That is achieved by the player's fingers shortening (stopping) the strings.

An expertly crafted violin, strung with an appropriate set of strings, and played with a good-quality bow, will produce a better tone than a poorer quality instrument set up with the same bow and strings. Unlike wind instruments, the tone quality of string instruments is largely a product of the quality of the material used in the construction of the body of the instrument and of the design and craftsmanship used in making it.

The violin, viola, cello, and double bass share most of the same technology and combine to make the most versatile choir of instruments in the contemporary music world. These instruments are similar in design, acoustical function, construction, and history. They enjoy a romantic quality that has resulted in their being considered collectibles, works of art, a three-century-old mystery story, and the heart of the modern symphony orchestra.

GLOSSARY OF STRING INSTRUMENT PARTS

This glossary will help the reader define terms that are related to string instrument parts. See the discussion above for more in-depth information on these items.

Back The back of the body of a string instrument, also referred to as the back plate.
Bass bar A carved strip of wood located on the underside of the top of an instrument, reinforcing the top while supporting the great force exerted by the tension of the strings. The bass bar distributes the vibrations from the strings throughout the top of the instrument.
Belly The top of a string instrument, also called the top plate.
Block A wooden block placed at key points in the structure of a string instrument to strengthen the unit. One block is placed in each corner where the upper and

lower bouts meet the C bout. One block is placed at the bottom of the body to reinforce the end pin, and one block is placed at the top of the body to reinforce the neck contact.

Body The name given to the main part of a string instrument. The body (front, back, and sides) amplifies the sound produced by the vibrating strings.

Bout The term used to identify the three sections of a string instrument's body. The upper third is called the upper bout, the mid-section, the C bout, and the lower third is called the lower bout.

Bow An arc-shaped staff made of wood or a man-made substance, strung with horse-hair or fiberglass hair substitute. The ribbon of hair is drawn across the strings of an instrument to produce sound.

Bow hair A ribbon of about 200 horse hairs, which make up the part of a bow that comes in contact with a string to generate sound.

Bow quiver An oblong case, usually made of leather, designed to hold double bass bows conveniently and safely. Can be used for all other bows.

Bridge A carved hardwood piece that supports the strings on an instrument and transfers sound from a vibrating string to the body of the instrument.

Bridge adjuster Screws on each foot of a bridge, which facilitate raising and lowering the bridge.

Chin rest An appliance designed to provide a comfortable and secure placement of a player's chin when holding a violin or viola in playing position.

Electronic tuner An electronic mechanism that provides a pitch, a series of pitches, and/or a visual illustration of the accuracy of a pitch being sounded for tuning purposes.

End button A wedge-shaped cylinder of wood inserted in the end of a violin or viola on which a tail gut is hooked to hold the tailpiece in place.

End pin An adjustable rod extending from the bottom of a cello or double bass to permit the player to raise or lower the instrument to a comfortable playing position.

f hole Sometimes called a sound hole, a decorative aperture resembling the shape of the letter "f" carved into the top of a string instrument. The f holes act as escapes for the sound vibrations that occur when a string instrument is being played.

Fine tuner A device designed to simplify tuning a string to the very slightest degree. Various iterations allow placement on a string, on a tailpiece, or built into a tailpiece.

Fingerboard A hardwood board (usually ebony) glued to the top of the neck. The fingerboard extends from the peg box over the body of an instrument to provide a surface against which the player can press the string to change pitches.

Lining Thin strips of wood glued around the inside edge of the ribs of an instrument to act as a support.

Machine head A worm-and-gear system used to tune the strings on a double bass.

Mute A device placed on a bridge to lessen the vibrations traveling from the string through the bridge to the instrument, altering the tone quality and volume of the sound.

Peg A wedge-shaped cylinder of wood used to hold one end of the strings on a string instrument. The string is inserted into a hole in the peg and, as the peg is turned, the string winds up and is tightened.

Pickup A microphone or electromagnetic contact device that transmits the vibrations from a string instrument to an amplifier and speaker setup. The three types of pickups are piezoelectric, omnidirectional, and bimorphic.

Purfling Two parallel strips of hardwood, usually ebony, inlaid into the surface around the edge of the top and back of a string instrument to strengthen its edges.

Rib The side of a string instrument.

Saddle A hardwood bar upon which the tail gut rests to prevent damage to the instrument's body.

Scroll The decorative carved figure at the top of the neck of a string instrument.

Scroll eye The center of a scroll.

Sound post A wooden dowel acting as a structural support for the top of an instrument. The sound post conducts the vibrations produced by the higher strings from the top of an instrument to its back.

String A length of wire, gut, plastic, or other material that is processed to produce a desired sound when properly installed on a musical instrument.

Tailpiece A device to which the lower end of the strings on an instrument are attached.

Wolf tone eliminator A device applied to a string to eliminate a sound (wolf tone) that can occur in some instruments where a particular note matches the natural frequency of that instrument.

6

Brass Instruments Defined

The term "brass instrument" is commonly applied to a musical instrument made of brass, which produces sound when the player expels air and buzzes his or her lips into a cup-shaped mouthpiece. This type of instrument is called an aerophone, which is any instrument that produces sound as a result of a stream of air activating a sound generator. In the case of brass instruments, the sound generator would be the player's lips vibrating into a mouthpiece. Two other names given to such "lip-vibrating" sound-generating instruments are labrosone, which means lip-vibrating instrument, and lip-reed, whose origin is obvious. For the purpose of this chapter, the term "brass instrument" refers to those contemporary labrosones that are made of brass, use a cup mouthpiece, and are commonly used as solo instruments and instruments in an orchestra, marching, symphonic, jazz, or dance band.

The individual names of brass instruments contain three terms that describe the kind of instrument, its practical performance range, and the overtone series upon which its acoustical design is based. An example is the B-flat soprano trumpet, which is (1) a trumpet, (2) plays in the soprano range, and (3) has a fundamental B-flat overtone series (see chapter 16).

Among the brass instruments currently in use are families of trumpets, trombones, French horns, tenor and baritone horns, and tubas. Each of these families consists of an assortment of instruments of a similar design and size with variations primarily in their range, transposition, and timbre. When combined, these instruments produce pitches that cover sounds ranging from D1, a twelfth below the bass clef, to C6, an octave above the treble clef.

Within each family there are several instruments with similar architecture that vary in size and pitch, thereby expanding the range of timbre or sound quality associated with that instrument. An example is the trumpet, which is made in B-flat, A, C, D, E-flat, low F, and G. Each of these trumpets functions in exactly the same manner mechanically but produces a slightly different tone quality or timbre, and plays in a different range.

BRASS INSTRUMENTS

The following are descriptions of the most commonly used brass instruments.

Trumpet—The B-flat trumpet is the most popular of the brass instruments (figure 6.1). The trumpet's effective amplification system is its body. A cup-shaped mouthpiece, usually made of brass and coated with silver, is inserted into a slightly conical-shaped tube called a leadpipe or mouthpiece receiver. This is connected to the main body of the instrument. The major portion of the trumpet tubing is cylindrical. Connected to this tubing are cylinders that house valves. The valves can be either of the piston or rotary type (see chapter 8 for more on valves). Following the main cylindrical section of the instrument is a bell section, which is conical and about one-quarter the length of the preceding cylindrical section.

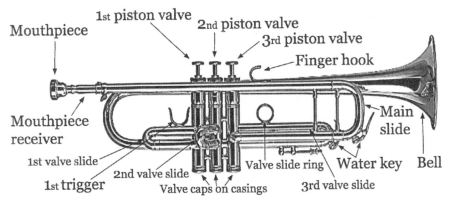

Figure 6.1.   B-flat Trumpet

The trumpet is designed with a tuning slide for each valve to accommodate inherent intonation problems. These slides can be adjusted in or out to modify the pitch that each valve produces. The trumpets being manufactured at present and used most commonly are the mezzo-soprano in C and B-flat; soprano in D; high E-flat; high F; sopranino in high G; piccolo in high B-flat; contralto in low E-flat and F; and tenor in C and B-flat.

Cornet—While the trumpet is primarily cylindrical with some conical parts, the cornet is almost totally conical. Sharing essentially the same design with the trumpet, the cornet begins with a cup-shaped mouthpiece somewhat smaller than that of the trumpet. That mouthpiece is connected to a cylindrical mouthpiece leadpipe which joins the remainder of the conical body. The overall appearance of the cornet is shorter than the trumpet because the cornet's tubing is usually bent into two loops. The combination of the smaller conical bore and the two turns in the tubing present greater resistance to the player, with the resulting tone being mellower than that of the trumpet. Currently in use are the mezzo-soprano cornet in B-flat and soprano in high E-flat.

Flugelhorn—This instrument is, in effect, a bass trumpet. It has the same range and pitch as the trumpet but demonstrates its unique characteristics in the contralto range, where it produces a rich mellow tone. The instrument is available in mezzo-soprano in B-flat and bass in C.

French Horn—French horns are manufactured in B-flat and F as single horns, and a combination of B-flat and F, called a double horn. Using a double horn, the player can switch from B-flat to F by pressing a thumb trigger, which turns a rotary valve to redirect the vibrating column of air from one section of tubing to another.

High notes on a French horn reside in the upper partials of the overtone series. Due to their close interval proximity, these notes present difficulties in tone placement. Switching from F to B-flat on a double horn enables a player to perform those notes more easily.

The single horn in F contains three rotary valves that open and close the various lengths of tubing. The double horn has a fourth valve. This operates the B-flat crook added to the single horn to make a double F–B-flat instrument. (More on this in chapter 8.) The bore of the instrument beyond the valves is conical up to and including the bell, which ends in a diameter of about eleven inches.

Mellophone—The mellophone resembles a French horn in appearance and is used as a substitute for the horn when an actual French horn is not practical or available. The mellophone has piston valves located for use with the right hand. This instrument is useful when a quick change from the trumpet or cornet to a French horn–like instrument is required. Mellophones are constructed in E-flat and F.

Slide Trombone—The slide trombone is the only brass instrument that can be played in perfect tune. This is so because instead of valves, the trombone uses a slide to create different notes by lengthening or shortening the instrument. If the player is capable of discerning proper pitch placement, there is no limit to the level of pitch perfection attainable since the slide can be placed at any point necessary to achieve accurate intonation.

Due to the slide design, the bore of the instrument must be primarily cylindrical. The exception occurs with the widening of the bell section, which flares out to approximately eight to nine inches at the widest point. This section of the instrument is equal to about one-third of the entire length of the instrument. Trombones come in an assortment of models, among which are the soprano in B-flat, alto in

E-flat, tenor in B-flat, bass in B-flat, contrabass in D, CC, or BB-flat, and the valve trombone in B-flat.

Valve Trombone—This instrument has the appearance of a trombone, except there are three piston valves incorporated into the slide design and the slide portion is stationary. The primary use of the valve trombone is to facilitate a lower brass player in doubling on the trombone. Because of the valves, these trombones suffer the same intonation problems as do other valve instruments.

Alto Horn—The upright E-flat alto horn is primarily a marching instrument and is often used in place of the French horn. Easy to carry, this instrument has a brassy tone and is predominantly used as a support to the rhythm section of the marching band. The alto horn is made in E-flat only.

Tenor Horn—More commonly used in central Europe, the tenor horn is so named for its range placement in the scheme of brass instruments. It is used for solo passages that require more virtuosity than those normally associated with instruments in the lower range. The tenor horn is built in the key of B-flat.

Baritone Horn—Representing the baritone voice in the brass family, the instrument is less versatile than the B-flat tenor horn and has a more mellow voice. The baritone horn is used most often in American concert bands and is built on the key of B-flat.

Euphonium—A form of tenor or baritone horn producing a rich mellow tone due to its large bore, the euphonium is best used to perform slow lyrical bass solos. Like the baritone horn, the euphonium is built in the key of B-flat.

Tuba—The tuba, lowest of the brass instruments, comes in several designs. The upright bell model is used primarily for concert work while the recording model, or bell front model, is used for marching. In addition there is the famous tuba designed for marching known as the sousaphone. This tuba is designed with its tubing in concentric circles to encircle the player, allowing the instrument to rest on the player's shoulder.

Tubas are built with three and four valves in either piston or rotary design. The various models available are the rotary or piston valve in BB-flat and CC, the three valve in BB-flat and E-flat, the four valve in BB-flat, and the sousaphone in BB-flat and E-flat.

Marching Band Instruments—A complete line of brass instruments called marching band instruments perform identically to the instruments mentioned above, except that the marching models are designed to be held in a horizontal playing position, as one would hold a trumpet. This design facilitates playing while marching.

Summary—The manner in which all brass instruments function acoustically, mechanically, and musically is almost identical. The materials from which they are made are the same. They all use the player's lips buzzing into a cup mouthpiece attached to a brass instrument body as an amplifying system. Valves fitted to the body are depressed to open tubing, which extends the length of the body and thereby lowering pitch. The slide trombone uses a slide to achieve the same result.

Unfortunately, this family of instruments also shares the characteristics, with the exception of the slide trombone, of having inherent intonation problems. These begin with the sound generator being the human lips functioning as a buzzing device. Through this system of sound generation, the brass player is restricted to the limitations inherent in his or her own lip and mouth configuration.

The brass player does not have the option of changing the components of the tone generator as do other instrumentalists. Single reed players can change mouthpieces, reeds, and ligatures. Double reed players have their reeds made to order or make them themselves. String players have a vast variety of strings, bows, and bridge configurations at their disposal. Whereas all other instrumentalists can select components with which they can customize their sound generators, brass players are born with theirs. The only outside assistance they can turn to is the cup mouthpiece. There are, therefore, numerous mouthpiece designs available to accommodate the infinite number of lip/mouth configurations. Brass players, unlike woodwind instrumentalists, cannot simply change their reeds.

Another problem that is unique to brass instruments, again with the exception of the slide trombone, is the change in valve-slide ratios as the pistons are depressed (see chapter 8). Devices such as the valve slide trigger and the addition of a fourth valve on some instruments, along with some creative concepts in bore construction, have helped improve the intonation problems. However, it is apparent that the valve system used on brass instruments at best provides an inexact system to perfect intonation.

Listeners have adjusted to these imperfect sounds by sheer exposure, tending to accept the sound of the brass section as being a product of timbre rather than of imperfect intonation. They have become accustomed to it and consequently find it acceptable. Of all the problems with instruments in use at this time, the brass player's most difficult plight is in the area of intonation. Good intonation on a brass instrument must rest with the ability of the performer to humor individual notes as required by each situation.

The brass choir provides the power and brilliance essential to the performance of band and orchestral music as it evolved with the works of Beethoven, Brahms, and Wagner during the Romantic period. Military, ceremonial, and entertainment bands could not fill their roles without the brass choir's dynamic character. So, as is the case with anything one loves and needs, one accepts it for its virtues and lives with its imperfections.

GLOSSARY OF TERMS RELATED TO BRASS INSTRUMENTS

This glossary will help the reader define terms that are related to brass instruments. See the descriptions above for more in-depth information on these items.

Baritone A designation for any musical instrument or voice that has a comfortable range lower than a tenor but above a bass, approximately from F below middle C (F2) to F above middle C (F4). See chapter 16 on scientific pitch notation.

Bass A designation for any musical instrument or voice in the lowest range of that musical group.

Bell The flared end of a wind instrument. The bell balances the instrument's intonation and tone quality.

Brass In music, a term used to describe any instrument that is made of brass and is a lip-vibrating sound-generating instrument (labrosone).

Cornet A brass valve instrument with a conical bore, very similar to a trumpet but with a mellower tone.

Cornetto A wind instrument dating from the Medieval period (1500) through eighteenth century. It was made of wood, played with a cup mouthpiece, and had tone holes for the player to alter the pitches.

Horn In colloquial speech the term "horn" is applied to almost any wind instrument. Its origin is from the animal horns that are considered to be the first labrosones.

Instrumentation The assortment of instruments used for a particular piece of music.

Intonation The accuracy with which a pitch is produced in relation to its prescribed cycles per second.

Leadpipe (pronounced leedpipe) The first section of the body of a brass instrument designed to receive the mouthpiece.

Mouthpiece A cup-shaped, usually metal device used by a brass instrument player to produce sound.

Post horn A brass instrument with a cupped mouthpiece and without valves used during the eighteenth and nineteenth centuries to announce the arrival and departure of a mail (post) coach.

Slide ring A ring or hook attached to a tuning slide on a brass instrument to facilitate the player moving the slide in or out.

Trombone A brass instrument in the tenor to bass range that changes notes by the player advancing or withdrawing a slide mechanism. Another type of trombone, called a valve trombone, is fitted with valves that function as do all other valves on brass instruments.

Trumpet A brass valve instrument with a primarily cylindrical bore, very similar to a cornet but with a brighter tone.

Valve A piston or rotary-shaped component on a brass instrument that when operated opens or closes tubing in order to change pitches.

Valve buttons The discs placed at the top of each valve stem upon which the player places his or her fingers.

Valve casing A cylinder in which a valve operates.

Valve slide The tubing connected to a valve casing that can be extended or withdrawn to adjust pitch.

Valve stem A metal cylinder that connects the valve buttons to the valve.

Water key (spit valve) A mechanism on brass instruments that allows the release of built-up condensation.

7

The History of Brass Instruments

EARLY LABROSONES

In chapter 6 a brass instrument is defined as a musical instrument made of brass, which produces sound by the player expelling air and buzzing his or her lips into a cup-shaped mouthpiece. These instruments are also called aerophones, labrosones, or lip-reed instruments. Although the ancient ancestors of contemporary brass instruments were not made of brass, they did fall under these latter categories because they utilized a lip-reed sound-generating process. The early history of instruments that produced sound by a player's buzzing lips, labrosones, is without documentation. The only possible early time line would have to be predicated on logical, deductive reasoning. What motivated primitive beings to create a device that would produce sound? What would that device look like? How would it be played? What purpose would it serve in a primitive society? How could all this come to be?

The history of brass instruments, and most other instruments for that matter, is replete with contradictions and vague references to what might have or could have happened. As one progresses through the time periods, information does become clearer with documentation, but not to the point where accuracy is the theme of the day. One might speculate that the first sounds were accidental. A reasonable scenario would be a person cleaning out a conch shell for its meat made a hole at the small end and blew into it to clear out the residual contents. His or her lips buzzed, a sound occurred, the player liked the sound, experimented with making other sounds, and so a labrosone was born. A similar scenario might have occurred with animal horns, hollowed-out sticks, and anything else that would produce such a result: "Wow! What a great sound. I can use this to call my tribe together. Hmm! If I tighten my lips, the sound goes up. Loosen them, down. If I blow real hard maybe I can summon the gods to help me get some rain or chase away the evil spirits."

This is speculation, but it is logical, and something that likely happened. Relics have been found that appear to be parts of such instruments dating back several thousand years B.C. to the Stone Age. During that period the primitive population was limited to the use of stone, wood, and other natural resources as the primary raw materials for creating implements for everyday use. Following the Stone Age was the Bronze Age, 3,000 B.C. to 1,000 B.C., when copper and bronze, an alloy of copper, came into existence. The period from 1,000 B.C. on is referred to as the Iron Age, completing the evolutionary sequence. With the development of those metals, mankind had the materials to make tools for survival, war, and entertainment. Evidence of instruments fabricated of various metal alloys begins to appear with the Bronze Age. Among them is the lur, discovered in the Nordic countries and northern Germany.

Lur—The lur was a labrosone in its simplest form. It had a trombone-like cup mouthpiece as its lip-reed sound generator. There were no valves, slides, or tone holes, so the player had to rely on embouchure to change pitch. A cup-shaped mouthpiece was connected to a conical pipe, which could be between four and six feet long. To accommodate their extreme length, some lurs were curved, shaped like an elephant's tusk. This configuration allowed the player to carry the instrument wrapped around his or her body as one would a modern sousaphone. The earliest known lurs, discovered primarily in Germany and Denmark, were from the Bronze Age and were made of bronze. Those found in Scandinavia were made of wood.

Roman Buccina—The buccina was a labrosone fabricated from an animal horn. As its popularity increased, the buccina was made from other materials and ultimately metal. Like the lur, the buccina took a circular shape which encompassed the player. The buccina was used to announce the changes of the guards and ceremonial events, both joyful and solemn.

Roman Cornu—This instrument, originally made from animal horn, then developed into a C-shaped brass instrument with a supporting brace crossbar. Like the buccina, it too was without valves or tone holes and relied on the player's embouchure to change pitches. As was true of many of the brass instruments of the time, their primary function was to sound alarms and signals for the military. The cornu served a similar function as a clarion call for social meetings, gladiator fights, and to announce the coming of the emperor.

Cornetto or Cornett—Not to be confused with the current-day cornet, this instrument was a labrosone (lip-reed) instrument that used a cup mouthpiece similar to that used on a trumpet, but made of animal horn or ivory. The cornetto was widely used for about 150 years beginning in about 1500. About two feet long, it was made in three different configurations called curved, straight, and mute. The curved model was made of wood in a very interesting manner. A block of wood was cut into a curve and split in half. A cone-shaped bore was then scooped out of each half. The halves were then joined back together to form the body of the instrument. There were six tone holes on the front of the body and one on the back, similar to the sound manipulation system used on today's woodwind instruments.

The straight treble cornetto was essentially the same instrument as the curved model, with tone holes and a bore. As the name implies, the instrument was straight, similar in appearance to a long recorder with a detachable cup mouthpiece but without a bell.

The mute cornetto was basically a straight treble cornetto with a built-in mouthpiece. There are many examples of this instrument dating back to the sixteenth century on display in museums throughout Europe.

Cornetti (plural) were also built in the tenor and bass ranges to complete the ensemble requirements of the time. Tenor cornetti were a bit longer than the treble model and sounded a fifth lower. The tenor's extra length required that a curve be incorporated into its body to facilitate holding it. This version had an additional tone hole with a key articulated by the pinky finger. The primary role played by the tenor cornetto was as the tenor or third voice in an ensemble. There is no evidence of its ever being a solo instrument.

The bass cornetto transposed a fourth of fifth below the tenor. This eight-foot-long cornetto was so large, it had to be serpentine in shape. It used a cup-shaped mouthpiece and woodwind-like tone holes to articulate the various pitches. Because of its serpentine shape, this instrument was also known as the serpent. One might consider it to be the tuba of the cornetto family. In liturgical music the bass cornetto provided the bass line. The bass cornetto was capable of producing such an offensive sound that it was used in the military to frighten the enemy. Three specimens of bass cornetti are displayed in the Musée de la Musique in Paris.

CONTEMPORARY BRASS INSTRUMENTS

The preceding is a brief overview of a few of the many labrosones that existed prior to the introduction of the "brass instruments" now part of the contemporary musical instrument inventory. These newer instruments have a more clearly documented history to provide facts on their origins and evolution. The brass instruments to be discussed are the contemporary trumpet, cornet, flugelhorn, French horn, trombone/sackbut, valve trombone, alto horn, euphonium/baritone horn, tuba, and sousaphone.

Trumpet—The term *trumpet* is widely used to label many labrosones from the past to the present. Some of these instruments were discussed in the preceding pages to give the reader some sense of the variety of lip-reed instruments that preceded the B-flat trumpet we now know and use. The early instruments were known as "natural" labrosones, since they were only capable of producing those pitches that were natural to the architecture of each instrument. There were no valves or slides, so players were entirely dependent on embouchure changes to produce different pitches. The instruments were used as signaling devices for social and military events.

Eventually some tone holes were added to the instruments and then the slide was born. Incorporated into the mouth pipe, the slide enabled the player to extend or contract the instrument's tubing, resulting in the ability to change pitches. Placing the hand in the bell, called hand stopping, was another method of changing pitch on a natural horn. Trumpet-like instruments were made with larger bells so that by closing the bell with the hand, the player was able to adjust the pitch up or down, thereby producing additional notes within the open tone series. Other attempts were made to change the pitch from the natural overtones through the use of keys similar to those used on woodwind instruments. The keys added pitches to the natural overtone series.

Another method of increasing the number of pitches on instruments without valves was through the use of crooks of different lengths. Players could change the effective length of an instrument by adding a shorter or longer length of tubing in the form of a crook to the main body of the instrument. Longer crooks lowered the pitch and shorter crooks raised the pitch. Through this method an instrument was able to play in different keys and, in so doing, be suitable for a greater variety of music. It was the invention of the valve that finally produced the complete chromatic scale.

The invention of the piston valve significantly advanced brass instrument development. The name Heinrich Stoelzel (1777–1844) is most often associated with that accomplishment. It is said that he and Friedrich Bluhmel were co-inventors of the device in 1814.

There is some question as to who invented the rotary valve. The names Nathan Adams, United States; Friedrich Bluhmel, Germany; Joseph Kail, Austria (Prague); and Joseph Felix Riedl, Austria (Vienna) are all associated in the history books with that invention. Organologists name Friedrich Bluhmel in conjunction with Stoelzel as the inventors. That said, Joseph Riedl is noted as the first to use valves on an instrument in 1832. By the end of the nineteenth century, the B-flat trumpet currently in use began to be the trumpet of choice. That transition occurred because of the trumpet's bolder, brighter sound, its ease of use with valves, and its improved intonation.

Cornet—It is generally believed that the cornet is a derivative of the post horn, a valveless labrosone which was used in the eighteenth century to signal the activities of mail coaches. The post horn was made of copper or brass and took either a circular or straight form. Jean Aste, an instrument manufacturer in the late 1820s, is said to have used the post horn as a model from which he created the cornet. There are some who speculate that Aste added the newly invented valves to a post horn and so appeared a cornet. This instrument shares the technology and playing experience of a trumpet. The difference between them is in the tone quality, the cornet being mellower than the trumpet. There is also a difference in the comfort level of holding the two instruments. Because the trumpet's design is straighter and longer than that of the cornet, the center of gravity differs from that of the cornet, making it easier to hold.

Flugelhorn—The original instrument that carried the name flugelhorn was a curved brass horn used in the eighteenth century to signal those on the hunt, a common pastime for the elite. It was the fluegelmeister who was charged with the task of keeping the hunters on the path of the hunted and he did so with a horn; thus the contemporized name, flugelhorn. The instrument was also used for signaling by the military.

The flugelhorn has a rather convoluted history, having gone through numerous modifications. It was built with different materials from wood to silver, and restructured with the addition of both piston and rotary valves. Over the years flugelhorns have been built in soprano, alto, tenor, and bass ranges in the keys of E-flat, B-flat, C, F, G, and A. As one looks back over the evolution of the instrument it becomes apparent that the term *fluegelhorn* was applied to an assortment of brass instruments with valves, thereby further confusing its history. If one were to examine that assortment of instruments from the past, the most likely parent for what is now known as a flugelhorn would be the keyed bugle.

French horn—The preceding paragraphs describe the various steps in the evolution of labrosones, beginning with instruments fabricated from natural resources such as sea shells, animal horns, hollow sticks, and the like. The French horn's origin is probably best associated with the lur (see above), a non-valve instrument that most closely resembled what is now the French horn.

Originally the French horn was valveless. Its concentric configuration permitted the player on the hunt to hold several feet of tubing with one hand while the other hand held the saddle horn. The instrument had a length of tubing that produced a predetermined set of pitches. As interest in the instrument increased, horn players would have several instruments with different tubing lengths at the ready to change when the music required different pitches. The next step in the evolution consisted of creating additional lengths of tubing called crooks for a particular instrument, which a player could exchange as the music called for different notes. Shorter crooks would raise the pitch; longer crooks, lower the pitch.

The natural harmonic series (chapter 2) consists of tones that begin with an interval of an octave, followed by a fifth, fourth, third, and then proceed in progressively closer intervals. Under these circumstances one is able to play a significant number of different notes in the upper register without using valves or changing crooks. This, in conjunction with the hand stopping technique (see trumpet above), permitted the experienced horn player to produce a significant number of chromatics. By the mid-eighteenth century, exchangeable crooks were devised for both the instrument's body and the mouth pipe so it was possible, although unwieldy, to play a complete chromatic scale.

How to solve that problem? Invent the omnitonic horn with all crooks built into the instrument and with a mechanism that would permit the player to transfer from one set to any of the others. This instrument was heavy, cumbersome, and had a short life, which ended with the adaptation by Francois Perinet of the Stoelzel piston valve to the French horn. It was now possible to play all the notes in a range of three octaves without having to have a plumber's license. This advance was succeeded by Riedl's rotary valve, so that by the late nineteenth century, rotary valves were the technology of choice.

It was at this time that the double horn was created by Fritz Kruspe, a German instrument maker. Kruspe built the double horn with a fourth rotary valve that allowed the player to shift from an F to a B-flat horn with the flick of a thumb. The original double horn was designed to add on tubing to increase the existing tubing's length. This configuration was and is still known as the compensating horn. The full double horn is actually a complete B-flat and an F horn sharing a single leadpipe and bell. The thumb trigger directs the air to the instrument of choice.

A third iteration of the French horn, called a descant horn, appeared at the beginning of the twentieth century. This was a smaller horn designed to facilitate playing the notes in the higher register. Pitched an octave above the traditional F horn, the descant horn places what would be the higher notes of the overtone series, which are more difficult to play because they are so close to each other, into the lower overtone series spacing, where the notes are farther apart. This spacing allows the player a bit more latitude when positioning the embouchure for those notes. The double descant horn concept was further expanded into the double horn concept in the middle of the twentieth century. The concept of a triple horn in F, B-flat, and high (descant) F followed, completing the ideal instrument to deal with all French horn players' needs.

Trombone/Sackbut—It is the opinion of some organologists that the trombone and sackbut are one and the same instrument, probably because there is no significant structural difference between them. The bell and bore sizes of the original sackbut/ trombone were somewhat smaller than those of contemporary instruments. The bells were rimless with a smaller flare of less than five inches. Due to the sackbut's smaller bore and more elongated bell, the tone is mellower and more sensitive than that of a trombone. Original sackbuts do not have a water key or slide lock, because those modifications were not yet invented.

In the mid-1800s the trombone became a permanent part of the instrumentation of full orchestras and bands. To balance the dynamics with the other brass instruments, trombones needed greater volume and a richer tone quality. This was accomplished by increasing the bore and bell sizes.

One might also reasonably speculate that the sackbut or early trombone was an offshoot of the slide trumpet. In an effort to produce chromatics on the "natural" trumpet (without valves), various attempts were made to incorporate a slide into either the leadpipe or other tubing locations to lengthen or shorten an instrument and thereby change pitches. Trumpets that were built in various sizes to cover the range desired included a bass trumpet. If one was built with a slide, it could have been the early makings of a slide trombone. There are indications through writings and artwork of the existence of such instruments dating back to the mid-fifteenth century. One of the dates given for the making of the oldest actual trombone is 1551, in Nuremberg, Germany.

Early trombones were primarily used to support the vocal bass line in church music. In an effort to expand their use, trombones were made in the keys of E-flat, B-flat, and F covering the alto, tenor, and bass ranges. With this advancement the trombone began to be included in opera scores, and ultimately by Beethoven in his Fifth Symphony.

During the Renaissance period the trombone was used primarily for social and liturgical occasions. In the Baroque period, J. S. Bach and G. F. Handel incorporated the instrument into some of their works. In Austria during the Classical period, the trombone began to be featured as a solo instrument in liturgical works by Mozart and Haydn while retaining a position in the opera and in church music. Trombones were used in duets with voice, and as an alto, tenor, and bass trombone trio.

It was the use of the trombone by Beethoven in his Fifth, Sixth, and Ninth symphonies that acted as the prime example for other composers to follow. In the nineteenth century all the renowned composers were including the trombone as part of the standard instrumentation for their works. It was not long before the trombone was no longer considered to be only an accompanying instrument for liturgical music, but rather took its place in the brass section of the full orchestra and band.

Valve Trombone—The Stoelzel piston valve invented in 1814 was applied to the slide trombone by Viennese instrument makers around 1820. The instrument gained immediate popularity in Germany and Italy, and its use spread throughout Europe, South America, and Asia primarily for popular band and theater orchestras. As mentioned above, the valve system used on any brass instrument has a series of inherent pitch problems. The slide trombone is spared those problems because of the total versatility of positioning the slide. Given a player's ability to discern perfect intonation, the slide can be placed in exactly the correct position to achieve that end. In the case of the valve trombone the player must deal with the idiosyncrasies of a valve instrument.

One further advantage the slide trombone has over the valve model is that when the outer slide is extended, because it has a larger bore than that of the inner slide, the total volume of the bore increases proportionately to the increase of the extension. This occurrence is absent in the valve model since there is no outer slide. For this reason, the slide trombone is often the instrument of choice.

Alto horn—Adolph Sax, the instrument maker from the mid-1800s who is famous for inventing all of the assorted saxophones, was also the inventor of brass instruments. Among these were the saxhorn and saxotromba, both labrosones made of brass with valve systems. Among these were a soprano in E-flat, an E-flat alto, a contralto in B-flat, an E-flat tenor, and a B-flat baritone. Having two E-flat horns, one alto and the other tenor, is believed to be the reason for the confusion that exists in the instrument world with the E-flat alto and E-flat tenor horns. In fact, today's alto and tenor horns are essentially the same instrument. The difference in nomenclature is due to the fact that in the United States, this horn is called the alto horn, whereas in Britain it is called the tenor horn.

Euphonium—The euphonium and baritone horn are often mistaken as being the same. Although they are similar and share a significant amount of technology, their differences are enough to qualify them as being different instruments. To establish the history of the euphonium it is necessary to go back to the serpent (see bass cornetto above), which is believed to be the euphonium's predecessor. The serpent led to the orphicleide, another labrosone in the bass range, invented by Jean Hilaire Aste in 1817. Also popular during that period, the orphicleide was made of brass and produced sound through the use of a cup-shape mouthpiece, but had pad-covered, keyed tone holes similar to those on a saxophone in place of the valves yet to be invented.

There is some confusion as to who invented the euphonium, since the credit is given to Carl Moritz in 1838, Ferdinand Sommer in 1843, and Adolphe Sax in the same year. Each of these gentlemen invented an instrument that fits the general description of a euphonium. To add to the puzzle are the saxhorn and the baritone horn, both instruments that have been confused with the euphonium.

When comparing the euphonium with the baritone horn in sound, the listener will note that the former has a more mellow sound. That occurs because the euphonium has a conical bore, whereas the baritone has a smaller, cylindrical bore. Conical bore instruments produce a mellow sound, whereas instruments with a cylindrical bore produce brighter sounds. The bore on both instruments is about nine feet long. However, the baritone's bore, in addition to being primarily cylindrical, is more closely configured, making the horn a bit more compact. Many distinguish the two by saying the baritone has three valves, whereas the euphonium has four. The fourth valve on the euphonium is used as a substitute for fingering the first and third valves, which cause inherent intonation problems. There are also baritone horns with four valves. Both instruments have the same fingering and range.

Added to the mix are a series of labrosones invented by Mr. Sax in various keys ranging from sopranino to contrabass. These instruments were the center of a controversy as to their names, and whether the instruments were copies of previous labrosones as opposed to being original to Mr. Sax. They were widely accepted by brass bands in the United States and Europe because they provided a compatible blend of like-sounding brass instruments with a complete range from sopranino to contrabass.

The serpent, orphicleide, and euphonium existed simultaneously for several decades until the euphonium eventually became the instrument of choice. Throughout the twentieth century, the major instrument manufacturers refined the euphonium's technology to the point where it is now a highly regarded member of the brass section in concert, ceremonial, and marching bands.

Tuba—The word *tuba* (Latin for trumpet) has been used throughout antiquity to name an assortment of labrosones, none of which is the tuba we know. Today's tuba evolved from the serpent, followed by the orphicleide, which was superseded by an assortment of brass lip-reed instruments, such as the saxhorn, saxtromba, and sax-tuba, all created by Adolphe Sax.

In 1835 a patent for a bass tuba was granted to Wilhelm Wieprecht and Johann Moritz. Similarly to already existing instruments, the patent was granted more on the basis of its name than its originality as an instrument. The bass tuba had three piston valves to be operated by the right hand and two additional valves for the left hand. The bass tuba supported the bass line in the brass, woodwind, and string sections of ensembles, so by the end of the nineteenth century it became a permanent part of the brass section of orchestras and bands. Today's tubas can have five and six valves in order to facilitate playing the complete chromatic scale with accurate intonation.

Sousaphone—This version of the tuba is believed to have been invented by the re-nowned march king, John Philip Sousa, but in fact the instrument already existed as the helicon. In about 1845 the helicon, which had the bell facing up as opposed to facing forward like on the sousaphone, appeared in Russia. The helicon was designed to be a marching instrument, and was produced by a Viennese, Ignaz Stowasser. In 1893, at the behest of Sousa, J. W. Pepper, a Philadelphia instrument maker, modi-fied a helicon into what is now the sousaphone. Pepper named the instrument after Sousa in appreciation for his idea.

Summary—"What's in a name? That which we call a labrosone by any other name would sound as splendid." *Guess who?*

Brass wind, lip reed, aerophone, and labrosone—all identify a family of instruments that provide the music community with a splendor and brilliance that can stand on its own as an ensemble, or significantly contribute to the sounds of any other combination of musical instruments. From the lur, buccina, and the cornu to the trumpet, French horn, and tuba, one must thank everyone, from those primitive individuals who made the first sounds to the inventors, musicians, technicians, and visionaries, who brought us to the point where society is now fortunate enough to enjoy a listening experience that has become a precious possession of our music world.

8

How Brass Instruments Work

TONE PRODUCTION

To produce a tone on a brass instrument, the player buzzes his or her lips into a cup-shaped mouthpiece (figure 8.1). The upper lip produces the primary buzz. Depending on the oral configuration of the player, the lower lip buzzes to a lesser degree. The lower lip also acts as a support or stabilizer for the vibration of the lips and controls the size of the opening through which the air passes into the mouthpiece.

Every conceivable opinion on the placement of the mouthpiece on the lips has been offered by experts. The only point of agreement is that the placement is unique to each embouchure and must ultimately be determined by the player. Beginning players are usually advised to place the mouthpiece in the center of the lips, with

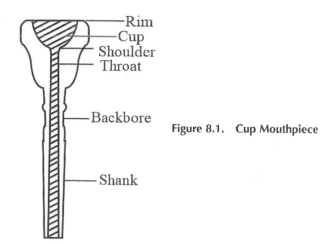

Figure 8.1. Cup Mouthpiece

equal amounts of the upper and lower lip in contact with the mouthpiece cup. It is then a matter of adjusting the mouthpiece placement up or down until the position that produces the best sound for that individual is determined.

The fundamental pitches produced on a brass instrument without the use of valves can be altered by increasing or decreasing the intensity of the buzz.

Valves—All brass instruments are similar in their acoustical and structural designs. With the exception of the slide trombone, brass instruments have a system of valves as part of their structure. There are two types of valves used on these instruments. The piston valve is used on most brass instruments. The rotary valve is used on the French horn and less frequently on other instruments.

A piston valve (figure 8.2) is a metal cylinder with ports that pass through the cylinder at different points. The cylinder is set in a casing, which also has ports that line up with those of the valve. The ports in the casing are connected to different tubing on the instrument and also with other adjacent valves. When a valve is in its rest position, certain ports are lined up with those in the casing. This alignment permits air to pass through a prescribed part of the tubing of an instrument. A series of tones can be produced with the valves in rest position. These sounds are called open tones. When a valve is depressed, different ports line up with other ports in the casing, diverting the air flow to a different set of tubing. By depressing the correct valve at the correct time, a player is able to open and close tubing and in so doing increase or decrease the length of the instrument. Longer instruments play lower tones. Shorter instruments play higher tones. Valves can be used individually or in combination to lower open tones to produce other tones.

A rotary valve (figure 8.2) works on the same principle as the piston valve except that there is a rotor in place of a piston. The rotor turns inside a casing configured

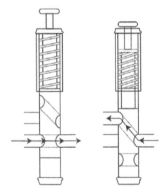

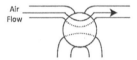

Flow of air before valve is activated

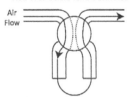

Redirected flow after valve activated

Figure 8.2.   Piston and Rotary Valves

to accommodate the rotor. The same procedure of port alignment as described above relates to the ports in the rotor and its casing.

Fingering Patterns—All brass instruments with valves can produce a series of open tones with no valves depressed. The open tones on a trumpet are C4, G4, C5, E5, G5, and C6 (see chapter 16 on scientific pitch notation.) By depressing valves, the open tones can be lowered in half-step increments to produce the tones that exist between each open tone:

To lower an open tone one half step, a minor second, depress valve 2.

To lower an open tone two half steps, a second, depress valve 1.

To lower an open tone three half steps, a minor third, depress valve 3 or valves 1and 2. *Note:* For better intonation the preferred fingering for these notes is 1 and 2.

To lower an open tone four half steps, a major third, depress valves 2 and 3.

To lower an open tone five half steps, a perfect fourth, depress valves 1 and 3.

To lower an open tone six half steps, augmented fourth or diminished fifth, depress valves 1, 2, and 3.

The Slide Trombone—This instrument uses a slide instead of valves to adjust the length of its tubing. Extending the slide down will lower the fundamental pitch from an open tone in half-step increments. The approximate distances the slide must travel for each position are as follows: first position: closed, second position: 2.5", third position: 6.5", fourth position: 8.25", fifth position: 13.5", sixth position: 19", seventh position: 24".

Review—The valves on any brass instrument can be used individually or in combination, lowering an open tone to produce all the other tones that exist below the open tones. The pattern is as follows:

Valve 1 = whole step or a second

Valve 2 = half step or minor second

Valve 3 = step and a half or minor third

Valves 1and 2 = step and a half or a minor third

Valves 2 and 3 = two whole steps or a major third

Valves 1 and 3 = two and a half steps or a perfect fourth

Valves 1, 2, and 3 = three whole steps or a diminished fourth

These principles also apply to the valve trombone. The slide trombone produces the same descending half-step progressions by extending the slide to the positions described above.

How Brass Instruments Are Tuned—Because all brass instruments with valves have inherent intonation problems, it is almost impossible to realize tuning perfection. Tuning a brass instrument is achieved by moving slides in or out. The main tuning slide, which is located at the end of the mouthpiece pipe, is used to tune the instrument's basic pitch. Additional slides on each valve casing are used to tune the notes related to the use of each valve. Extending a slide will lower the pitch. Drawing in a slide will raise the pitch.

Some euphoniums and BB-flat tubas are structured with an auxiliary set of tubing used to compensate for the natural rise in pitch inherent in the low register of these instruments. By depressing a fourth valve, additional tubing is opened to lower the pitch for that particular note. This mechanism does not affect the other registers on the instrument.

Summary—Sound is produced on all labrosones, lip-reed brass instruments, by a player buzzing his or her lips into a cup-shaped mouthpiece. Using this procedure one is able to play a series of open tones that are basic to the instrument. With the exception of the slide trombone, brass instrument use valves to convert the basic open tones into all the other tones needed to play music. The slide trombone uses a slide to do this.

GLOSSARY OF TERMS RELATED TO
HOW BRASS INSTRUMENTS WORK

Some terms from the chapter 6 glossary are repeated for the convenience of the reader. See the chapters on brass instruments for more in-depth information on these items.

Bell The flared end of a brass instrument. The size and shape of a bell can affect the timbre of the instrument. Smaller bells produce brighter sounds and larger bells produce mellower sounds.
Brass instrument A wind instrument (labrosone) made of brass that produces sound by the player blowing air and vibrating his or her lips into a cup-shaped mouthpiece.
Cup-shaped mouthpiece The name ascribed to the concave shaped mouthpiece used to play a brass instrument.
Embouchure The shape of one's lips, teeth, mouth, and facial muscles when combined to play a wind instrument.
Fingering A term used to define the placement of a player's fingers on an instrument to produce a given note.

Intonation The accuracy with which a pitch is produced in relation to its prescribed cycles per second.

Leadpipe (pronounced leed pipe) The first section of tubing on a brass instrument into which the mouthpiece is placed.

Pinky rest A metal hook soldered onto the body of a brass instrument in an appropriate place for the player to hook his or her pinky finger as a stabilizing force when holding the instrument.

Piston valve A metal cylinder set in a cylindrical casing, both having openings that can be aligned. The cylinder can be pressed down or released up to realign the openings and redirect the air to pass through different parts of an instrument (see figure 8.2).

Rotary valve A metal rotor in a casing, both having openings that can be aligned. By pressing a key the rotor can rotate to realign the openings and redirect the air to pass through different parts of an instrument (see figure 8.2).

Valve A piston or rotary-shaped component on a brass instrument that when operated, opens or closes tubing in order to change pitches (see figure 8.2).

Valve buttons The discs placed at the top of each valve stem upon which the player places his or her fingers (see figure 8.2).

Valve caps Threaded cylindrical caps that screw onto the bottom of a valve casing (see figure 6.1).

Valve slide The tubing connected to a valve casing that can be extended or withdrawn to adjust pitch (see figure 6.1).

Valve slide rings Metal rings attached to valve slides into which the player inserts his or her finger to facilitate moving a tuning slide. Drawing in a slide will raise the pitch. Extending the slide will lower the pitch (see figure 6.1).

Valve stem A metal cylinder that connects the valve buttons to the valve (see figure 8.2).

Water key (spit valve) A mechanism on brass instruments that allows the release of built-up condensation (see figure 6.1, third valve slide).

9

Woodwind Instruments Defined

Woodwind instruments are aerophones, instruments that rely on a flow of air to produce a sound. Most woodwind instruments use a thin blade of material such as cane (bamboo), metal, or plastic, called a reed, that will vibrate when subjected to a flow of air. The vibration agitates the column of air contained within the body of the instrument, resulting in a sound. Clarinets, saxophones, oboes, and bassoons are some instruments that use reeds. Two types of reed configurations used on woodwind instruments are the idioglot, in which the reed is carved from part of the instrument, and the heteroglot, in which the reed is made separately and then connected to the instrument.

Single reeds—Throughout history, woodwind instruments have been designed with various types and combinations of reeds connected to an instrument in different ways. Single reed instruments such as the clarinet and saxophone have an oblong rectangular reed that is flat and tapered to become very thin at its top (figure 9.1A). The reed is attached to a mouthpiece (Figure 9.1B) by a band called a ligature (figure 9.1C). When a player blows a column of air into the mouthpiece and across the reed, it vibrates to produce a sound.

Figure 9.1.   Single Reed, Mouthpiece, and Ligature Compared to Double Reed

Double Reeds—Double reeds are two reeds bound together (figure 9.1). When set into motion by a stream of air, the two reeds vibrate against each other, producing a sound. Double reed instruments use the double reed in place of a mouthpiece. The most common double reed instruments are the oboe and bassoon. Other iterations of the oboe are the oboe d'amore, the English horn, and the shawm. The bassoon is joined by the contrabassoon and the sarrusophone.

Windcap—Bagpipes are also a well-known double reed instrument, but the reeds are covered with a windcap. This cylindrical device encompassing the reed has an opening at the top into which the player blows air to set the double reed into motion. The player has no direct contact with the reed. Figure 9.3 shows a crumhorn with the reed in place and the windcap removed. Next to the crumhorn is a cross-section of a windcap and reed in place.

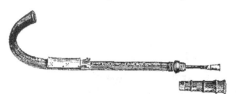 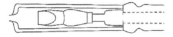

Figure 9.2. Windcap with Double Reed

Free Reeds—Free reed instruments have a reed that does not come in direct contact with the player. The reed is a blade of wood, metal, or other man-made material attached at one end only to a frame so that the blade is free to vibrate when activated by a stream of air passing over it. The pitch that a free reed produces is determined by its length, breadth, density, and flexibility. Each free reed unit produces only one pitch.

The two types of free reed design are those that have the reed constructed separately and attached to a frame (heteroglot), and those that have a reed carved out of the frame itself (idioglot). The most common example of free reeds can be found in pitch pipes and harmonicas. Familiar keyboard instruments that use a free reed system are the harmonium, accordion, and the concertina.

The thickness and taper of reeds can vary in order to provide players with increasing degrees of resistance to accommodate for individual embouchures. Reed strength is measured numerically in half degrees from numbers one through five, with five being the thickest. These classifications are proprietary so that a specific number thickness by one manufacturer may not be the same for another.

Flat Edge—An alternative method used to produce sound on woodwind instruments is to direct a stream of air at a sharp flat edge. When striking the edge, the air stream undulates above and below the edge to produce sound. The transverse flute and recorder are two different types of flat-edge instruments. More on this later. The configuration of the flat edge mouthpiece can take the form of an open-edge system or a closed-edge system.

Open Edge—The transverse flute is an example of an open-edge system, in which the player blows a stream of air across a hole to strike the edge opposite that of the air stream. The air stream striking the edge undulates above and below it, setting the column of air within the flute into motion and thus producing a sound (figure 9.3). It is the challenge for the player to direct the stream of air so that it strikes the edge exactly as needed to create the desired results.

Closed Edge—The recorder is an example of a closed-edge system, also called the fipple system (figure 9.3). This consists of a mouthpiece with an opening at its end into which the player blows air. The air is conducted by a duct (B) to strike a sharp shelf-like edge (C) where the undulating process takes place. Using this system, a player can blow into the opening with less proficiency than that needed to direct a stream over an open-edge system.

Figure 9.3. Open Edge Flute Compared to Closed Edge Fipple System

Material—Although woodwind instruments are often made of wood, they can also be made of brass, metal alloys such as nickel silver, sterling silver, gold, plastic, or glass. These instruments are given the woodwind name because of the wooden reed used to play most of them. An exception is the flute, which is most often made of metal and which has no wooden reed. There are some wooden and glass flutes but those are not commonly used.

GLOSSARY OF TERMS RELATED TO WOODWIND INSTRUMENTS

This glossary will help the reader define terms that are related to woodwind instruments. See the descriptions above for more in-depth information on these items.

Aerophones Instruments that rely on a flow of air to produce a sound.
Bagpipe A windcap reed instrument with a leather air bag attached to a melody pipe for note articulation and additional pipes to produce drone notes.
Bass For woodwind instruments, the word bass is an adjective preceding the name of the instrument to identify it as being in the lower register of the family.
Bassoon A double reed woodwind instrument that performs in the lower register of the woodwind section.
Clarinet A single reed, almost totally cylindrical woodwind instrument performing in the range from E3 to G6 (see chapter 16 on theory).
Double bassoon A large bassoon that completes the range of woodwind instruments by performing an octave lower than the bassoon.

Double reed Two reeds bound together, which when set into motion by a stream of air, vibrate against each other to produce a sound.

Edge tone A sound-generating process on a flute in which the player directs a stream of air across an embouchure hole to strike the edge of the tone hole opposite the player's lips.

English horn A double reed woodwind instrument a bit larger but similar in appearance to an oboe, and sounding a fifth lower.

Flute A metal cylindrical woodwind instrument with side holes covered by keys. Sound is produced on a flute through the edge tone sound-generating system.

Free reed A reed that does not come in direct contact with the player.

Heteroglot A reed that is connected to an instrument.

Idioglot A reed that is carved from part of the instrument it serves.

Oboe A member of the woodwind family, the oboe resembles a clarinet in appearance, has a double reed for a mouthpiece, and produces a somewhat more penetrating timbre than that of the clarinet.

Oboe da more (Italian, "oboe of love") An alto oboe in A sounding a third below the oboe.

Reed A reed in music is a thin blade of any material such as cane (bamboo), metal, or any other man-made product that will vibrate when subjected to a flow of air.

Saxophone A quasi-inverted, S-shaped, conical brass woodwind instrument using a single reed to produce sound. The saxophone was invented by Adolphe Sax to bridge the gap between the brass and woodwind instrument sections of the orchestra by combining the features of both.

Windcap A cylindrical device encompassing a double reed. The device has an opening at the top in which the player blows air to set the double reed in motion. The player has no direct contact with the reed.

10

The History of Woodwind Instruments

At last count there were 141 woodwind instruments, past and present. This begs the question, "How does one write about the history of 141 woodwind instruments?" The answer? In a very long book. This is not a viable option since only one chapter of this book is assigned to the topic. Therefore, a survey of the history of the flute, clarinet, saxophone, oboe, and bassoon, the five most popular woodwind instruments now in use, will follow.

THE FLUTE

Evidence of flute-like instruments dates back as far as 43,000 years. In Slovenia, a cave bear's femur (thighbone) configured as a primitive flute with several tone holes was discovered. Another such instrument found in Germany, fabricated from a vulture's wing bone, is estimated to be about 35,000 years old. Other artifacts resembling a primitive flute suggest that very early on, mankind was becoming aware of the fact that a stream of air passing over and through a vessel can produce sound.

Comparatively simple flute-like instruments dating back to the pre-Christian era have been discovered in numerous countries. Simple wind instruments made from crane bones dating back 9000 years and others of bamboo from 433 B.C. were discovered in China. In 2004 in southern Germany, one of these instruments made from a mammoth tusk, along with two other similar instruments made from swan bones, were discovered. One can find depictions of individuals playing flutes in ancient art works along with references to such instruments in literature. When these pieces of evidence are added to the discoveries of actual instruments on various continents, one can easily conclude that this type of instrument was growing in popularity in many locations throughout the world simultaneously. That being the case, there is no definitive way to assign an accurate time or location to the "invention" of the flute. One must be satisfied with the concept that it evolved over millennia.

By the sixteenth century these instruments had been developed into one-piece cylindrical units with as many as six tone holes. By covering the holes with the fingers, the player was able to produce different notes within a limited range. To compensate for that limitation, the instruments were made in different sizes to produce a greater variety of pitches. Larger instruments produced lower sounds, whereas smaller instruments produced higher sounds. That evolution reached a point in the eighteenth century where technology was sophisticated enough for flute makers to refine the architecture and key systems of the instruments. To that end we now enjoy a flute that can respond to the virtuosity and musical demands of present society.

Jacques-Martin Hotteterre (1674–1763), renowned flautist and instrument maker of his time, is credited with improving the transverse flute by devising the three-piece design with a separate head joint, body, and foot joint structure. See chapter 11 for more on this. From that period on through the early 1800s, improvements were made relocating and resizing the six tone holes and adding keys. This all resulted in improved intonation and a greater capability to perform chromatics.

In the early 1800s, jeweler and goldsmith **Theobald Boehm** (1794–1881), an accomplished flautist and flute maker, determined that larger, properly spaced tone holes would produce a better tone quality and improved intonation. Over a period of approximately twenty years he redesigned the instrument, producing a key system on a three-piece cylindrical body that, with slight modifications, became the instrument we know today.

SINGLE REED INSTRUMENTS

Single reed instruments of the idioglot version, in which the reed is carved from part of the instrument, date back three millennia B.C.

Zummara—Native to Egypt, the zummara had the reed enclosed in a wind cap (see chapter 9). The zummara had two pipes, one functioning as a drone and the other used to play the melody. The player was required to finger both pipes by spanning the holes on each pipe simultaneously. Intonation was dreadful.

Aulos—Another early woodwind instrument, the aulos took two forms. One configuration was similar to that of the transverse flute, with the player holding the instrument horizontally. Historians have deduced from images depicted in various ancient art works that both single and double reed versions of the aulos existed. The single reed iterations were often idioglots because of the simple structural design required to produce such a sound generator. By cutting a triangular slit in a reed (plant), one could blow into it and produce a sound. So appeared the first reed woodwind instruments.

Chalumeau—The term *chalumeau* (plural, chalumeaux) was used as early as the twelfth century throughout central Europe for a variety of single reed instruments. The early chalumeau lacked musical sophistication in both intonation and tone quality, so its use and repertoire were relegated to folk rather than classical compositions. Eventually improvements were made to the instrument so that by 1700, the chalumeau evolved into a single reed woodwind instrument with seven tone holes on the front, one on the back, and two keys. Its range, from F3 below middle C to A4 above middle C, was equal to that of the present-day clarinet's lower so-called chalumeau register. This more sophisticated chalumeau gained acceptance throughout France and Germany and became part of the popular instrumentation.

Because the chalumeau had a range of only twelve notes, the players were required to use as many as four different models to cover the range from F3, a fifth below middle C, to B-flat5 above the treble staff. At this time at least eight original chalumeaux are in existence. These are being used as models for contemporary makers who produce chalumeaux to satisfy the present market.

Clarinet—Along with his son Jacob, **Johann Christoph Denner** (1655–1707), an instrument maker, is credited with advancing the technology of the chalumeau by first adding two keys and then gradually changing the size of the tone holes to improve intonation. Johann Christoph then relocated and added keys and a bell, increasing the length of the instrument. The result was the Baroque clarinet, which had an extended range.

The four ranges of the contemporary clarinet, starting with the lowest note, are the chalumeau, E3 to F-sharp4; throat tones, G4 to B-flat4; clarion, B4 to C6; and altissimo, C-sharp6 to C7 depending on the player. Notes in the clarion register parallel the intensity of those of a trumpet. In the Middle Ages the word *clarion* was applied to the trumpet. Combined with the chalumeau or lower register and eventually extending the range up to the higher (altissimo) register, by 1800 the Baroque clarinet became the single reed instrument of choice, thereby relegating the chalumeau instrument to a diminished status.

From that point on, a series of artist/instrument makers modified the instrument over a period of about 300 years to where it is now, the contemporary clarinet. During that period Ivan Müller, Hyacinthe Klosé, Auguste Buffet, Theobald Boehm, Heinrich Joseph Baermann, Eugène Albert, and Adolphe Sax each contributed modifications that would result in the contemporary clarinet with a key system consisting of seventeen to twenty-two keys and four to six rings.

Ivan Müller (1786–1854) invented the air-tight pad, making possible the addition of enough keys to facilitate the playing of chromatics on the clarinet. Müller pads replaced the flat brass keys with leather pads, which were not effective in covering the tone holes. Müller also invented the metal ligature, which replaced the use of string or wire used up to that point to secure the reed to the mouthpiece. An interesting note is that to date there are still some clarinetists who prefer the use of string in place of a ligature. In addition to these two very important achievements,

Müller redesigned the clarinet to contain thirteen keys to service the redesigned tone holes. The result was greater facility for the player and improved intonation. Müller's system had no ring keys.

Eugène Albert (1816–1890) was a Belgian clarinet maker who developed a key system based on the Müller thirteen-key system, but with the addition of two ring keys. Adolphe Sax, also a clarinet maker and inventor of the saxophone, was Albert's tutor. Sax was responsible for adding the two ring keys to Albert's key system. Subsequent to that, Albert added an additional two rings, resulting in the "Albert System" with thirteen keys and four ring keys. This arrangement further enhanced the intonation of the clarinet and once again facilitated fingering and cross-fingering for accidentals.

Albert's clarinets were very well received because of their excellent craftsmanship and intonation; however, there was one limitation. The instruments were made to pitch A = 452 vibrations per second, meaning the general intonation was higher than the standard A = 440. Albert's son, also a clarinet maker, seeing his father's instruments going out of favor, built a clarinet to tune to A = 440, thereby extending the popularity of the Albert System clarinets into the twentieth century.

Hyacinthe Klosé (1808–1880), August Buffet (1789–1864), and the Boehm System—The Boehm key system, originally invented by Theobald Boehm for the flute, served as a model for Hyacinthe Klosé and August Buffet to create a key system for the clarinet. Over a period of about four years starting in 1839, they modified ring keys and side keys, enabling clarinetists to articulate chromatics and difficult passages with comparative ease and a much improved intonation. Theobald Boehm had no part in this transition except to have been the inspiration for what is called the Boehm clarinet key system. In the last quarter of the nineteenth century, Buffet introduced what he called the full Boehm system, which is accepted worldwide and has replaced the Albert System.

Clarinet technology, having developed to a point where a player was able to perform at a high level technically, prompted a need to further improve intonation and tone quality. **Oskar Öhler** (1858–1936) was able to achieve this by repositioning the tone holes, modifying the fingering, and adding keys up to a total of twenty-eight. He also reduced the diameter of the bore and extended the length and decreased the diameter of the mouthpiece. Öhler's concepts for tone improvement were carried on by his students and, eventually, into the late twentieth century by the Wurlitzer manufacturing company, whose clarinets are most popular in Germany.

Saxophone—The saxophone can be considered the first woodwind instrument that was actually invented as opposed to being an offshoot of some instrument from the past. Adolph Sax (1814–1894), born in Belgium, was a flautist, clarinetist, and instrument maker who received recognition for improving the timbre and key system, and extending the lower range of the bass clarinet. He was also noted for making the ophicleide, a brass instrument played with a cup mouthpiece but having tone holes fitted with as many as twelve woodwind-like keys. With this background, one might speculate that the stage was set in Sax's mind for a single reed woodwind instrument that would produce the sound characteristics of a brass instrument. It was also Sax's intention to design such an instrument to overblow at the octave rather than at the twelfth, as does the clarinet, in order to permit the player to use the same fingering in all registers. And so appeared the saxophone.

Sax designed and built a series of fourteen saxophones, spanning the tonal range from sopranino to contrabass. In 1846 he was granted a patent on these instruments, making him among the first instrument makers to purposely design, build, and produce a woodwind instrument, rather than his work resulting from the evolution of a series of previous such instruments.

After the patent expired, the saxophone was improved by several other makers who enhanced the key system to facilitate playing legato passages and chromatics, changed the bell, and extended the instrument's range down to B-flat. A significant modification in the key work replaced what were two octave keys, which operated the two octave vents, with one key controlling both vents. The saxophone now holds an important position in all categories of instrumental music.

DOUBLE REED INSTRUMENTS

Shawm—The shawm, dating back to the twelfth century, was a double reed, conical-bore instrument with eight tone holes, seven on the front and one on the back. The reed on some ancient shawms was surrounded by a windcap (see chapter 9) called a pirouette. With this device in place the player's lips had no direct contact with the reed, thereby making it possible to play the instrument while on horseback or marching. The disadvantage to this arrangement was the player's lack of control of intonation, expression, and volume normally afforded by direct contact with the reed. The resulting sound was piercing and very rich in overtones. Its strident tone was intended to compete with and accompany trumpets and percussion instruments.

As the shawm evolved, the tone quality was modified to some degree by a change in its architecture. The range was increased by an octave, and the bore and tone holes were reduced in size. Various sized shawms were made to cover the range from soprano to bass, the latter being less than successful due to its inconvenient size. The shawm enjoyed popularity up to the middle of the seventeenth century, at which time the oboe began to make its presence known.

Oboe—The oboe is a derivative of the shawm, but with a refined key system that permits the player to display virtuosity with reasonable ease. The removal of the windcap gives the player direct contact with the double reed, improving intonation, timbre, and volume control. The result is an instrument that is compatible with those of a modern orchestra, as opposed to the shawm which produces a more "independent" sound.

The oboe body was divided into three parts for convenient transport and to facilitate repairs to the body. Damage to one section of a three-piece body is easier to deal with than damage to a one-piece body, since the damaged piece could easily be replaced without having to replace the entire body.

In determining who invented the oboe and when it was invented, one can only speculate on the basis of anecdotal evidence from individuals in the European music world of the seventeenth century. I believe there is no sense in pursuing that sort of speculation. What is of interest is the various iterations of the instrument that appeared throughout Europe. As the oboe evolved, it went through four stages of development, labeled the Baroque, Classical, Viennese, and conservatory models.

The original Baroque oboe was a simple instrument with three keys and a range from C4 to D6. In order to move to a higher register, the player had to increase the intensity of the air stream.

The Classical period oboe had additional keys, a decreased bore diameter to ease playing in the upper register, and a vent key (not quite an octave key as we know it), which served to shift up an octave more easily. It was later in the oboe's evolution that a true octave key was devised. The Classical oboe range increased to F6.

The Viennese oboe began to appear in the last quarter of the nineteenth century. It had a larger diameter bore and used a wider reed, resulting in a forceful, more powerful double reed sound. The upper register was also stronger in both timbre and projection due to the increase in upper partials. Overall, the Viennese oboe might be considered the bridge from the antique to the contemporary instrument. The Viennese oboe is still in use today.

The conservatory oboe, developed about the same time as the Viennese oboe, had a key system modeled after that of the Boehm flute system. This system was not very popular, but did act as the next step in the development of the instrument to reach the point of the modern full conservatory system now in use. The full conservatory system has forty-five keys, some with rings and others with plateau keys. These oboes have a range from B-flat3 to A6.

A number of other oboes have been developed to form a family of instruments that range from the piccolo oboe to the contrabass oboe. These include the oboe d'amore, a mid-range oboe with a modified tone; the cor anglais in F, encompassing a range a perfect fifth lower than that of the soprano oboe, and the bass oboe, a full octave below the soprano oboe and twice its size.

Bassoon—The dulcian, considered to be the forerunner of the bassoon, was popular for about two hundred years beginning from the mid-sixteenth century. Like the bassoon, the dulcian used a double reed connected to a bocal. The bore was conical and long enough to have to be folded upon itself; however, unlike the bassoon, the dulcian was carved from one piece of maple. The tone holes had to be drilled at an angle so that on the inside of the bore they were placed according to the acoustical requirements, while on the outside of the instrument they would accommodate a normal finger span of the player. During its period of popularity, eight different-size versions were developed to complete the soprano to bass range. The instrument had eight tone holes and two keys. The dulcian continued to be popular as the bassoon began to make its appearance.

Martin Hotteterre (1657–1712), a prominent flautist, composer, and Renaissance man in the music world of his time, is credited with being one of several individuals responsible for inventing the bassoon. As a member of a large family of instrument makers, one might speculate that Hotteterre was able to use his musical ability, experience, and creativity in conjunction with the skills of his instrument maker family members to develop and build an early bassoon. Hotteterre increased the size of the bell, extending the range of the bassoon to B-flat, and designed the instrument in four sections so the bore could be more accurately machined.

Carl Almenraeder (1786–1846) designed a bassoon with seventeen keys, which was able to play a four octave range chromatically. Almenraeder joined **J. A. Heckel** (1812–1877) in producing what would ultimately become the German Heckel system bassoon. Heckel went on to expand the range of the bassoon and to create a contrabassoon. Both of these were prototypes for the bassoons used today.

Advances in technology for musical instrument manufacturing, and an increased understanding of the principles of acoustics, enabled instrument makers to provide for the increased demands of the performance community. And so evolved the Heckel or German system and the Buffet or French system bassoons. These are two distinctly differently designed instruments which, to date, serve two differing viewpoints on what a bassoon should be.

The Buffet (French) design has a simple twenty-two key system joined with a narrow bore. The results are less complicated articulation requirements and a more lyrical, mellifluous tone quality. The Heckel (German) system features a more complicated key system with up to twenty seven keys joined with a wider bore, producing a fuller sound. The Heckel system bassoons currently enjoy popularity throughout most of the world while the Buffet model has greater popularity in France, Spain, and Canada.

Summary—Woodwind instruments, which are not all made of wood and some of which have not a piece of wood in their entire makeup, are the most mechanically complex of the acoustic orchestral instruments. As such, their evolution had to consist of a greater concentration on the technical and mechanical aspects of their inventors' creativity than was the case with creators of the other acoustic instruments. Artistry, musicianship, and creativity, combined with a sensitivity to the science and esthetics of music production, all play a role in the creation of all musical instruments, but one might sense that the mechanical aspects of those creative efforts took a more dominant role in the evolution of woodwind instruments.

11

How Woodwind Instruments Work

THE FLUTE

A fully assembled flute is approximately 26½ inches (67.3 cm) long. The head joint of the flute is a slightly tapered tube containing a lip plate into which a hole called an embouchure hole is bored (figure 11.1). The tube is stopped at one end with a crown assembly consisting of a decorative threaded piece called a crown (A). This is screwed onto a threaded screw (B) upon which there is a first round metal disc (C) followed by a tubular cork (D) followed by a second round metal disc (E).

Figure 11.1.   Flute Head Joint

The head joint added to the body and foot joint of the flute form a cylinder or tube, in which there are a number of holes that can be opened or closed by key mechanisms.

When a flute is played, the column of air within the body of the instrument is set into motion by the player blowing a stream of air across the embouchure hole in the head joint (figure 11.2). The stream of air will set the column of air within the flute vibrating. The vibrating column of air will extend to the point where the first open tone hole on the flute's body occurs. At that point (arrow), the motion is interrupted and the vibrating air column ends.

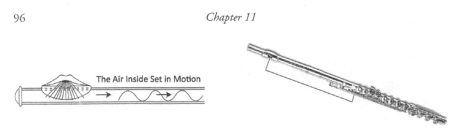

The Air Inside Set in Motion

Figure 11.2. Vibrating Column of Air

The length of the vibrating column determines the pitch of the tone being produced. The shorter the vibrating air column, the higher the pitch; the longer the vibrating air column, the lower the pitch. The performer can shorten or lengthen the effective length of the tube or body of the instrument by opening or closing the side or tone holes on the body with the use of padded keys and levers. The player can close holes to lengthen the flute and produce lower notes, or open holes to shorten the flute and produce higher notes.

Sound Production—Sound is generated on a flute when the player, resting the lip plate against his or her chin just below the lower lip, directs a stream of air across the embouchure hole (see figure 11.2). As the stream of air strikes the edge of the embouchure hole opposite the player's lip, that air stream undulates above and below the edge, exciting a pattern of vibrations within the head joint. These in turn set the air contained within the body of the flute into motion, resulting in a flute sound. A tone produced in this manner is often referred to as an edge tone.

The position of the player's lower lip on the lip plate and the shape of the player's lips and facial muscles in forming a space through which the air is blown make up the embouchure. Since all players have slightly different-shaped mouths, it is necessary for each embouchure to be developed as dictated by the player's individual oral structure.

Flute manufactures are able to control the sound their flute design produces by using different shapes, sizes, and locations for the embouchure hole and the lip plate. The shape of the embouchure hole can be either rectangular with rounded edges or oval.

The sound that is produced by the process described above will only be that sound fundamental to the instrument's design. In order to provide the option of producing an assortment of sounds, the instrument must be designed to enable the player to alter the length of the vibrating column at will and with versatility.

The Key System—The laws of physics dictate the location and size of the tone holes on the body of a woodwind instrument. Unfortunately, the requirements set by these laws do not coincide with the structure of the human hand, and so in order to fulfill the increasing demand for more notes and greater versatility, mechanical means had to be found to extend the potential span of the fingers. Thus began the introduction of keys for woodwind instruments. Using the modern key system, it is now possible to control the opening and closing of tone holes regardless of their location on the body of an instrument.

Key systems for all woodwind instruments use the same principles of leverage, and are described by the same terminology. There are two basic types of keys. These are called open and closed. The terms "open" and "closed" are not to be confused with similar terms used to describe the open hole, French, or perforated keys, or the closed hole, or plateau, keys of the flute.

An open hole key on a flute actually has a hole in its middle (figure 11.3). It is necessary for a player to place his or her finger in precisely the correct position on the key in order to cover the opening. Most musicians believe that open hole (French) keys produce a better sound than the closed hole (plateau) keys, since the open design strengthens the upper partials of each note, thereby enriching the sound.

Figure 11.3. Open Hole and Closed Hole Flute Keys

A plateau or closed hole key on a flute is solid and covers a hole completely (figure 11.3). This allows the player a bit more latitude in finger placement.

The term open key, when used in the broadest sense, refers to a key that, when at rest, is not covering the hole it services (figure 11.4). With the key at rest, that hole is open, but has a key to cover it when necessary.

Figure 11.4. Open Flute Key and Closed Flute Key

The term closed key, again when used in its broadest sense, refers to a key that, when at rest, covers and seals the hole it services (figure 11.4). Both types of keys, when activated, produce the inverse effect their names imply, that is, when activated, a closed key opens the hole it services, whereas an open key closes the hole it services.

Flute Keys—Flute keys of modern design follow basic principles of leverage, using a fulcrum as a pivot point on which the key rocks back and forth when activated. There are three parts to a key mechanism (figure 11.5). The part in contact with the player's finger is called either the paddle, spatula, or finger (A). On the opposite end

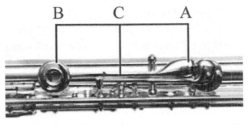

Figure 11.5. Flute Key Parts

of the key is the pad cup (B). This cup contains a pad, most often made of felt, which is covered with leather, fish skin, or sheep skin. The pad covers the tone hole. The paddle and cup are joined by a stem called an arm, which in turn is connected to a hollow tube called a hinge tube (C). That tube is connected to the flute by two posts.

Key Springs—Two types of springs are used to provide the tension required to return a key to its position of rest. These are wire springs or flat springs (figure 11.6).

Wire springs (A), as the name implies, are wires usually made of an alloy cut to the length required by its position on the instrument. These are inserted into a hole in the post that holds the flute key in place.

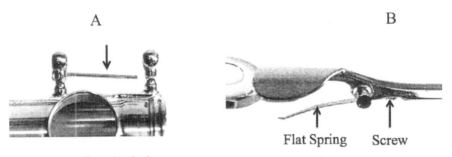

Figure 11.6. Flute Key Springs

Flat springs (B) are also made of various metal alloys and are shaped and sized to fit their position on the instrument. A flat spring is shaped to lie flat on the underside of a key. The spring has a hole in the contact end where a screw is inserted to hold the spring on the key.

Tone Holes—Tone holes on flutes extend out from the body, whereas tone holes on other woodwind instruments are usually drilled into the instrument's body. The flute tone hole can be constructed independently of the body and then soldered into place, or it can be drawn from the material of the body itself.

The process used to construct drawn tone holes consists of drilling a small hole in the body of the flute and then pulling a series of balls of increasingly larger size through the hole. The drawing process pulls the material from the inside of the body upward, forming a cup-like projection that extends from the flute body. The resulting projection is then leveled and its edge is rolled, providing a smoother surface on which the pad can rest. This process creates a smoother extrusion, which is thought by some to produce less resistance to the air flow and, therefore, a better tone.

The Flute Family—At this time only four members of the flute family are commonly used in contemporary orchestras. The concert flute in C is the most common and easily recognizable. This instrument has a prominent role in orchestral, concert band, and marching band repertoires as well as in solo works.

The piccolo in C is a small version of the C flute, sounding one octave higher. The piccolo is often used to double with flute and/or violin melodies, adding brightness or an "edge" to the sound. Another use for the piccolo in C is to add a decorative upper melody to a selection. This technique can best be heard in some of the more popular marches by John Philip Sousa.

Next in order of descending sound below the C flute is the alto flute in G. This instrument sounds a fourth lower than the written note while maintaining the same written range in the score. The alto flute is not particularly effective in the higher register, but in the middle and lower registers it produces a very mellow rich tone.

At the lowest end of the range of the flute family is the bass flute in C. This flute sounds an octave lower than the written note while it shares the same written range with the C flute. Due to the extraordinary size of this bass instrument and the comparatively large size of the embouchure hole in the head joint, some players may have a difficult time adjusting to the bass flute after playing the other instruments of the family. A great deal more airflow is required to generate the vibrations that excite the air column within the body of this instrument. However, the resulting sound is a rich and haunting tone which is most useful for special effects.

Three additional flutes are available but seldom used. These are the treble flute in G, the soprano in E-flat, and the tenor in B-flat. These instruments are sometimes used for special effects or to satisfy the needs of a particular score.

Summary—Sound is generated on the flute through the use of an edge tone–type head joint. The sound generated is amplified through the body of the flute and manipulated by a side hole–shortening keyed system.

Flutes are made of a variety of materials including wood, crystal, and numerous metals and alloys. Of greatest importance is the fact that the tone quality of a flute is almost entirely the product of the design of the head joint, embouchure hole, and body. The material used in the construction of the body and keys of the flute have little effect on its tone quality.

THE CLARINET

The clarinet is a single reed, mostly cylindrical tube about 26 inches (66 cm) long. The body of the instrument is not totally cylindrical but instead flares out slightly at its lowest segment to accommodate a bell, which continues the flared shape to the end of the instrument. The mouthpiece is tapered toward the tip so that the entire instrument, although cylindrical for the most part, actually starts out small, and ends up larger.

The B-flat soprano clarinet (figure 11.7) consists of a mouthpiece with reed, ligature, and cap (A), a barrel (B), upper joint, (C) lower joint (D), and a bell (E). All of the sections are connected by cork-covered tenons (F), which fit into sockets. The upper and lower joints are fitted with keys in the form of open rings and levers attached to padded keys (G).

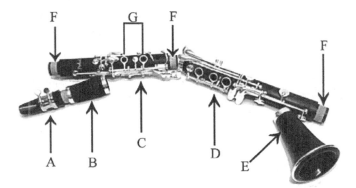

Figure 11.7.   B-flat Soprano Clarinet

The range of the contemporary soprano clarinet is from E3 below middle C, to G6 two octaves above middle C. This range is divided into three sections. The lowest register from E3 to B-flat4 is called the chalumeau. The middle register, called the clarion, has a range from B4 to C6. The altissimo is the highest register spanning from C-sharp6 to G6. As the notes of each register are played, the timbre of the tone in the registers differs. Chalumeau register sounds are full bodied, and can be mellifluous or powerful depending on the intensity with which the player attacks the notes. As the notes progress upward, the timbre can be delicate, but has the potential to become more strident.

The clarinet, like the other woodwind instruments, is constructed with a basic set of six tone holes on the front of its body. The six tone holes are covered by the index, middle, and third finger of each hand, with the left hand covering the top three holes and the right hand, the bottom three holes. Additional tone holes exist in appropriate locations on the body to complete the notes on the instrument. These holes are covered by keys with pads in them and are articulated by the thumb, pinky fingers, and the sides of the index fingers between the first and second knuckle on each hand.

When playing the clarinet, the effective length of the instrument is as long as the distance between the mouthpiece and the first open hole (figure 11.8A). As the holes are covered, the effective length of the instrument becomes longer and the sound

Figure 11.8. Clarinet Tone Holes

lower (B). In addition to the six tone holes, there are the side keys which, when activated, alter the tone produced when any or all of the six open holes are covered.

On the back of the clarinet at the left thumb position is a register key that is unique to that instrument (figure 11.8C). Other woodwind instruments have an octave key in the same location which, when engaged, will raise the note being played an octave. The clarinet has a register key in place of the octave key, which raises the pitch of the note being played a twelfth instead of an octave.

The Key System—The mechanism or key system of the clarinet went through about two centuries of evolution before becoming what is now referred to as the Boehm system, named after Theobald Boehm. However, Boehm had little if anything to do with the development and design of the key mechanism. His primary accomplishment was in determining the placement of the tone holes in the body of the instrument to allow the laws of acoustics to be satisfied. The actual mechanism was developed by Klosé and Buffet (see chapter 10). Since Boehm's research findings required placement of tone holes that rendered playing with the human hand impossible, Hyacinthe Klosé, a teacher of clarinet at the Paris Conservatory, and Louis-Auguste Buffet, still a well-known name in clarinet manufacturing, collaborated to invent a key system that would accommodate Boehm's design.

The current Boehm model clarinet has twenty-four tone holes that are controlled by seventeen keys and six rings. These rings are actually open circles of metal that encircle tone holes. When the tone hole is covered by the player's finger, it depresses the ring, which activates a reciprocal action that in turn covers one or more additional holes. A number of modifications have been made on the key system, primarily intended to facilitate the player transition from one note to another, or to produce a trill that may be particularly awkward to execute.

Sound Production—Sound is generated on the clarinet by means of a single cane reed attached by a ligature to a well-designed and carefully constructed mouthpiece.

As a player initiates a stream of air flowing through and against the reed/mouthpiece combination, the reed is set in motion, vibrating against the mouthpiece. This causes the column of air within the body of the instrument to vibrate, producing a sound. Current research in the technology of musical instruments offers voluminous evidence to indicate that the quality of sound produced by wind instruments is more the result of the mouthpiece/reed combination than any other factor or combination of factors incorporated in the design or construction of the instrument.

Clarinet mouthpieces have been made of practically every material imaginable. However, over the centuries, trial and error encouraged the industry to settle on the use of wood, glass, crystal, plastic, or hard rubber. Although the material used is of some consequence, its importance must be judged in conjunction with other design considerations in making a mouthpiece. In the broadest terms one might say that extremes in the design of any aspect of the mouthpiece should be avoided, if the designer is to provide for the average player. Conversely, at the top level of professional performance, a highly specialized design can be obtained through the combined efforts of the performer and the mouthpiece maker.

Although there are trends that seem to indicate that certain materials and dimensions are more effective than others for general use, one should bear in mind that all recommendations for such designs must be subject to the needs and physical individuality of the player. All rules must allow for exceptions.

The Barrel, Joints, and Bell—The first phase of the voyage of the column of air that has been excited into motion by the sound generator, that is, the mouthpiece and reed, takes place within the barrel of the instrument (see figure 11.7). The barrel is a short cylindrical section used to join the mouthpiece to the body of the clarinet. Although the original Boehm patent did not have a barrel, making the upper joint one piece, the barrel became a part of all instruments to date. The rationale to its persistence is that it can function as an aid to tuning. The player can extend or contract the overall length of the instrument by moving the barrel slightly in or out of the upper joint, thereby raising or lowering the instrument's overall pitch.

Of equal importance is the fact that the barrel is the first part of the body of the instrument to receive the flow of warm moist air from the mouthpiece. It is, consequently, subjected to the greatest amount of expansion and contraction from the constant humidity and temperature changes, which often result in cracking the wood. In such a case, a simple replacement of the barrel will resolve the problem as opposed to having to repair or replace the entire upper joint of the instrument.

Following the mouthpiece and barrel, the third and fourth sections of the clarinet are the upper and lower joints. These are essentially cylindrical in shape, though there is some flaring in the lower joint, starting anywhere from the fourth-lowest side hole to the last hole. Flaring is necessary to accommodate the bell, which compensates for the acoustical inconsistencies inherent in the clarinet design.

The bell of the clarinet is the lowest portion of the body. This section serves as an extension of the sound amplification system. It also compensates for the absence of subsequent open holes when all holes are closed to play the lowest note on the instrument. When a note other than the lowest one is played, some side holes are closed, with the remainder left open. The last two or, at most, three of these remaining open holes allow the tone to radiate from the instrument, thereby enhancing tone quality and amplification. When the lowest note on the instrument is reached, these successive open amplifying holes no longer exist, causing the tone quality and amplification to suffer. The addition of the bell compensates for the absence of the amplifying holes by acting as an extension of the amplification system.

Characteristic Sound—The tone quality or timbre of any instrument is a result of the intensity of the overtones (harmonics or upper partials) produced in relation to the fundamental (see chapter 2, figure 2.4). The quantity and intensity of these overtones superimposed on the fundamental result in the timbre that is identified with any particular instrument. In the case of the clarinet, the even-numbered upper partials (i.e., the second, fourth, sixth, etc.) are present in a relatively smaller amplitude than the odd-numbered partials (i.e., the third, fifth, etc.). This imbalance accounts for the characteristic clarinet sound.

Material—The material used in constructing a clarinet has little or no effect on the tone quality. Empirical studies strongly indicate that those involved in the selection of musical instruments, in this case clarinets, should direct most of their attention to the sound-generating aspect of the outfit while giving less attention to the material from which the body is made. The mouthpiece and reed on a clarinet deserve the greatest investment, while the materials from which the remainder of the instrument is constructed are of less importance.

The Clarinet Family—The inventiveness of the human mind has resulted in the creation of numerous clarinets of assorted sizes and transpositions. At this time in our musical evolution, some of the many choices of clarinets in common use are A-flat and E-flat sopranino; B-flat soprano; A soprano; F basset horn; E-flat alto; B-flat bass; EE-flat contra-alto; and BB-flat contrabass. For all clarinets, the sound generators, bodies, mechanisms, and acoustical principles are essentially the same. The significant differences are in their size and transposition, the shape of the bell, and the coupling devices connecting the mouthpieces to the main bodies of the instruments.

Summary—Studies clearly indicate that the essence of the clarinet's sound quality is primarily the product of the mouthpiece, and all that follows serves merely as a means to amplify and manipulate that sound. The clarinet is an acoustically complex instrument. Its cylindrical design lessens the intensity of the even-numbered upper partials in relation to the fundamental, and emphasizes the odd-numbered partials. Since it functions as a cylinder as opposed to a cone, the acoustical balance of nodes and anti-nodes (points of interrupted vibration and of greatest vibration) results in the instrument overblowing at the twelfth instead of at the octave, as do the other woodwinds. This then increases the complexity of the tone hole placement and size so that accurate intonation relationships among the registers become virtually impossible. The solution is found in placing and sizing the tone holes in such a way that none of the registers is radically out of tune, yet never truly in tune.

THE SAXOPHONE

The saxophone (figure 11.9) is a quasi-inverted, S-shaped, conical brass tube beginning at about the size of a dime, and ending with a bell about the size of a teacup saucer.

Unlike most other musical instruments, the saxophone was conceived and invented by one individual, the Belgian clarinetist Adolphe Sax. It was his intention to bridge the gap between the brass and woodwind instrument sections of the orchestra by combining the features of both. The result was a brass instrument with holes in

Figure 11.9. Saxophone

the body which, when opened and closed, shorten or lengthen the effective sound-producing length of the instrument. The saxophone generates sound by a single-reed mechanism similar to that of the clarinet (see figure 9.1). Due to Sax's unique, perhaps even radical concept, there was and still continues to be a wide difference of opinions regarding the virtues and shortcomings of the instrument.

The saxophone has a written range from B-flat3 below middle C to F-sharp6 an octave above the treble staff. The instrument shortens or lengthens the vibrating column of air that produces sound through the use of from eighteen to twenty-one tone holes and two vent or octave keys. The saxophone is a hybrid instrument that can produce such a variety of timbres that it can be used in jazz bands and symphony orchestras alike, and can even accompany the human voice.

The Mouthpiece—The mouthpiece of the saxophone appears to be very similar to that of the clarinet. The differences are not in the labels given to the parts nor in the general appearance of the two mouthpieces, but rather in the detail of the specifications of construction. Whereas a clarinet mouthpiece is specifically designed to produce a distinct clarinet sound, when used by a professional, saxophone mouthpieces can produce a wide variety of sounds that demonstrate the acoustical versatility of the instrument.

The facing on a mouthpiece, the flat side where the reed is placed, is one of the most important parts of any reed instrument, for it is the facing in conjunction with the reed, and the juxtaposition of the two, that ultimately produce the sound. The facing can be short, medium, or long. Following the basic concept that runs through all of musical instrument design, that is, the bigger the instrument, the lower the sound, then longer facings favor lower sounds, shorter facings favor higher sounds, and medium facings strike a balance. The obvious conclusion is that a medium facing will probably be best for most students.

A vast number of changes have been made in the design of the saxophone's mouthpiece since its inception in 1840. It has been lengthened, shortened, enlarged, made smaller, cored out, tapered, colored, and reshaped using every sort of material conceivable. The materials from which the mouthpieces are made are similar to those of the clarinet, namely, wood, glass, crystal, plastic, and rubber, along with some use of metal such as gold and silver. Each of these changes has contributed to the wide variety of opinions on the saxophone's sound, since each change in mouthpiece design resulted in a change in tone quality or timbre.

Because the saxophone produces tones that include overtones up to the sixteenth partial, greater in number than in any other instrument, the mouthpiece must not only act as a medium to supply sound, but also as a device to control the abundance of sound that results from the design of the instrument.

The 1930s saw the evolution of the era of the large dance band, which brought a demand for a sound that would be more compatible with brass instruments. At that time the reed and brass instruments were distributed equally in bands, necessitating strengthening the sound of the reeds to match that of the brasses. Since sophisticated devices for sound evaluation were not yet available, it was necessary for those involved in research and development to rely on their ear and instinct to find remedies. Experimentation with materials of various densities and expansion coefficients resulted in redesigning the structure of the mouthpiece interior. This experimentation produced a number of mouthpieces so unsatisfactory that they led to the decline of the reputation of the saxophone as a serious instrument.

During that time one mouthpiece was developed that was a modification of the original and produced a richer tone with stronger emphasis on the upper partials. This event helped the saxophone regain some of its original popularity. Subsequently, the industry developed an additional design modeled on the contours of the clarinet mouthpiece. The new mouthpiece produced an extraordinarily powerful and penetrating sound, gaining favor with those performers of dance band music who were in competition with their brass-playing counterparts. Simultaneously, the saxophone was removed from use by classical musicians, due to the instrument's increasing incompatibility with symphonic sounds.

Further experimentation with the aid of more advanced technological sound evaluating devices led to smaller chambers, which proved to be unsatisfactory, and then to the double-tone chamber, which had a tapered cylindrical bore and a smaller tone chamber and throat. This mouthpiece produced a very aggressive sound, enabling a player to literally blast out the notes, but creating a greater likelihood that the less-experienced player might lose control of tone quality and intonation.

A mouthpiece that seemed to strike a suitable balance, incorporating most of the attributes mentioned above and in proportions that produced a tone acceptable to most "classical" musicians, was designed in France. Featuring a round chamber, it produced a smooth, mellow tone yet included sufficient upper partials to still be bright.

Progress in the study of the technology of musical instruments increasingly shows that a woodwind instrument's source of sound holds the primary responsibility for the quality of that sound. To reiterate, the mouthpiece is the major contributing factor to the quality of the tone produced. For the saxophone, the mouthpiece has proven to be such an extreme example of this position that players select theirs with great care and consideration for their individual aptitudes, physical characteristics, embouchures, and playing experience.

The Body—The mouthpiece of the saxophone is coupled to the instrument's body through an L-shaped neck (figure 11.9). The neck provides a convenient angle for placement of the mouthpiece in relation to the player's embouchure, and an appropriate placement for the primary octave or vent key. The main body of the instrument is made of brass, is conical in shape, and utilizes a series of side holes that increase in size as they descend on the main structure. The body ends in an upturned bell with tone holes incorporated almost to the very end of the structure.

The Key System—The key system of the saxophone uses principles that are similar to those of other woodwind instruments. One difference is that the pads on the keys of the saxophone are usually covered with leather instead of fish skin or sheepskin as used on other woodwind instruments. This covering is necessary because the large size of the tone holes and the force of the strike of the key against the tone holes result in increased wear on the pads. The large size also causes the pads to be more susceptible to the accumulation of moisture from the player's breath, making them subject to more rapid deterioration. Leather pads are stronger and hold up better under those conditions.

In order to produce the upper octave on a saxophone, it is necessary to divide the vibrating air column in the body of the instrument at the midpoint. This division is achieved through the use of two octave vents strategically placed to allow for acceptable but not perfect intonation on all notes. Technically, if one were to create a saxophone that played every note in tune, it would be necessary to have an octave vent for each note. The complexity of such a mechanism would make it impractical, and so, only two vents are used.

The Saxophone Family—The saxophone family has ten variations of the same instrument. Five currently in use are the B-flat soprano, E-flat alto, B-flat tenor, E-flat baritone, and the B-flat bass. The other five variations less commonly used are the F and E-flat sopranino, C soprano, F mezzo-soprano, C melody, and the E-flat contrabass. While all ten instruments belong to the saxophone family, the second five are not readily available, and are not commonly found in the scores of much music.

All saxophone models are almost identical in fingering and playing requirements, with only some adjustment needed by the player to accommodate for the different size of the instrument and mouthpiece. These changes are minor and easily adapted to by the player. Key systems and fingering are the same, and all instruments are written in the treble clef in spite of the soprano, alto, tenor, baritone, and bass classifications. Notation is, therefore, identical, and the player can easily switch from one instrument to another without any concern for clef changes.

Summary—The saxophone holds a unique position in the woodwind family for a number of reasons. It is not made of wood but usually of brass (although there have been some made of silver and others of plastic); it is the only single reed, conical instrument; it overblows at the octave; its tone quality can be radically changed by changing the mouthpiece; its intonation has so wide a range that the experienced player can capitalize on varying the pitch for special effects, though the amateur might have difficulty controlling pitch; and it can find a place in symphony, opera, and jazz, either as part of an ensemble or as a solo instrument, all with equal prominence. It has come to be very widely known, and both loved and hated. The saxophone might be considered the only instrument capable of being all things to all people.

THE OBOE

The oboe resembles the clarinet in appearance but is in many ways more closely related to the flute and to the saxophone. The oboe is a derivative of the shawm, an ancient woodwind instrument (see chapter 10). As with the shawm, the sound on the oboe is generated by a double reed that excites a column of air contained within a conical shaped body. The instrument can be made of a variety of hardwoods, plastic, or, less often, metal.

The body of the oboe is designed with tone holes covered with a key mechanism consisting of levers, cups, and pads similar to, but more complicated than, those of the clarinet (figure 11.10).

Figure 11.10.   Oboe

The cone-shaped bore of the oboe starts at the point of entry of the reed and is small in comparison with other woodwind instrument bores. Being conical, the oboe overblows at the octave. Because the cone is so small, it produces a tone that is rich in upper partials (see chapter 2) in relation to the fundamental. In fact, the instrument is capable of producing as many as twelve or more upper partials. These partials are extremely intense and, in some cases, are even capable of overpowering the fundamental. This is not to say that the fundamental is not audible to the listener, for the human ear, in conjunction with the central nervous system, is able to distinguish the intended pitch in spite of the ratio of the fundamental to its partners in sound. The oboe's small conical bore and proportionately small side holes, together with the forceful nature of a double reed sound generator, produce an intense, reedy sound that is distinctive and peculiar to the oboe.

Sound Production—The oboe has no mouthpiece. Its sound generator is a double reed, that is, two cane reeds bound together onto a metal tube called a staple. The staple is covered with cork and joins the reed to the body of the instrument (see figure 9.1). When the reed is placed between the player's lips and air is blown into the ()-shaped opening formed by the two blades of the reed, the blades vibrate against each other, activating the air column already present in the body of the instrument (figure 11.11). The sound produced is then modified by the body and keys of the instrument.

The oboe reed is simple in design. It is, however, the subject of much dismay, frustration, conflict, and despair among oboists. With the exception of the bassoon, the sound generators of other instruments are mouthpieces that are easily obtained. Unfortunately, oboists cannot go to the local music dealer and select a mouthpiece

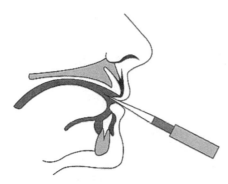

Figure 11.11. Oboe Player's Embouchure

from an assortment of designs, materials, sizes, and shapes. Oboists are relegated to either making their own reeds which will, incidentally, have a relatively short life, or depending on a reed maker for a steady supply. This dependence is unique to double reed players.

Although single reed users also suffer anguish related to reed usage, their plight is less onerous than that of the double reed user, since it is the mouthpiece of the single reed instrument and not the reed alone that plays the most significant role as the true sound generator. The double reed, which is constructed of cane, is by its very nature inconsistent. Each reed is unique in its structure. The same instrument played by the same performer can never reproduce exactly the same tone quality when a different reed is used.

The Single Reed Oboe Mouthpiece—One attempt at circumventing the inconsistency of the double reed was the introduction of the single reed mouthpiece designed for use on a double reed instrument. This mouthpiece copies the general structure and design of a clarinet mouthpiece, but is adapted to the size and needs of an oboe or bassoon. The purpose of the device is to enable a clarinet player to double on the oboe "in a pinch." When the music requires a short passage for an oboe, and the budget does not allow an oboist to be hired, the single reed mouthpiece can be used by a clarinetist. The single reed oboe (or bassoon) mouthpiece is also very convenient for younger students who may not be musically or physically mature enough to deal with all of the challenges of using a double reed.

The use of the single reed mouthpiece on an oboe has stirred some controversy. It is this writer's opinion that there is a place for the mouthpiece in the overall scheme of music study and performance and that, given certain circumstances, such a device can prove to be useful and can possibly even "save the day." Pragmatic but sparing use of any device that will extend the performance of music to those who need such aids is certainly advisable. But the user must also bear in mind that the single reed oboe mouthpiece is not a permanent substitute for the original double reed.

An in-depth look into oboe reeds requires complex and lengthy research and experimentation, and leads to inconclusive results. Writings by experts who specialize in the area of oboe sound production indicate that there are still no definitive recommendations regarding what will produce the best sound on a double reed instrument. There are still no final answers.

The Key System—During the past century and a half, a number of different key systems were tried in attempts to maximize the potential of the basic conical double reed instrument. These were simple systems such as a thumb plate system; non-automatic octave keys; low B–C connections; an articulated E-flat; a forked F vent; an articulated G-sharp thumb plate action; a half-hole plate; a semi-automatic octave key; and a full automatic octave key. These names in themselves have little meaning to the reader, but are listed just as an indication of how many different attempts have been made in this quest. Other devices were added to and subtracted from the key system of the oboe in France, Germany, England, Spain, and other countries. The many key systems that were developed enjoyed varying degrees of success and longevity.

All of the above evolved into what is now referred to as the conservatory system developed by Lucien Lorée and George Gillet during the years between 1900 and 1906. Today it is generally referred to as the plateau or French system. But, in fact, the saga does not end there, for there are a number of variations of this system. These are the basic conservatory, modified conservatory, standard conservatory, and full conservatory models. They are all modifications of the original design of Lorée and Gillet.

A point of interest is that, in spite of the preference for plateau keys by professional performers, the ring-type key (similar to that found on the clarinet) is recommended for school use. The ring system is less likely to go out of adjustment and is found to be more suited to the physical stress to which a school instrument may be subjected.

The oboe key system has an insatiable desire to be adjusted. Due to the complexity of the system and the variety of possible accessory keys, the instrument can have as many as seventeen adjustment screws. Each of these screws regulates two or more keys so that their reciprocal function will be operational. Adjustments must be made judiciously and only by a professional technician, if possible.

The Oboe Family—In addition to the oboe in C there are four other similar instruments, often referred to as deep oboes. These are the oboe d'amore in A, the cor anglais or English horn in F, the bass oboe in low C, and the heckelphone in low C. All of these instruments transpose below the oboe in C by the interval of the key named. They share almost all of the characteristics of the oboe in C, using a double reed on a conical body controlled by a complex key system over a side-hole system.

Summary—The oboe comes from one of the oldest methods of woodwind instrument music making. It evolved from the primitive act of squeezing together the ends of a cut reed, and blowing air through the small space remaining to excite a vibration. It developed into a highly complicated woodwind instrument, producing sounds of great intensity, and is regarded by many as one of the most sophisticated of the modern orchestral instruments. It is challenging to learn, difficult to play, expensive to purchase, and demanding in its maintenance requirements, but still the tonal jewel of the ensemble.

THE BASSOON

The bassoon (figure 11.12) shares many of the historical, physical, and mechanical characteristics of the oboe. The body of the bassoon has a conical bore and uses a body tone-hole system served by a mechanical padded key system like that of all other woodwind instruments. Bassoons are considered by many to be acoustical enigmas and, as such, are the instruments most challenging to understand, build, and play. The instrument is about 8 feet (2.5 m) long, and is separated into five sections that are assembled using the tenon design similar to that used in the clarinet and oboe.

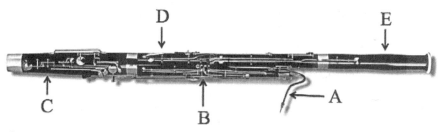

Figure 11.12.   Bassoon

The smallest section of the bassoon is the bocal (A). Made of metal, it serves as the receiver for the reed and connects that sound generator (reed) to the body of the instrument. The bore at the bocal is about ⅛ of an inch (3 mm) in diameter. The bore progresses through the body or amplifier, which consists of the wing joint (B), boot joint (C), bass joint (D), and bell joint (E). The bore ultimately reaches a final diameter of about 1½ inches (3.8 cm) at the bell. Because the bassoon is about 8 feet long, it is folded in half at about the midpoint by the boot joint, which has a U-bend in it. These sections of the bassoon are usually made of maple, although other woods, ebonite, and occasionally metal are used.

Bassoons are now made in two types, the long-bore and short-bore models. The long-bore instrument produces a darker tone and is believed by many to produce truer intonation. The short-bore bassoon is more difficult to control and, therefore, is less consistent in its intonation.

A design feature peculiar to the bassoon is that the tone holes at some points need to travel as far as 2 inches (5 cm) from the outside of the body to reach the bore. These must be drilled at an angle so that the bore end of the hole will be positioned at the correct acoustical position inside the bore to achieve the desired pitches, while the player's fingering end of the hole enables him or her to span the distance with the fingers on the exterior of the body. This particular requirement results in a weakening of the venting (interrupting the vibrating column of air to reach upper registers), which allows a great portion of the energy to travel to the lower section of the instrument. The result is the strong resonance that is unique to the sound of the bassoon.

Sound Production—The sound generator for the bassoon is the double reed (see figure 9.1). Like the oboe, the bassoon has no mouthpiece and so it shares all of the problems of the oboe's sound production, but with a few additions.

Bassoon reeds are consistently inconsistent. One can expect no two reeds will be alike. Therefore, there will be no two reeds producing exactly the same sound, even though they are used by the same performer and on the same instrument. This is due to the fact that good bassoon reeds are most often individually made by hand and are the product of the skills or limitations of the maker. In addition, the raw material, cane, is by its very nature lacking in consistency, and is so delicate that the life span of a bassoon reed is relatively short. This combination of factors creates a potential for problems of sound production on the bassoon that require much dedicated attention and expertise.

Bassoon reeds are made in a variety of sizes, shapes, densities, and designs. There are usually ten parts to the design or shaping of the reed. If one were to multiply the number of variables by the number of parts where those variations might occur, the likelihood of arriving at a clinical prescription for making a bassoon reed becomes almost impossible. One should be aware of the design, structure, fabrication process, and assorted possible styles of reeds commonly in use. This information can serve as a base from which to work in developing a point of view and for gathering additional knowledge on the subject.

Bassoon reeds, like the instruments they serve, are classified as being either German or French in construction. The difference between them is primarily in the thickness of the lay, or heart, of the reed. German reeds tend to be thicker in the heart, whereas French reeds have a more gradual and even taper. This difference can be seen by holding the reed up to a strong light. One will notice that the center of the lay of the German reed is shadowed, whereas on the French reed, the light passes through more evenly. This difference can also be felt by gently passing the heart of the reed between the thumb and index finger. The German reed will have a bulge down the center of the lay, while the French reed will feel flatter. As a result of this structural difference, the French reed produces a thinner, more penetrating sound, while the German reed has a more haunting, darker sound.

Another characteristic that must be considered when examining a bassoon reed is the longitudinal contour of the lay. There are three possible contours that are used in double reed manufacturing. These are the parallel contour, the wedge contour, and the double-wedge contour.

The parallel contour is constructed so that both blades are of equal thickness throughout. This design is not commonly used, for it is difficult to make, and presents a problem to the player in maintaining control of pitch and tone quality.

The wedge contour, where the blades gradually taper or thin out toward the tip, is used primarily in the construction of the French-style reed. This design is more popular and easier to fabricate.

The double-wedge contour, used primarily for the German design reed, has many variations because it uses two degrees of taper. The first section of the blades shows a very slight taper or, sometimes, none at all. The second section of the blades then tapers more abruptly toward the tip of the reed. The length of the two sections of taper can vary significantly according to the needs of the player and the design used by the reed maker.

The Key System—The two different types of bassoons currently in use, the German system and the French system, are similar in appearance. However, there are considerable differences in the number of keys and how they are utilized. The manner in which the individual keys function is for the most part the same as that of the other woodwind instruments. Padded cups cover holes, and the cups are interconnected and controlled by the player depressing spatulas or finger plates. Posts, pivot screws, screw rods and tubes, wire springs, and flat springs are all present in some form, and all of these conform to the descriptions of the key systems for instruments discussed earlier (see "Flute Keys" above).

In spite of all the similarities of design, there remains one profound difference between the French and German key systems. The German system bassoon contains many more keys, especially in the boot joint (figure 11.12). Specifically, the German system, sometimes referred to as the Heckel system after the family of the same name that owns the world's most famous bassoon factory, will contain from twenty-one to twenty-four keys, depending on the sophistication of the model. Additional features are assorted rollers to facilitate a smooth transition from one key to another, an automatic whisper key, assorted trill keys, ring keys, key guards, joint locks, an extended range, posts and springs that are locked in place with screws, metal-lined tone holes, extra octave keys, and the partially covered half-hole keys such as those found on the oboe.

All of the extras on this rather lengthy list are "extra" only in the sense that a bassoon could be played without most of them. They are available on the Heckel or German model bassoon, facilitate playing the instrument, and improve its intonation and life span. These parts are fabricated of nickel silver, German silver, or brass.

The French key system permits the player to perform the same music, but the system is mechanically simpler and relies more on the player's virtuosity to achieve the transitions from note to note. The French instruments also contain trill keys, finger plates and rings, rollers, and many of the other devices found in the German design. However, many notes are attainable only by using cross fingerings, half holing (rolling the finger to cover only half the hole), or trilling certain notes by means other than trill keys specifically designed to facilitate a particular trill. In spite of the fact that the German system appears to be the system of choice, a significant number of bassoonists in Europe still use bassoons built on the French system. American bassoonists almost exclusively use the German system.

The Bassoon Family—The only additional relative to the bassoon currently in use with some degree of regularity is the double bassoon or contrabassoon, which sounds an octave lower than the bassoon. There have been several other bassoons developed during the past century. Among them are the tenor, tenoroon, and soprano bassoons. These instruments are not commonly in use at this time.

Summary—The bassoon provides the lower notes of the woodwind choir. Considered by some to be the clown of instruments because of its ability to produce sounds that can evoke humor in the musical psyche, it is far from humorous in its design or on the demands it places on its players. On the opposite side of the spectrum is its ability to transmit solemnity, graphically demonstrated in the opening measures of Tchaikovsky's Sixth Symphony, the *Pathétique*.

In spite of the bassoon's large size, the successful work of its developers has made it possible for a skilled bassoonist to manipulate the instrument musically. There are many passages that are impressively rapid and complex and can be performed confidently and competently by the professional bassoonist.

Technologically speaking, the instrument is consistent with its woodwind relatives in terms of the maintenance demands of its sound generator, sound amplifier, and key work. The only possible exception might be that the keys are long and numerous and, therefore, may need more frequent regulation. Considering the acoustical and technological complexities created by the use of a double reed on a large, conical instrument, it appears that the bassoonist must function in an atmosphere of compromise in order to have the instrument respond effectively.

The bassoon cannot operate for more than one octave without sacrificing quality, and so the reed, which cannot be changed in mid-passage, must be designed to function reasonably effectively in all registers, at the expense of not being at its best in any one given register. Does this mean that becoming involved with a bassoon as a technician is to make a commitment to a life of challenge and frustration? Perhaps not! This may be one of the areas of musical instrument technology for an aspiring technician to make a mark in the industry by creating a redesigned bassoon that will produce the unique sound for which it is known without all of the negative characteristics inherent in the present instrument.

A GLOSSARY OF WOODWIND INSTRUMENT PARTS LISTED BY INSTRUMENT

This glossary will help the reader define terms that are related to woodwind instruments. See the discussion above for more in-depth information on these items. *Note:* Because woodwind instruments have a greater number of parts that are not universal to the family, the listings are divided by instrument.

Flute Parts

Adjustment screw Small screws strategically placed to facilitate adjusting the system.

Body (middle joint) The middle section of a flute.

Closed hole (plateau) key A closed hole or plateau key that is solid and covers a tone hole completely.

Crown A cap placed on the closed end of a flute head joint.

Embouchure hole A hole in the lip plate of a flute head joint across which the player blows a stream of air to produce a sound.

Embouchure plate A plate on the flute head joint upon which the player rests a portion of his or her lower lip.

Flat spring A spring that has a flat shape, used to rebound certain keys on woodwind instruments.

Foot joint The third or bottom section of a flute.

Gizmo A supplementary key on the foot joint used to facilitate fingering low B.

Head Joint The first section of a flute.

Head receiver The first section of the main body (middle joint) into which the head joint fits.

Hinge tube A tube that acts as a housing for the screws that hold the keys onto the posts.

Lip plate See embouchure plate.

Low B-flat key A key at the end of a flute that extends the range of a flute down to B-flat.

Open hole key A key that has a hole in its middle.

Post A post attached to the body of a flute onto which the hinge tubes and keys are attached.

Rib A strip of metal soldered on the body of a flute as a support onto which the posts are soldered.

Tenon The end portion of a section of a flute, which is reduced in size to fit into another section.

Tone holes Holes in the body of a flute covered by keys that enable the instrument to produce the different notes.

Wire spring A spring made of wire, used to rebound certain keys on a flute.

Clarinet Parts

Baffle (beak) The outer part of a clarinet mouthpiece upon which the player's teeth rest.

Barrel The second section of the five parts of a clarinet.

Bell The fifth section of a clarinet and the flared end of any wind instrument.

Bell ring A metal ring placed around the edge of a clarinet bell to reinforce that part.

Bore The cylindrical inner tube of a clarinet's body and of a clarinet mouthpiece.

Bridge key The key on a woodwind instrument that joins the key system at the point where two sections of the body of the instrument are connected.

Facing The gradually curved, upper section of the flat, reed side of a clarinet mouthpiece, from the table up to the tip.

Ligature A band, usually of metal or other man-made material, used to hold a reed on a woodwind instrument's mouthpiece.

Lower joint The fourth lower section of a clarinet.

Mouthpiece The part of an instrument that is placed in the player's mouth to produce sound.

Reed A piece of bamboo configured to produce sound on a woodwind instrument. Reeds are of different sizes and configurations for different instruments. They can also be made of metal, plastic, or any other material that will respond with the flexibility needed.

Register key The key on the back of a clarinet which, when pressed, shifts the notes up an interval of a twelfth.

Side rail The edge on either side of the window of a clarinet mouthpiece.

Table The flat surface on a clarinet mouthpiece upon which the reed lies.

Tenon The end portion of a section of the body of an instrument where it is reduced in size to fit into another section.

Tenon ring A metal ring put around the edge of a clarinet tenon to reinforce that part.

Throat The beginning part of the inner chamber of a clarinet mouthpiece.

Tip The very top edge of a clarinet mouthpiece.

Tone holes Holes in the body of a clarinet that are covered by keys, which open and close to produce different notes.

Upper joint The third section from the top of a clarinet.

Window The opening on the flat side of a clarinet mouthpiece over which the reed is placed.

Saxophone Parts

Bell The flared end of the body of a saxophone.

Body The main structure of a saxophone, to which the keys are attached.

Bow The bottom curve on the body of a saxophone.

Key guard Metal plates configured to the shape needed to protect the lower side keys on a saxophone.

Ligature A band, usually of metal or other man-made material, used to hold a reed on a woodwind instrument's mouthpiece.

Mouthpiece The part of an instrument that is placed in the player's mouth to produce sound.

Neck The first section of the body of a saxophone. The neck receives the mouthpiece.

Neck cork The cork wrapped around the top of the neck that acts as a gasket for the mouthpiece to connect to the neck.

Neck screw Screw that holds the neck in place on the main body of a saxophone.

Octave key The key on the back of a saxophone which, when pressed, raises the notes an octave.

Spatula keys Keys on the side of a saxophone that have an extended flat surface for the player's fingers.

Tone holes Holes in the body of a saxophone that are covered by keys, which open and close to produce different notes.

Oboe Parts

Adjustment screw Small screws strategically placed to facilitate adjusting the system.

Bell The bottom, flare-shaped section of an oboe.

Bridge key The key on a woodwind instrument that joins the key system at the point where two sections of the instrument meet.

Double reed Two reeds bound together, which serves as a mouthpiece for an oboe.

Lower joint The lower half of an oboe body.

Octave key The key that, when pressed, raises the notes being fingered an octave.

Reed socket The orifice on the top of an oboe body that receives the reed.

Staple The part of a double reed made of cork that connects to the body of the instrument.

Upper joint The upper half of an oboe body.

Bassoon Parts

Bass joint (long joint) The third and longest joint of a bassoon.

Bell The flare-shaped bell at the end of a bassoon's body.

Bell joint The fourth joint of a bassoon which ends in a flared bell.

Bocal (crook) A curved metal tube that joins the reed to the body of a bassoon.

Boot joint (butt or double joint) The bottom joint of a bassoon, in which the bore is turned around to travel up the remaining part of the instrument.

Crutch A hand rest attached to the side of a bassoon to assist the player in holding the instrument securely.

Double bassoon (contrabassoon) An instrument larger than a bassoon and sounding one octave lower.

Double reed Two reeds bound together, which serves as a mouthpiece for a bassoon.

Wing joint (tenor joint) The first joint of a bassoon, to which the crook is connected.

12

Percussion Instruments Defined

Percussion instruments produce sound by reacting to any type of agitation, such as being struck, scraped, or in the case of something with sound-producing particles in an enclosed vessel, shaken, or by being activated by a stream of air, as in a whistle. By definition then, almost anything can be labeled a percussion instrument. This results in the percussion section being the largest category of musical instruments in the industry.

Percussion instruments play an essential role in most music performing groups. But these instruments do not share the complexity in design, playing challenges, acoustics, sound-generating characteristics, and mechanical intricacy that one finds in a woodwind, brass, or string instrument. The chapters to follow will elaborate on this point of view.

CLASSIFICATION

A broad classification used for percussion instruments is by the type of sound they produce. These are either tuned or definite pitched, as in a bell or timpani, or not tuned or indefinite pitched, as in a snare or bass drum. A more general set of classifications uses the terms idiophone, chordophone, aerophone, or membranophone to categorize the manner in which the various acoustical musical instruments produce sound. Each family of instruments falls into one of these categories. The percussion section is unique in that there are instruments in that family that fit into every one of those four categories.

Idiophones—Idiophones are instruments that, when activated, produce sound through the vibration of the entire instrument. An example would be cymbals, bells, and chimes. When struck, these instruments respond with their entire structure to produce sound. Idiophones can be made of almost any material that can vibrate. Certain rocks or stones, which when struck react by producing sound, are considered to be idiophones. A percussion instrument made of such stones is called a lithophone.

Chordophones—In the percussion family chordophones are those instruments that use strings as their sound-producing source. In order for a chordophone to be classified as being in the percussion family, the strings must produce sound by being struck with a mallet or other hammer-like item. A hammered dulcimer and a piano are examples of chordophones.

Aerophones—Aerophones are instruments that produce sound by a flow of air from any source. In the percussion family, whistles and sirens fall into this category. One might argue that these instruments are actually wind instruments, and that may in fact be true; however, these particular instruments are almost always made part of the percussion section in an instrumental ensemble.

Membranophones—Membranophones contain some form of membrane as part of their structure and produce sound when that membrane is struck or agitated in some way. Drums are membranophones, since they are constructed with a membrane stretched over a shell.

An additional unofficial category of percussion instruments is a catch-all to cover the countless items that are not necessarily musical instruments, can produce sound by any means, and are used in some manner in music performance. These items can fall into any one of the four above-mentioned categories, but with somewhat dubious justification for being called a musical instrument. Included would be anvils, pots and pans, car horns, and almost anything that will make a sound when agitated in any manner. Percussion instruments of this nature are most commonly used in twentieth-century contemporary or popular compositions.

The unique position percussion instruments hold among their counterparts results from the fact that there is a large enough variety of percussion instruments to have them appear in each of the four major musical instrument categories. Whereas woodwind and brass instruments are strictly aerophones and the violin family of instruments is strictly made up of chordophones, percussion instruments exist in every category.

PERCUSSION INSTRUMENTS

Snare Drum—The snare drum is a membranophone (see figure 14.1). It consists of a shell upon which a membrane called a head is attached on both ends. The head is attached with a rim, which is bolted down to the shell with screws called tension rods. These are screwed into lugs or threaded metal receivers connected to the shell. The tension bars can be tightened or loosened with a drum key.

The shell or body of a snare drum can range in size anywhere from three to ten inches in depth and generally between twelve to fourteen inches in diameter. The snare from which the drum is named is a curled metal or plastic set of wires stretched across the bottom head of the drum. This addition produces the rattle-like brilliance associated with the typical sound of a snare drum.

Drum Head—Drum heads are made of animal hide or some form of polyester. Plastic heads can be found in single- or double-ply and in various thicknesses measured in millimeters, or one thousandth of a meter. Single-ply heads are most popular and can be bought in 7, 7.5, 10, and 12 mm thicknesses.

The axiom, common to all things musical, that smaller produces higher sounds and larger produces lower sounds applies here in that thinner heads produce higher upper partials with a resulting crisper sound, while thicker heads produce a fuller, warmer sound. The caveat here is that the single ply is thinner and as such, less durable.

Double-ply heads are made with two layers of Mylar, a form of plastic that can have the same thickness or differing thicknesses. In addition to the standard single- and double-ply heads, there are numerous designs that produce special effects. Among these are coated heads, which are sprayed with a variety of translucent or colored coatings to produce different sounds. Any addition to the surface of a drum head will have the effect of muffling the sound to some degree. This is not necessarily a negative and, for certain musical effects, may be desirable. Should a muffled sound be required, heads are made pre-muffled or with built-in mufflers. This effect is achieved by adding a layer of some substance on top or under the head, or having a two-layer head with oil between the layers. The variety of options is limited only by one's imagination.

Bass Drum—Bass drums are used in three different venues and, therefore, come in three different designs. They are all membranophones and adhere to the construction pattern of the snare drum, except that they are bigger and have no snare. The largest bass drum is used for concert bands or symphony orchestras. These range in diameter from thirty-two to forty inches, with an average depth of about twenty inches. The sizes can vary significantly depending on the desires and needs of the individual situations for which they are to be used.

Another type of bass drum, referred to as a kick drum, is used as part of a dance band or "trap" set of drums. This bass drum is constructed in the same pattern as the others, is played with a beater connected to a pedal, and can also vary in size.

A third type of bass drum is used for marching bands. It is lighter in construction and fitted with a harness to facilitate carrying. Marching bass drums are also constructed as those described above.

Cymbals—Cymbals are used to enhance and color music of every type. They can produce an endless variety of effects depending on their design, the material from which they are made, and the process by which they are manufactured. A cymbal is circular in shape and has a hole in its center for mounting on a stand or for installing a handle used to carry the cymbal. Cymbals are categorized by their size and weight because these two factors affect the quality and strength of the sound they produce. Larger and heavier cymbals produce louder sounds. Thinner cymbals produce a richer, more sustained sound.

The material from which cymbals are made is generally a type of alloy flexible enough to be formed into the shape and density desired by the manufacturer. These are referred to as sheet cymbals because they are formed from sheets of metal. Better-quality cymbals are fabricated from bell bronze and are forged or hammered by hand.

As is the case with many of the percussion instruments, the number of types of cymbals and variations of those types is endless. There are cymbals called bell; china; clash; crash; hi-hat; ride; sizzle; splash; swish; orchestra; suspended; marching; and finger, just to mention some. These all have a saga of evolution, design, material, and use, which can fill volumes.

Timpani—Timpani (timpano in the singular) are definite pitched instruments. They share many of the structural characteristics of the other drums but with a more sophisticated technology. Timpani are built on a copper, brass, or fiberglass shell shaped like a kettle and thereby comes the nickname "kettle drum." The kettle is fitted into a frame, which often has two wheels to facilitate transportation. Also fitted to that frame is a pedal used to make quick adjustments in pitch to the heads.

Timpani are made with bowl sizes ranging from twenty to thirty-two inches in diameter. As is the case with all musical instruments, the larger the instrument, the lower the pitch. Larger bowl timpani have a lower pitch and smaller bowl timpani produce a higher pitch. A full classical orchestra or concert band will usually have at least two timpani and as many as five when the score calls for them.

Mallets—Mallets consist of a stick or shaft made of wood or a man-made product to which a head is attached. The head can be made of almost anything, from soft material such as cotton or felt to wood. The choice of the mallets to be used is entirely up to the performer, the requirements of the music to be played, and the wishes of the music director. It is not uncommon for a timpanist to own a large variety of mallets of all strengths, head densities, and different shaft materials in order to be prepared for all possible music requirements (see chapter 14).

Drum Sticks—Drum sticks are made in a variety of sizes and of hard woods such as oak, hickory, or maple. Aluminum and various forms of plastic, fiberglass, and carbon fiber are also used to make these sticks. A drum stick is usually about 1¼ inches around and about 14 inches long. The sticks come in such a wide range of sizes, thickness, densities, and weights that any effort to categorize them would be futile. Suffice it to say that each different size and weight stick used on the same instrument will produce a different sound.

Brushes—Brushes are used for special effects on snare drums and cymbals. Brushes are made of metal or plastic bristles connected to a rigid wire, which is fed through a hollow handle. A loop on the end of the wire is used to pull the bristles in or out of the handle. When the wire is pushed into the handle, the bristles fan out the opposite end of the handle, and the brushes are ready for use. In this manner the player can adjust the spread and flexibility of the brushes to achieve different effects, and then collapse the brushes for easy transportation.

The Drum Set—A drum set, sometimes referred to as a trap set or drum kit, consists of a combination of different drums and cymbals. A three-piece set would be made up of a snare drum, bass drum, and floor tom-tom, a ride cymbal, crash cymbal, and a hi-hat cymbal. Cymbals are not included in the count of a trap set. Adding two side or mounted tom-toms would result in a five-piece set, providing the player greater performance versatility. This equipment requires appropriate stands and hardware and usually includes a throne (stool) for the drummer. The hi-hat cymbal and bass drum are activated with a foot pedal while the drummer plays with both hands.

Smaller Percussion Instruments—An array of smaller instruments can be added to a drum set to extend its versatility. Among the most common are the triangle, wood block, and the cow bell.

Electric Drum—With the evolution of the electronic synthesizer, the drum industry has been able to develop an electronic drum that can produce a variety of prescribed percussion sounds. The extraordinary flexibility of this apparatus allows a performer to duplicate both tuned and non-tuned percussion instruments. The set can be used with full amplification for a realistic percussion sound, or it can be used with earphones for practice with very little sound audible to the surrounding environment. These devices do have a level of contrived sound which can only be judged acceptable or not by the player and the circumstance in which the set is to be used. Additionally, the feel of the set to the drummer, although closely resembling that of a traditional membranophone, does fall a bit short.

Practice Pads—Practice pads were conceived of as a way to provide a student or drummer with a piece of equipment on which to practice that would be mobile, inexpensive, quiet, and yet have the feel of a drum or set of drums. The music industry has responded with a variety of contrivances ranging from a wooden square with a rubber pad attached, to a complete set of circular pads with surfaces that in some way will respond with the feel of a drum without producing much sound.

PITCHED MALLET INSTRUMENTS

Mallet instruments are named so because they are played by being struck with some type of mallet. The mallets used have heads that are graduated in hardness to the degree needed to produce the percussive effect desired. These mallets have been described previously. Generally, the mallet instruments described below produce sound idiophonically by the player striking a series of tuned bars composed of various natural and man-made materials. Among these are rosewood, padauk (a type of pea-wood), fiberglass, and some metals. A product called vibrail is used to fabricate bars of a composite lamination using various combinations of metal, wood, plastic, and rubber.

Xylophone—The xylophone is one of the more popular instruments in the mallet percussion family. The instrument is designed with tuned wooden bars in the form of a piano keyboard. There are some manufacturers who produce xylophones with rosewood bars. When struck with a mallet the bars respond idiophonically, that is, vibrating in their totality. Xylophones are transposing instruments with the notes sounding one octave above the written note. The range of the instrument generally starts at F3 (below middle C) and, depending on the instrument model, can extend up from two and a half to as much as four octaves (see chapter 14).

Marimba—The marimba is considered to be one of the solo instruments in the percussion family. It is designed with African padauk wooden bars laid out in the form of a piano keyboard and is generally played with four moderate to soft-headed mallets, two in each of the player's hands. The marimba produces a rich, warm sound that is less percussive than that of the xylophone. Depending on the size of the instrument, marimbas have a range of between four and five octaves, the lowest note being C3, or the second space C in the bass clef, and the highest C7, three octaves above middle C.

Vibraphone—The vibraphone is the most sophisticated of the mallet instruments. It has the same piano-like keyboard as that of the xylophone and the marimba, except that the bars on the vibraphone are made of aluminum instead of wood. Vibraphones are equipped with resonators, which are metal tubes that modify the basic sound produced by the bars (see chapter 14). A note struck on a vibraphone will sustain much longer than one on the other mallet instruments. The range of most vibraphones extends from F3 (F below middle C) to F6, or about three octaves up. Larger, more expensive models are expanded by as much as an additional octave, going from C3, an octave below middle C, to C7.

Glockenspiel—The glockenspiel (German for play-bells; see figure 14.4) is a smaller, more portable tuned mallet instrument with bars set out in a piano keyboard format. The sound produced is very bright and well sustained. It is, therefore, sometimes necessary to moderate the enthusiasm of the player to meet the requirements of the music being performed.

Glockenspiels are tuned in the key of C, have a range of about two-and-a-half octaves, and transpose at the octave, sounding an octave above the written note.

How all of the above instruments work is covered in more detail in chapter 14. Some information in this chapter will be repeated in chapter 14 for the convenience of the reader.

13

The History of Percussion Instruments

The definition of percussion instruments includes anything that produces sound by being hit (drum), rubbed (guiro), or shaken (maraca). On that basis, one can confidently speculate that the earliest percussion instruments most likely existed with the earliest presence of humankind. Percussive sounds could be produced by clapping hands, striking any part of the human body, stamping feet on a responsive surface, or striking or rubbing anything that will produce a sound. Some of these could have been a hollow log, lithophone (see below), or a multitude of other idiophones (see chapter 12). It is, therefore, not feasible for one to establish a specific time reference for the beginning or invention of percussion instruments. We know when the saxophone was invented, and can calculate the approximate date of the beginning of non-fretted string instruments such as the violin, but there is no distinct point of reference for the first percussion instrument. There is, however, a significant amount of information on the development of certain percussion instruments. More on that later.

Numerous drums evolved throughout the ages, some of the earliest dating back millennia. One will find groupings of similar types of percussion instruments associated with particular ethnic societies throughout history. A lithophone was discovered in 1949 in Vietnam. This is a marimba-like instrument constructed of rocks, which produce sound when struck. It appears that these idiophones could have been among the first mallet instruments. An assortment of such instruments has been found primarily in Africa and the Far East.

Studying the history of early percussion instruments is complicated by the paucity of source recorded history, the vast number of different items that can be classified as percussion instruments, and the universality of their evolution. They have been everywhere, at every time, and utilized in every way for almost every reason. It is more advantageous to focus on some of the more popular percussion instruments for which there is at least some concrete indication of a designated starting point to their lives.

Turkish Percussion Instruments—Several important members of the percussion family had their start in Turkey. These are the bass drum, kettle drum, bells, cymbals, triangle, and tambourine. Responsible for this occurrence was the royal bodyguard, called the Janissaries. This group combined drums, bells, triangles, and cymbals to form what was probably the first percussion section.

Western composers of the late eighteenth to early nineteenth centuries, intrigued by these instruments, began to incorporate them into their compositions. This began the inclusion of a percussion section in the classical orchestra. At first, percussion instruments were used simultaneously as a group producing a distinctive sound. Over time the instruments were modified and took on their own individuality so that they became entities unto themselves, no longer dependent on each other. These instruments were to be used in scores by such luminaries as Mozart, Haydn, Gluck, and Beethoven.

Bass Drum/Davul—The davul is probably the earliest example of a drum from which the current bass drum evolved. Its origins are believed to be in Asia Minor, now part of Turkey, and in Central Asia. The instrument became part of the culture and tradition of the percussion instruments of Turkey. It is still in use today at Turkish ceremonies, sports events, and festivals.

The davul consisted of a cylinder-shaped shell open on each end, upon which animal skins were stretched. The skins were secured by hoops that were held onto the shell with ropes. Unlike the modern bass drum, the skins on the davul were of different densities. The drum with the thicker head made of sheepskin was held on the player's right side. The drum with the thinner head of goat skin was held on the left side. These were each struck with different beaters. The thicker skin was struck with a beater called a tokmak, similar to a present-day mallet. The thinner skin was struck with a lighter stick or brush-like implement made of twigs called a ruthe. Because the sound produced by this drum was significantly more forceful than that of other drums of the time, the davul became the instrument of choice for military signaling.

The davul is one of the ancient percussion instruments most closely related to today's bass drum. The similarity is in that they both have skins on both sides held on with hoops and produce percussion sounds primarily in the lower register. On the contemporary bass drum, skins or heads of the same thickness are secured with tension rods (see chapter 12) instead of ropes. The tension rods permit one to adjust the tension of the heads by turning knobs.

Snare Drum—Paintings and drawings from the twelfth to the sixteenth century indicate that a form of drum called a tabor, a name given to several types of drums, could be considered to be the precursor to the modern snare drum. Early graphics depict tabors consisting of a cylindrical shell with a hide head on each side. These were mounted on hoops connected with ropes running in a "W" pattern traveling up and down the drum shell. The two-headed tabor was fitted with a gut snare, which could be adjusted for different effects. There was, however, an inconsistency in how these drums were built since some so-called tabors had only one head and no snare. One might speculate as to whether that inconsistency was in the architecture of the drum or in the name given to those instruments.

Tabors are often pictured being played by one individual who is also playing a recorder-like instrument simultaneously. This combination was noted as far back as the twelfth century and continues to be in effect today in Spain and France. The wind instrument was constructed with two holes in the front and one in back for the thumb, allowing the player to handle the instrument with one hand. A smaller version of a tabor was strapped on the player and was played with the other hand. There is also evidence of the tabor/recorder or fife combination being used by the Swiss military during the fifteenth to sixteenth centuries.

Throughout the eighteenth and nineteenth centuries, improvements to the instrument's snare assembly, the introduction of coiled wire snares, developments in the drum shell size, the material from which it was made, and the introduction of the plastic batter and snare heads eventually resulted in the modern snare drum architecture.

Timpani (Kettle Drum)—As is the case with most percussion instruments, the origin of the timpani is unknown. The common belief is that it had its beginnings in ancient Middle Eastern territories where primitive forms of membranophones are evidenced in the iconography of the time. Animal skins were stretched over clay pots or other such vessels to form simple shallow bowl drums. By the twelfth century, evidence of an assortment of larger hemispheres fabricated of clay, metal, or other substances began to appear throughout Asia, Africa, and then Europe. These could be shaped into increasingly larger shells that were then fitted with animal-skin heads and became drums. The sizes increased until a prototype of the contemporary timpano (singular for timpani) in its simplest form evolved. These kettle-shaped drums were attached, one on each side, to horses or other beasts of burden to be used by the military in various kinds of ceremonies.

From the thirteenth through fifteenth centuries, kettle drums worked their way to Europe through the Crusades until, by the sixteenth century, they began their technological evolution into the more sophisticated timpani. It was at that time that improvements in the tuning mechanism using screw-like arrangements evolved into what are now tension rods (see chapter 12). By the seventeenth century the kettle drum/timpani became an accepted member of the orchestra.

Cymbals—The onset of the Bronze Age in Mesopotamia some 5000 years ago provided those few who were involved in the expansion of percussion instruments with the raw material needed to advance their agenda. In Turkey it became a material of choice for the military and, ultimately, for the fabrication of percussion instruments. Thus, the early cymbal was born to become a fixture in the Turkish music world.

As trade routes expanded, the use of cymbals became part of the instrumentation of orchestras throughout the world. The evolution of the drum set in the twentieth century completed the validation process of the cymbals by making them part of the percussion ensemble and transitioning them into the popular music genre. Today Turkish cymbal makers are recognized by many as the ultimate producers of fine cymbals as they continue to develop and modify their products to satisfy the needs of the contemporary music world.

Prior to the development of ensemble music as we know it today, cymbals were used in ancient civilizations in the Middle and Far East for ceremonial events. The configuration of the cymbals in Asia fell into two categories: large, broad-rimmed cymbals were used to crash together, and smaller, less intense-sounding cymbals held in a vertical position were struck to create a softer sound. Additionally there were small cymbals of specific pitches that dancers attached to their fingers as part of their performance. In China, small cymbals with a slightly different configuration from that of the Turkish "finger" cymbals were used ceremonially at weddings and funerals.

By the eighteenth century, cymbals had been developed that produced a variety of different sounds, so they became a permanent member of the percussion section of the orchestras of Haydn, Mozart, Beethoven, Wagner and ultimately all the composers to follow.

Triangle—Evidence of the existence of a triangle dates back to the tenth century, where it is mentioned in writings. From that point on its appearance spread throughout the East. In the early years it was used as a sound-producing ornament, then associated with a flute-like instrument called the pipe and ultimately as part of small musical groups. The Crusades brought the triangle from the East to Europe where it grew in popularity and eventually became a permanent part of the percussion section. By the beginning of the eighteenth century, the triangle began to be part of the instrumentation of orchestras in the opera houses of Europe.

Throughout its evolution, the triangle was not always triangular in shape. Depictions of the triangle show it as a trapezoid; others show it as being part of an Egyptian rattle called a sistrum. Some triangles included in their structure metal discs that jingled when set into motion. Others were both open- and closed-ended, the closed form producing a definite pitch and the open-ended model an indefinite pitch.

Tambourine—There has been little change in the structure of the tambourine since the first versions which date back to ancient times. The instruments consisted of the rim alone, with metal discs built into it that jingled when shaken; the rim with one animal-skin head and two sets of discs; and a rim with or without the heads with bells attached. In some cases the head would have a snare made of coarse animal hair or other fibrous material.

Tambourines can be found in the iconography of most Middle Eastern cultures throughout early history. The instrument eventually migrated to Europe where, in the nineteenth century, it began to appear in orchestras and in the opera. An interesting note in the history of the tambourine is its conspicuous absence in the music of the Baroque and Classical periods in music history.

Mallet Percussion Instruments—Percussion instruments of definite pitch date back to several millennia B.C. when man first discovered that certain stones or pieces of wood would produce a sound when struck. Thus the concept of the idiophone (see chapter 12) was discovered.

In addition to the marimba-like instrument discovered in Vietnam mentioned above, similar instruments have been discovered in the Far East and in Africa. This demonstrates that, as is the case for many items in their earliest form, these innovative musical instruments were appearing in various parts of the world simultaneously. The xylophone is one example. It is estimated by the Vienna Symphonic Library that the xylophone's earliest appearance took place in the ninth century in Southeast Asia, whereas similar finds are purported to date back to 2000 B.C. in China.

Bells—It may be possible, but not practical, to determine how many different kinds of bells there are. Their origin dates back millennia as they appeared on all continents throughout the world. Because bell sounds are able to travel great distances, it is likely that originally, bells were used as a means of communicating and signaling. The improvement in understanding the science of metallurgy provided the raw materials needed to craft different types of bells to create different sounds. Bells of differing timbre were used to chase evil spirits, announce religious events, direct activities for the military, and for celebrations and rituals.

In China during the Ming and Qing dynasties beginning in 1416 and spanning some 500 years, different types of bells were designated to represent certain levels of society and its activities. Some bells were associated with the Buddhist and Taoist religions, others bells were allocated to the emperor's court, and still others were used for alarms, entertainment, and other more mundane activities. One particularly interesting use of bells in China was showing the number of bells one had on either side of one's home as representative of one's social status: four bells for the emperor, three for a duke, two for a minister, and one for a government official.

The popularity of bells in Europe began during the fifth century in Italy when Benedictine monk experimentation resulted in significant improvements in bell sound quality and endurance. Three centuries later in England, bells began to be used at funerals and later at other religious events. With the Renaissance came the church bell towers, giving bells a credible permanent home. It was also during that period that bells became a part of orchestral instrumentation.

Bells exist in every size, shape, pitch, and timbre possible, and they are being used in every imaginable way in every part of the world. One can wonder what other classification of musical instrument enjoys such universal popularity.

Summary—It is evident that any attempt to focus in on a particular time or place for the beginnings of a particular early percussion instrument is quite impossible.

One can only accept speculation in place of fact that these instruments evolved in various parts of the world at similar times in history concurrent with the evolution of humans. Actual documented source material for the invention of such instruments did not start to occur until industrialized society began to modify and manufacture those early instruments. The number of percussion instruments beginning from the first to the present is immeasurable. One can safely speculate that percussion instruments were first in the chain of musical instrument discoveries by virtue of their simplicity of design in conjunction with humans' natural instinct to express themselves rhythmically.

14

How Percussion Instruments Work

Since anything that produces sound by being hit (drum), rubbed (guiro), or shaken (maraca) can be classified as a percussion instrument, this section will be limited to the percussion instruments found in the contemporary symphony orchestra.

DRUMS

The term "drum" can be applied to any instrument in the percussion family that has a shell, either cylindrical or bowl shaped, over which a membrane is tightly stretched. The membrane can be attached to either one or both ends of the shell, depending on the type of drum.

Drum Head—Animal hide, the original material used for drum heads since the beginning of time, is sensitive to changes in temperature and humidity. Warm humid air will cause the skin to soften and lose its brilliance. The reverse happens with cold dry air, which shrinks and tightens the skin. In the middle of the twentieth century, a polyester film called Mylar was developed and has taken the place of animal hides to a great degree. Mylar does not react to ambient atmospheric changes unless they are extreme, and so the percussionist now has some stability in his or her drum head inventory.

Drum Shell—The drum shell is the body of the instrument, the hub to which all the parts of the drum are connected. Drum shells can be made of wood, various plastics, fiberglass, or metal. Wood is the material of choice for acoustical reasons, while metal or plastic is the material of choice for practical reasons.

Shells are built in different diameters and depths. Bigger shells produce lower sounds and smaller shells produce higher sounds. The most popular snare drum diameters range from ten to fourteen inches, with a possible outside range of six to sixteen inches for special effects. The depths of these instruments can range from three to ten inches.

The remaining parts of a drum (figure 14.1) are the rim or hoop, lugs, tension rods, and in the case of snare drums, a snare.

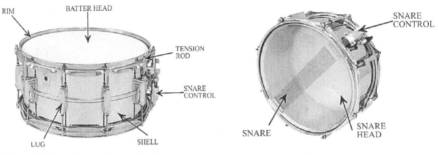

Figure 14.1. Snare Drum Parts

The rim or hoop holds the head in place on the shell.

Lugs are metal units with a female thread into which male threaded tension rods are screwed. Tension rods are long screws that hold the hoop in place.

The hoop holds the head in place.

The head is a membrane that is stretched across one or both open sides of the shell.

The snare is a set of wires configured into spirals attached in direct contact with the bottom head (snare head) of a drum.

When the drum is struck on the upper (batter) head, the snare produces a rattling sound, which is amplified by the drum's shell and snare head. Snares can be adjusted by means of a snare adjustment mechanism attached to the side of the drum. The snares can also be released by flipping a lever at the same location. Releasing the snare on a snare drum will result in a tom-tom-like sound.

Tightening or loosening the tension rods adjusts the tension on the head, thereby tuning the drum. The number of lugs on a drum can vary so that more lugs provide better tension distribution while better maintaining the drum's tuning. Fewer lugs provide less tension stability.

Snare Drum—The snare drum is the primary instrument in a percussion section. Each part of the drum has some effect on the sound produced. The upper drum (batter) head is the main source of sound. When struck, the head vibrates, setting the air inside the drum shell vibrating. This activates the snare (bottom) head and the snare itself into motion, thus producing the snare drum sound. This action is called sympathetic vibration, defined by the *Merriam-Webster Dictionary* as "a vibration produced in one body by the vibrations of exactly the same period in a neighboring body."

Indefinite Pitch—Although snare drums are instruments of indefinite pitch, they still must be tuned if they are to respond properly to the player's stick articulation. There is a school of percussionists who profess that snare drums of indefinite pitch should indeed be tuned to pitches. When tapping a snare drum lightly, one can hear a definite pitch. Depending on the depth of the shell and the tension of the heads, the pitches heard can range from G to B; however, these definite pitches are never heard in performance.

Those in the "pitch camp" further propose that the snare or bottom head should be tuned to sound a fourth or fifth above the pitch of the batter head. It is their contention that this highly sophisticated level of tuning a drum of indefinite pitch will provide the best level of performance for that instrument. The player can decide to what degree he or she wishes to carry the tuning process.

Tuning—The procedure used to tune a drum is essentially the same for all drums. The tension or tightness of the head will determine the nature of the sound produced. The head is tightened by turning the tension rods in a clockwise direction. To loosen the head, turn the tension rods in a counterclockwise direction.

Adjusting the tension of the heads changes the sound produced and simultaneously changes the feel of the drum sticks as they strike the head. Tighter heads produce crisper, higher-pitched sounds with a more resilient stick rebound. Looser heads produce mellower, lower-pitched sounds with a less resilient stick rebound. The choice is entirely up to the performer and should be determined by the type of selection being played and the venue in which the performance is taking place.

Tuning a drum head requires a bit more than just random tightening or loosening of the tension rods. In order to achieve balance on a drum head a percussionist will:

1. Release the snare by flipping the lever on the snare release.
2. With the head loose but securely in place with little but equal tension on the tension rods, depress the center of the head to assure it is firmly seated on the shell. The player will ensure that all the tension rods are turned into the lug so that an equal amount of each tension rod is visible.
3. Select any tension rod as a starting point. Lightly tap the head with a drum stick about two inches from the rim opposite that tension rod and simultaneously tighten it to the degree where the head begins to show some resistance and the sound begins to change.
4. Repeat the process on the tension rod directly opposite the first one. Tighten that one until the sound being produced at that point on the head resembles the sound at the first location.

5. Repeat the process on the tension rod next to the first one.
6. Repeat the process on the tension rod directly opposite that one.
7. Continue that procedure around the drum until all tension rods have been tightened to the desired degree.

On a six-lug drum, the tightening pattern of the tension rods should be 1–4, 2–5, and 3–6. Overtightening heads will reduce their productivity.

The degree to which the tension of the batter and snare heads should match each other is an issue yet to be resolved. For a brighter sound, the snare head should be somewhat tighter than the batter head. The choice remains that of the performer.

This process can be used with both indefinite and definite pitched drums. The result to be achieved for indefinite pitched drums should be a percussive sound appropriate to the type of music to be performed. Definite pitched instruments should be tuned to the pitch indicated in the music to be played.

Bass Drum—Bass drums are large drums that produce indefinite pitches in the lower range. In a symphony orchestra or symphonic band, the bass drum is an essential part of the percussion section. The bass drum is placed on a bass drum stand and is stationary. The drum's primary use would be to establish primary accent beats and to enrich special effects. The drum functions like those described above. The acoustical process, structure, and tuning are all similar to that of the snare drum, but larger.

Timpani (Kettle Drums)—Timpani are large, kettle-shaped drums that are tuned to a definite pitch. In addition to knowing all the percussion playing rudiments, a timpani player must have an acute sense of pitch along with the knowledge and ability to translate that information into the actions required to keep and play a set of timpani in tune.

The Timpani Pedal—Timpani are used to produce a variety of pitches throughout a performance. To facilitate this process, a pedal mechanism is installed in the instrument, allowing the timpanist to immediately change pitches within certain parameters without having to go through the tension rod turning process described above. When the pedal is depressed, cables inside the shell of the drum pull down on the rim to tighten the head. When the pedal is depressed, this tightening occurs and the pitch is raised in a glissando (sliding up or down) in an interval of approximately a fifth above the fundamental tone. The player can stop the pedal at any point when the desired pitch is reached.

The timpani pedal must be properly adjusted for it to hold the position set by the player. To adjust the tension of the pedal, the player proceeds as follows:

1. With the head properly tuned to the fundamental tone prescribed and the pedal in the heel-down position, the pedal is depressed toe down to its maximum position. When the foot is released from the pedal, it should remain in that position.

2. If the pedal moves back on its own, the adjustment knob located just above the pedal must be turned to the right to tighten the tension spring.
3. Conversely, if the pedal in the heel-down position moves up on its own, the adjustment knob must be turned to the left to loosen the spring tension.
4. A properly adjusted pedal should remain at any point in its range without having to be held in place by the player's foot.

Timpani Tuning—Timpani have two levels of tuning. There is a fundamental tuning where, with the pedal in the heel-down position, the heads are tuned to a particular pitch prescribed by the size of the timpani and the music to be played. The tuning process is similar to that of the snare and bass drums described above except that the ultimate goal is to achieve a specific pitch. Tuning a drum head requires a bit more than just random tightening or loosening of the tension rods. The reader may wish to refresh his or her memory by re-reading the tuning process described in the snare drum section above. With the exception of the first step of releasing the snare, the same process is applicable to the timpani.

The following is a list of the notes to which the different-size timpani can be tuned and the approximate ascending range of notes that can be produced with the use of the pedal.

A 30- to 32-inch kettle can be tuned to C2 and pedaled up to F3.
A 28- to 29-inch kettle can be tuned to F3 and pedaled up to D4.
A 25- to 26-inch kettle can be tuned to B-flat3 and pedaled up to G-flat4.
A 23- to 24-inch kettle can be tuned to D3 and pedaled up to B-flat4.
A 20- to 22-inch kettle can be tuned to F4 and pedaled up to D5.

CYMBALS

Cymbals are metal discs that when struck or crashed together produce a metallic crashing sound, which has some duration. Cymbals can be played in several ways:

They can be hand held and crashed together.
They can be mounted on a pedal-operated stand called a high-hat stand, which holds two cymbals horizontally facing each other. When the pedal is depressed the two cymbals crash against each other.
A stand called a ride cymbal stand holds one cymbal suspended. A player can strike it with a drum stick, play it with brushes, or achieve special effects by using different density mallets for the strike.
One lesser-known technique is running a heavily rosined bass bow in a perpendicular up-and-down motion along the edge of the cymbal for a special effect.

The point at which a cymbal is struck significantly affects the resulting sound. Striking the same cymbal in different places creates different sounds. When viewed from the side, a cymbal will evidence a gradual and then a more sudden elevation in the upper surface. The center area of the cymbal where the hole is located is raised to form a cup shape called the bell (see figure 14.2A). When struck, the bell area produces a sharp penetrating sound of short duration. The larger area from the outer edge to the sudden elevation is called the bow. The size of the bow determines the cymbal's pitch. The greater the bow, the higher the pitch. A player must determine where to strike the cymbal in order to produce an appropriate sound for the music being performed.

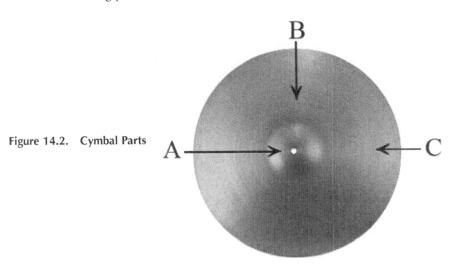

Figure 14.2.   Cymbal Parts

The bow has two strike areas. The section closer to the bell is called the ride area (figure 14.2B) and because of its thickness, offers a bolder sound. As the bow tapers out to the thinner section called the crash area (14.2C), the sound becomes brighter and self-sustaining.

The first issue of importance to a cymbalist is the size and weight of the cymbal. As stated previously, cymbals are categorized by their size and weight because these two factors affect the quality and strength of the sound they produce. Larger and heavier cymbals produce louder sounds. Thinner cymbals produce a lighter, more sustained sound. It is, therefore, the percussionist's task to have available and use cymbals that would be appropriate for the music at hand. In view of all of the above, it should be evident that playing the cymbals is not as easy as it may appear.

DRUM STICKS

The feel of a drum stick in a player's hands has a significant effect on his or her performance. Therefore, careful selection of a stick most suited to the player and the music being performed is essential. The three factors considered in stick selection are the strength, weight, and density of the stick. These are all determined by the material used to make the stick and its size.

Material—Oak sticks are the heaviest and strongest due to the density of the wood. The strength provides durability and strong contact with the strike for the player. The weight will produce a strong sound.

Hickory is more commonly used due to its strength and lighter weight. It is believed by some that hickory sticks produce a better percussion sound that other woods or materials.

Rosewood is a very dense wood offering durability and a heavier product. Rosewood is the most expensive wood in common use for drum sticks.

Maple is the lightest wood used for sticks and, therefore, may be best to produce a quick, light, percussive effect.

Synthetic products such as aluminum and carbon fiber are also used to make drum sticks. These are usually more durable than wood and offer an unlimited variety of ways to satisfy the needs of drummers with different "feels" to their sticks.

Drum Stick Tips—Drum stick tips are either a continuation of the material from which the stick is made or are made of nylon and added onto the stick. Nylon tips produce a crisp sound and are particularly effective on cymbals, whereas wooden tips produce a warmer, more subtle sound. Also available are rubber tips, which can slip over the original tip and are useful for practice when a drum is not available or when little sound is desired.

Percussionists sometimes refer to a labeling system used for drum sticks that uses a combination of numbers and letters to identify stick sizes. Unfortunately, this system is far from standardized. Many manufacturers use their own proprietary labeling, which adds to the confusion.

The three most common size markings that enjoy a reasonable degree of accuracy are 7A, which is thin and light; 5A, a bit heavier and most used for beginners; and 5B, the heaviest of the three, used for big bands and rock music. Any effort for more specific guidance would lack validity and be non-productive.

MALLETS

Mallets are sticks or shafts with a bulbous head attached to one or both ends. The shafts and heads of mallets are made of a variety of materials. The shafts can be made of different types of wood or plastic or other man-made material. The head can be made of almost anything from metal to soft wrapped cotton, and can be any degree of hardness depending on the mallets' intended use.

Bass drum mallets are often called beaters. Their heads can be made of wood or cotton depending on the degree of hardness required for the music being played. These beaters also come with a double head, that is, a head on each end of the stick. The two heads are usually of different sizes and can be of different hardness. Two-headed beaters permit the player to quickly change the quality of the sound by using one head or the other. They can also be used to produce a bass drum roll by the player holding the beater in the center of the shaft and rapidly rotating the wrist from left to right.

Timpani mallets are constructed in the same design as that of other percussion instruments. The mallets consist of a stick or shaft made of wood or a man-made product to which a head is attached. The head can be made of almost anything, from soft material such as cotton or felt to wood. The choice of the mallets to be used is entirely up to the performer, the requirements of the music to be played, and the wishes of the music director. It is not uncommon for a timpanist to own a large variety of mallets of all strengths, head densities, and different shaft materials in order to be prepared for all possible music requirements.

Tuned percussion instruments with bars that must be struck to produce sound, such as orchestra bells, the glockenspiel, or the xylophone, require hard-headed mallets. These can be made of wood, nylon, metal, or hard rubber. Other tuned percussion instruments that produce a less percussive sound, such as the vibraphone, use softer mallets. These have a hard core that is wrapped with a softer material like cotton, nylon, yarn, or other form of corded fabric.

Summary—The heads of mallets are made of a variety of materials from the softest substance to steel, depending on the type of sound desired and the instrument for which its use is intended. The choice must be made by the performer and the requirements of the music being performed. The shafts can be made of various types of wood, plastic, or other man-made material.

PITCHED MALLET INSTRUMENTS

Mallet instruments are those percussion instruments which are of definite pitch and produce sound by being struck with a mallet. These instruments duplicate the structural design of a piano keyboard by using a layout of the tone-producing bars or bells in a pattern similar to that of the white and black keys, sharps and flats, on a piano. A player will strike the bars with mallets that are appropriate for achieving the desired sound.

As stated in chapter 12, the mallets used have heads that are graduated in hardness to the degree needed to produce the percussive effect desired. The material from which the heads are made can range from a winding of soft cotton to denser cotton, felt, wood, plastic, or steel. Figure 14.3 shows three different pitched mallet instruments: the xylophone, the marimba, and the vibraphone.

Xylophone **Marimba** **Vibraphone**

Figure 14.3. Mallet Instruments

Xylophone—The xylophone is the most common instrument in the mallet percussion family. The instrument is designed with tuned wooden bars in the form of a piano keyboard. When struck with a mallet, these bars respond idiophonically, that is, vibrating in their totality (see chapter 12).

Two mallets, one for each hand, with heads of the density appropriate for the music to be played, are used to strike the bars. The mallets used can have heads of hard plastic, acrylic, or hard rubber but, depending on the effect to be achieved, softer core cotton-wrapped mallets change the effect to a more mellow sound. Four mallets can also be used, two in each hand, to perform music requiring this technique.

Xylophone bars produce a sound that is not long sustained. To increase the duration of the sound, some xylophones are built with resonators under the bars to hold the otherwise shorter sound the bar alone would produce. Xylophones are transposing instruments with the notes sounding one octave above the written note. As stated previously, the range of the instrument generally starts at F3 (below middle C), and, depending on the instrument model, can extend up from two-and-a-half octaves to as much as four octaves.

Marimba—The marimba is also one of the solo instruments in the percussion family. It is designed with wooden bars in the form of a piano keyboard and is generally played with four moderate- to soft-headed mallets. The marimba produces a rich warm sound that is less percussive than that of the xylophone. The mellow sound is attributed to the fact that the bars are made of wood and that each bar is fitted with a tube-shaped resonator hanging below. The tubes are graduated in size and modified in shape to accommodate the pitch of the bar it services. When the bars are struck, the vibrations they produce travel down into the resonators, which act as amplifiers of the sound much as a violin body amplifies the vibrations of its strings. As stated previously, marimbas have a range of between four and five octaves, the lowest note being C3, second space C in the bass clef, and the highest C7, three octaves above middle C.

Vibraphone—This mallet instrument differs from the other mallet instruments in that it has a sustaining pedal that is used to control the sustained sound. Vibraphones are equipped with a damper system operated by a pedal, much like that of a piano. When the pedal is depressed, felt pads in contact with the sound bars are released and the bars are free to vibrate. When the pedal is released, the pads resume contact and the vibration is stopped.

Vibraphones are also equipped with resonators, metal tubes open at the top and closed at the bottom. These tubes contain discs run by a motor or, in the more sophisticated models, controlled by a computer. The discs rotate within the resonator, resulting in the unique vibraphone sound. There is a resonator under each bar. When a bar is struck, its vibrations travel down the tube-shaped resonator to the closed bottom and then bounce back up to the bar to repeat the process. This action increases the intensity of the fundamental within the note, producing the vibraphone sound.

Vibraphones use an electric adjustable-speed motor and pulley assembly mounted on one side of the instrument to drive the discs in the resonators. The more advanced models have motors that are computerized to provide greater control over the discs in the resonators.

The basic mallets used to play a vibraphone have a slim hardwood or plastic shaft with a head of hard rubber wrapped with a soft cotton or synthetic cord. Because the density and resilience of the mallet head have a profound effect on the quality and timbre of the sound produced, players generally keep a wide variety of mallets in their quiver. By doing so, the players have the ability to produce any type of sound, from piercing and metallic to amorous and mellifluous.

One extraordinary albeit seldom-used sound-generating process replacing the use of mallets on a vibraphone is the use of a cello or double bass bow. When drawn along the edge of the bar, the percussive character of the sound generated is turned into a smoother, purer tone.

Glockenspiel—The glockenspiel is among the smaller, more mobile of the tuned mallet instruments. It comes in two configurations, both played with the same technique and producing the same sound. The bell lyre-shaped glockenspiel (figure 14.4) is easily carried with the use of a harness for marching situations or can be placed on a stand for stage performances.

The encased glockenspiel (figure 14.4) sits on a stand and is best used for staged performances, for obvious reasons.

The bars of the glockenspiel, like other tuned mallet instruments, are configured as a piano keyboard. The bars are struck using nylon, metal, or other hard-tipped mallets, and the sound produced is very bright and well sustained, making the instrument a valuable contributor to marching bands. Music written for the instrument generally ranges from G3 a fourth below middle C to C6, two octaves above middle C.

Marching   # Encased

Figure 14.4.   Glockenspiels

PERCUSSION EQUIPMENT

Drum Set—Drum sets, also called trap sets, are assembled to allow one player to play all the instruments in the set from one seated position. These sets are primarily used in small ensembles such as dance bands, rock bands, and jazz bands. Being surrounded by an assortment of drums enables one player to control a snare drum, bass drum, various cymbals, several tom-toms, and any assortment of lesser percussion instruments such as a cow bell or wood block.

Electronic Drums—Electronic drums can have all the features found in a drum set with the addition of giving the player the ability to adjust both volume and timbre electronically. Pads with a resilient drum head–like surface contain a sensor which, when struck, sends an electric impulse through a cable or midi connection to a sound-producing and amplifying system. The individual pads can be designed and programmed to replicate various types of drum, cymbal, or other percussion sounds. Different-sized pads are set up on stands in the same configuration as that in a trap set, so the player can experience the drumming process as one would on an acoustic drum set. Another advantage to this setup, when compared to a traditional acoustic drum set, is the ease of portability and storage the former offers.

Practice Pads—Used in place of a drum, practice pads are a means to practice in relative silence without all of the drum paraphernalia associated with drum playing. These simple pads come in a variety of sizes, shapes, and designs, are comparatively inexpensive, and are very effective, if not totally satisfying, substitutes for a real drum.

Brushes—Brushes (see chapter 12 for a description) are used for special effects on snare drums. Rather than emitting a percussive sound as do drum sticks and mallets, brushes can produce a swishing sound, a staccato sound, or a combination of both. The general effect can be one of a relaxed ornamentation to any melodic or harmonic sounds being presented by the other instruments of the ensemble. Brushes, like salt in food, are an essential but little-recognized member of a total end product. When they are present they are not noticed, but when absent, they are sorely missed.

GLOSSARY OF TERMS RELATED
TO PERCUSSION INSTRUMENTS

This glossary will help the reader define terms that are related to percussion instruments. See the descriptions above for more in-depth information on these items.

Bass drum A large drum which produces sounds of indefinite pitch in the lower register.
Beat An underlying, repetitious pulse that acts as the base on which different rhythms are established. In 4/4 time there would be four beats in a measure on which the rhythm is built.
Brushes Metal bristles connected to a rigid wire fed through a hollow handle in a splayed configuration. Brushes are used to create special effects, usually on a snare drum or cymbals.
Cymbal A metal disc that produces a metallic crashing sound of some duration.
Drum A cylindrical shell, made of wood or other man-made material, covered on one or both ends with a tightly stretched membrane. To produce sound the player strikes the membrane with a drum stick.
Drum head A membrane made of treated animal hide or a man-made product that is tightly stretched over one or both ends of a drum shell (body). The head is struck to produce a percussive sound.
Drum shell The body of a drum.
Electronic drums Drums that are fitted with any type of electronic pickup that is attached to an amplifying system and speakers.
Glockenspiel A portable percussion instrument with idiophonic metal bars that sound when they are struck with a mallet. Glockenspiels are built in a lyre-shaped frame for marching or in a trapezoidal-shaped case for use on stage.
Gong A bronze disc with a turned-in edge designed to produce a full, resonant, sustaining sound when struck with a felt-covered mallet.
Indefinite pitch A sound that cannot be identified as a particular note or pitch.
Mallet A short stick, ten to twelve inches long, made of wood or plastic with a head made of felt, wood, metal, or plastic used to strike percussion instruments to produce sound.

Marimba An instrument designed with wooden bars in the form of a piano keyboard and generally played with four moderate- to soft-headed mallets, two in each of the player's hands. A marimba produces a rich, warm sound that is less percussive than that of the xylophone.

Percussion The act of striking. In music, percussion instruments produce sound by reacting to any type of agitation such as being struck, scraped, or in the case of something with sound producing particles in an enclosed vessel, shaken.

Pitch Pitch refers to the highness or lowness of a tone.

Practice pad A pad, usually made of rubber, which is used for practice in place of a drum.

Snare A set of parallel spiral-shaped wires attached in direct contact with the bottom head (snare head) of a drum to produce a rattling sound when the drum is struck.

Timpani Large, kettle-shaped drums that are tuned to a definite pitch.

Trap set (drum set) A set of drums consisting of a snare, bass, tom-tom, ride, and high-hat cymbals in any quantity, along with assorted special-effects percussion items needed for the music at hand.

Tuning Adjusting the pitch of a musical instrument.

Vibraphone An idiophonic percussion instrument with aluminum bars and resonators that extend the duration of each note.

Xylophone An idiophonic percussion instrument with wooden bars.

15

Form in Music

Musicologists and theorists have analyzed the structure of music throughout the ages, and some of these scholars having approached the subject with fairly elevated degrees of sophistication and complexity. As a result, a reader may be confronted with rather intricate detailed diagnoses of the structure of a work, or a somewhat esoteric definition, such as the one offered in the tenth edition of the *Oxford Companion to Music*. There, Percy Scholes defines form as "a series of strategies designed to find a successful mean between the opposite extremes of unrelieved repetition and unrelieved alteration." This definition may be valid but, perhaps, a bit much for us poor mortals.

Form in music refers to the manner in which a composer structures the elements of a work. Form is created by combining melodic shape and harmonic architecture. One can state a melody and then repeat it exactly, modify it, or follow it by an entirely different melody. The composer creates a melodic line, combines it with a rhythmic structure, adds harmonies to establish a key, and a form takes place. These components can be combined to make sections as short as a few simple measures, or increasingly larger sections of extended length and complexity.

The use of a particular form by a composer does not preclude his or her digressing from that design, modifying it, completely abandoning it, and then perhaps returning to it at some point later in a composition. Musical forms are skeletons upon which a composer can build the body of a work.

A convenient way to label elements in music is with the use of letters of the alphabet. Sections of a piece that consist of a melody followed by a second melody, and that followed by the first melody repeated, can be labeled A for the first melody, B for the second, and then A for the repeat of the first melody. The prime symbol (') added to a letter indicates a section is repeated with some variation. For example, a piece labeled A, B, A'' would have a first theme, second theme, and then the first theme repeated with some variation.

The following are terms used to identify basic forms in music. These definitions have been accepted by the music community as being sufficiently descriptive to identify those forms. But the reader must bear in mind that every form can be modified in any conceivable manner and can then be categorized and labeled in a variety of ways by the scholar du jour. So, here are a mélange of labels for forms, ranging from a simple couple of letters to a treatise of intricate classifications of the parts of the work under study.

Binary Form—A musical form that combines two sections, each of which can be repeated. Binary form can take several shapes.

Simple Binary Form—The sections may differ and be labeled with the letters A and B, so a work in simple binary forms will have a section A followed by a section, possibly in a different key, labeled B. Each section may be repeated, in which case it would be labeled A, A, B, B. This was a common form used for dances in the eighteenth century.

Modified Binary Form—Binary form can be varied, modifying the various sections by adding material from one section to another, or altering a section melodically, rhythmically, or harmonically. These designs can be labeled "rounded binary" where part of section A is added to section B, and "balanced binary" where the harmonic structure of the cadence (the conclusion of a phrase) from section A is added to section B.

Ternary Form—This form consists of three parts, which can be handled in several ways. Simple ternary form can be A, B, A. That can be expanded to A, A, B, A where the first theme is repeated, followed by a second theme, after which the first theme reappears to close the pattern.

A more expanded iteration of the ternary form is known as the sonata allegro form, likened to the form used to write a paper. This form is divided into three sections: the exposition, the development, and the recapitulation. The labels almost tell the entire story.

In the exposition, a statement of a major theme is presented in a given key. This is followed by a secondary theme, often in the dominant key, which is a fifth above the original key. The exposition then concludes with a return of the first theme in the original key.

The development section is exactly that. The themes are developed to whatever degree and extent the composer desires. This section provides an opportunity for the composer to demonstrate his or her creativity.

The recapitulation consists of the themes from the exposition repeated, but this time with no change in key.

Sometimes a short introduction precedes the exposition and an ending section is added on to finalize the piece harmonically and thematically. The final section is called a coda.

Rondo Form—The rondo form consists of a primary theme, which is repeatedly stated as the hub, after which differing additional themes occur. The result can be an A, B, A, C, A, D, A, E, A pattern, or an A, B, A, C, A, D, A, B, A pattern, where the final three sections duplicate the first three. The primary (A) theme is called a refrain, while the differing additional themes are called episodes. Such a series can be developed with variations and repeated multiple times.

Fugue—A fugue begins with a subject theme performed in one voice, instrument, section, or keyboard register. At different points during the statement of the subject theme additional voices introduce the same theme, but at different pitches so that ultimately a blend of all the voices are performing the same theme simultaneously but at different points in the melody. Fugues often follow the ternary or sonata allegro form where there is an exposition, development, and recapitulation.

Through Composed—This is a term used for a selection that has no discernible sections. Such music can be classified as being rhapsodic, telling a story, or describing visual images through sound. It is a continuous, cohesive progression of music intended to create a specific effect or image in the mind of the listener.

Strophic Form—In strophic form all verses are musically the same. A, A, A, A, A, A. Strophic form is used with a series of different texts applied to each repetition of the reoccurring verse.

Variation Form—In variation form a theme is established followed by a series of variations on that theme: A, A', A'', A''', and so on. The extent of the variations is limited only by the versatility of the composer. The themes can be melodic, rhythmic, harmonic, structural, any combination of, or all included.

Summary—Forms in music as described above are not hard-and-fast rules to which a composer must adhere. These are general outlines used as an organizing design on which to build the subject piece. In certain types of vocal music such as opera, oratorio, and the Mass, the form is set by the requirements of the libretto. The content of the text dictates the form and structure of the music. Other forms, such as the symphony or sonata, call for a more restrictive organization; however, this does not necessarily imply that the composer does not have license to stray or, at his or her discretion, completely break with the defined structure. Specific forms help the composer create a selection and help the listener identify it. Form should be a tool for the music participant, not a constraint.

GLOSSARY OF TERMS RELATED TO FORM IN MUSIC

This glossary will help the reader identify items and define terms that are related to form in music. See the discussion above for more in-depth information on these items.

Anthem An inspirational song intended for a specific group that can be either religious or secular.

Bagatelle A simple short piece of unassuming character, usually for the piano.

Ballad A short instrumental piece to depict a folk narrative.

Barcarolle A song that is harmonically and metrically designed to replicate the flow of a boat in motion.

Basso continuo A system of music composition common during the Baroque period, in which a bass line called a figured bass was transcribed with numbers to indicate the harmony that should be used to accompany each bass note. The bass line was played by one of the lower non-fretted string instruments, with a keyboard instrument improvising the upper parts.

Berceuse A song in 6/8 time or other triple meter with the gentle lilting qualities of a child's cradle song.

Canon A technique used in counterpoint (below) where a primary melodic theme is stated, followed by additional participants entering with the same theme at different times.

Cantata A substantial musical work for chorus and orchestra with vocal solos based on a sacred or secular libretto. (Canta is the Italian word for sing.)

Chamber music A musical composition written specifically for performance in a small chamber by a correspondingly sized instrumental ensemble.

Chamber orchestra A small orchestra. See orchestra below.

Chorale A term applied to a church hymn and also used to denote a vocal ensemble.

Chorale prelude A musical preface to a chorale.

Coda An additional passage of music added onto the end of a piece.

Concertante A musical work that contains solo parts for individual or for a small group of instruments. Concertante can be the diminutive of a concerto.

Concerto A major work for orchestra, with a solo instrument or instruments prominently featured.

Concerto grosso Italian for "big concerto, a concerto featuring a group of soloists as opposed to a single soloist.

Continuo see basso continuo.

Counterpoint A system of composing, popular during the Baroque period, in which a primary musical line or melody was combined with additional lines establishing harmonic compatibility while maintaining each line's individuality. Countering one melody with others within a system of exacting guidelines.

Da capo Return to the beginning. The letters "D.C." are often substituted for the words da capo.

Da capo al fine Return to the beginning and replay or sing to the end.

Da capo al segno Return to the sign and play or sing to the end.

Divertimento A lighthearted form of music developed in the eighteenth century for a small instrumental group. The music had no particular form and was intended as entertainment for social occasions.

Duet (duo) A composition for two vocal or instrumental performers.

Elegy A composition written in a somber despondent mode to express musically a solemn situation.

Etude Originally intended as an exercise to improve technique, this French term developed into a label for significant compositions demonstrating a performer's technical skills.

Exposition A statement of the principal themes in a major work. See sonata allegro form.

Fantasy Originating in the sixteenth and seventeenth century, the term was applied to music of no particular form but rather a product of the composer's fancy.

Fugue A form of counterpoint where a subject theme is imitated in different keys by additional voices or instruments entering at various times as the subject theme progresses.

Gregorian chant Liturgical text sung in unison with multiple repeated notes and a rhythmic design dictated by the meter of the text.

Harmony The study and management of two or more notes being performed simultaneously, usually to provide support to a single theme or melody.

Humoresque A music form in a lighthearted vein, evoking an atmosphere of casual humor rather than a more intense comedic experience.

Impromptu A free-wheeling form of composition giving the impression of an extemporaneous improvisation as opposed to a predetermined structured composition.

Improvisation A spontaneous musical response to a given set of conditions.

Instrumentation The distribution of instruments assigned to a music composition.

Interlude A short musical selection performed in between two more significant pieces of music.

Intermezzo As is an interlude, an intermezzo is a short selection performed between two longer selections or as an interruption to a longer piece. The term has also been used as a label for a movement in chamber music.

Invention A short contrapuntal selection, usually in two parts for keyboard.

Leitmotif A German term for a melodic or rhythmic theme associated with a particular individual, idea, or action.

Lied German for song.

Mass The Catholic worship service to celebrate the transformation of bread and wine into the body and blood of Christ. The ordinary of the Mass, which consists of the parts of the Mass that reoccur during every celebration, has been set to music throughout the ages. The Bach B-Minor Mass may be considered the quintessential work in this category.

Mazurka A Polish dance.

Minuet A French dance in triple meter.

Missa Latin for mass.

Motet Thirteenth-century choral music used for secular texts in a liturgical setting. Over the centuries the motet evolved into a contrapuntal composition for full vocal scoring and included both secular and liturgical texts.

Nocturne A musical selection that is harmonically, rhythmically, and expressively suggestive of the night.

Opera A play set to music. See chapter 18.

Opera buffa (Italian; opera comique in French) Comic opera. See chapter 18.

Opera seria (Italian) Serious opera. See chapter 18.

Operetta Light opera. See chapter 1.

Opus Latin for work. The term is often used as part of a numbering system to organize the work of prolific composers. The plural of opus is opera.

Oratorio A composition based on a religious story line and performed by solo voice, chorus, and instruments in a concert setting.

Orchestra A combination of string, woodwind, brass, and percussion instruments. An orchestra can number from about fifty to over one hundred, depending on the music to be performed.

Orchestration An arrangement of music in preparation for an orchestra or other ensemble.

Overture An introductory piece often containing themes from a major work to follow, such as an opera.

Partita See suite.

Passacaglia An early form of theme and variations built on a basso ostinato or repeating bass figure. This form first appeared in Spain in the early 1600s.

Passion An account of the death of Jesus Christ set to choral music.

Pastorale A musical selection expressing through rhythm, tempo, melodic inference, and/or harmonic structure the relaxed, idyllic ambiance associated with life in a peaceful environment.

Plainchant A form of medieval church music consisting of a liturgical text chanted a capella in unison with a free rhythm prescribed by that of the text.

Polyphony Music in two or more parts.

Postlude The antithesis of a prelude. Music played at the end of a piece.

Prelude Music preceding a work. Similar to an overture, which is an introductory piece often containing themes from a major work, such as an opera, to follow.

Programme music Music composed to represent in sound a story line. The form and the melodic and harmonic structure of such music is designed to tell a story in sound rather than follow a particular music architecture.

Psalm A sacred song predicated on biblical writings, originally sung in the style of plainchant. In later times the text was applied to a more structured form of music composition.

Requiem Mass A mass for the dead.

Rhapsody A work unrestricted by the formal rules of composition, allowing the composer to express him- or herself freely through the medium of sound.

Rondo A form in which a principal theme reappears after each of a series of subordinate themes.

Sarabande A Spanish dance form in triple meter, used during the Baroque period as the third movement in a four-movement suite.

Scherzo In Italian, the literal translation is "joke." In music it has come to mean a lighthearted movement in a major work such as a symphony.

Serenade A derivative of sereno, Italian for calm, a serenade is a serene work often dedicated to one's significant other.

Sinfonia The term used for an orchestral introduction to an opera.

Sinfonia concertante A concerto for two or more solo instruments.

Sinfonietta The diminutive of symphony.

Singspiel German for a musical rendition of a play with spoken words. Perhaps the original musical.

Sonata A two- to four-movement piece for solo instrument or small instrumental ensemble.

Sonata allegro form An exposition where the themes are stated, a development where those themes are expanded to the degree and in a style of the composer's choice, and a recapitulation where the original themes are restated. Added to those three main parts can be an introduction preceding the exposition and a coda following the recapitulation.

Sonata da camera A dance suite for multiple instruments with continuo. Originally from the Baroque era.

Sonata da chiesa An instrumental piece from the Baroque period in four movements alternating in tempi (plural) from slow to fast and then slow and fast again. Usually played by violin or flute for the melody, with basso continuo.

Sonatina The diminutive of a sonata, a small sonata-like piece.

Suite Originally a combination of short dances, the term *suite* eventually grew to apply to any combination of short pieces.

Symphony An extensive composition for orchestra, usually containing four movements in various forms that are structured to follow a predetermined format.

Vocalise A work for voice where the music is sung with vowels and random syllables in place of words. This can be done to create a special effect or as a vocal exercise.

Waltz An instrumental piece in triple meter, intended as a dance.

16

Music Theory

This chapter deals with the fundamentals of music notation, rhythm, pitch, and harmony. As is the case with all topics in music, music theory is an intensely complex subject that requires a life's commitment to study if one wishes to understand it fully. This chapter will serve as an introduction to music theory. There is a lot more to it, but this is a start.

NOTATION

Note Names—Notes are named using a portion of the alphabet from A through G. In ascending order, the notes are named A, B, C, D, E, F, and G. To continue ascending the next letter name upward will begin again with A and continue with B, C, D, and so on. When descending, the pattern is reversed. A numeral following a note's letter name, such as C4, indicates that note's exact location in the entire music range. (More about this below under scientific pitch notation.)

The Staff—The basic format upon which all music notation is written is called the staff. It consists of five horizontal lines, between which there are four spaces (figure 16.1). The five lines can be expanded up and down by adding lines called ledger lines above or below the staff, called ledger lines. These enable one to write notes beyond the range of the basic staff.

The lines and spaces of the staff are numbered from the bottom up: first line, second line, and first space, second space, and so on. A series of symbols, to be discussed later, have been established to represent the various notes and rests. These are written on staves (plural of staff) to create a score from which musicians read to play music.

A   **B**   **C**

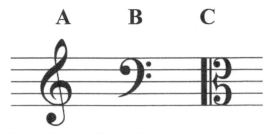

Figure 16.1.   Staff with Clefs

Clefs—Clefs are symbols used to assign a particular letter name to a line on a staff. Once the name of that line is established, all other lines and spaces are named in relation to the line established by the clef. The A through G alphabet established above is used to name these notes. If a clef establishes line two as being the note G, then the next space up would be A, the line above that, B, and so forth. Descending is the same in reverse. Below G would be F, and then E, and so on down. Three different clefs are used to expand the range over which one can write notes on staves. The three clefs are called the G clef, F clef, and C clef.

The G Clef—Figure 16.1A is a symbol called the G clef or treble clef. Note that the symbol appears as a somewhat modified letter G. The symbol encircles the second line on the staff, indicating that the line is to represent the note G4.

From that point on, the line and space names follow the sequence described above. Ascending from G, the next space would be A, the next line B, the next space C, and so forth. Descending from the G line the spaces and lines would read F, E, D, and so on.

The F Clef—Lower notes are written using the F clef or bass clef (figure 16.1B). Notice how the symbol draws attention to the fourth line of the staff by circling that line and placing a dot above and below it. That line will represent the note F3. The lines and spaces of the bass clef follow the same sequence of letters as those in other clefs. With line four being F, all other lines and spaces follow in order within the parameters of the letters A through G. From the fourth line F, the ascending sequence will be G, A, B, and so on. The descending sequence will be E, D, C, and so on.

The C Clef—This clef is movable (figure 16.1C). It is used to permit one to write music on the staff that, due to the music's range, would otherwise have to be written using numerous ledger lines. Whichever line the C clef embraces becomes middle C. All other lines and space are then relative to that C. The space above would be D, below would be B, and so forth.

The two most frequent uses for the C clef occur when it is on the third line. This is used for the viola and for the alto voice. Another common use is placing the C clef on the fourth line for use by the cello, bassoon, and the male tenor voice.

The Grand Staff—The grand staff (figure 16.2) is made up of two staves combined with a bracket. This configuration is used to accommodate an expanded range of notation. The grand staff is used for keyboard music and the harp. The upper staff generally, but not exclusively, is used for the notes in the upper or treble range played with the right hand. The lower staff is used for the lower or bass range, usually played with the left hand.

Figure 16.2.   Grand Staff with Middle C

Middle C—If one were to attempt to write an ascending scale starting from the bottom of the grand staff, the series would end with the note B, one space above the fifth line in the bass clef. Continuing in the ascending mode, the next note available after B one space above the last line in the bass clef would be D, one space below the first line on the treble staff. There is no place for a C to complete the sequence. The void is compensated for by the addition of a line called a ledger line situated between the staves to provide for the missing C. This note C is called middle C because it is situated in the middle of the two staves.

Scientific Pitch Notation—Among the several ways used to identify the register in which particular notes are written is with the use of an alphanumeric system, a combination of letters and numbers. Above, you have learned the letter names of notes. By placing a number following a letter, the register of that note in the entire range of notes is identified. An example would be middle C, whose alphanumeric name is C4. The C one octave below middle C is C3. The C an octave above middle C is C5. The notes ascending between these Cs maintain the C's numeral until the next C is reached.

An example would be C4, D4, E4, F4, G4, A4, B4, C5, D5, and so on. Figure 16.3 shows the alphanumeric symbols for all notes.

Figure 16.3. Alphanumeric Symbols

NOTE SYMBOLS AND THEIR VALUES

Music notation consists of a series of symbols used to indicate pitch and note duration. The position of a symbol on the staff indicates the pitch that is to be played. The various configurations of the notes indicate the duration of the note.

Note Duration—This is a matter of simple mathematics. The notes are named in fractions of a whole. A whole note is equal to two half notes, which are equal to four quarter notes, which are equal to eight eighth notes, which are equal to sixteen sixteenth notes, and on and on.

For each kind of note there is an equivalent rest. Figure 16.4 is a listing of the different note values and their equivalent rests indicated under the note values.

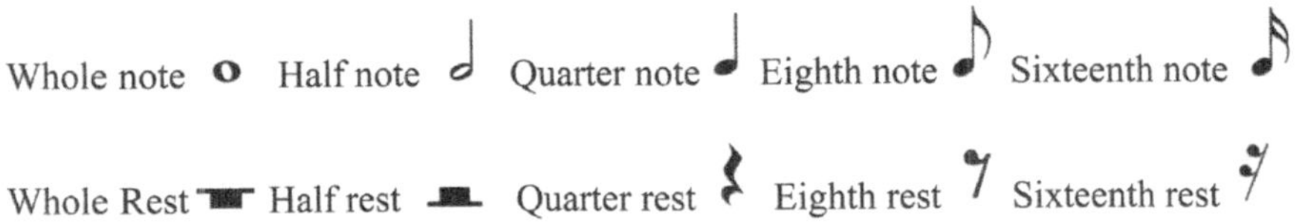

Whole note **o** Half note ♩ Quarter note ♩ Eighth note ♪ Sixteenth note ♬

Whole Rest ▬ Half rest ▬ Quarter rest 𝄽 Eighth rest 𝄾 Sixteenth rest 𝄿

Figure 16.4. Note Durations

Measures or Bars—In order to give note duration a structure, the notes on a staff are separated into units called measures or bars. The measures are divided by vertical lines called bar lines. Bars are assigned a particular number of beats, and the notes contained are assigned a time value. These are indicated by a time signature.

Time Signature—A time signature or meter signature is represented by a numerical fraction that appears at the beginning of a piece. The numerator or upper digit of the fraction tells how many beats there are in a measure. If the numerator is 2, there will be two beats in a measure. If the numerator is 4 there will be four beats in a measure. The number of beats in a measure is determined by the composer.

The denominator or lower number of the fraction tells the kind of note that is equal to one beat. If the lower number is 4, a quarter note will get one beat. If the lower number is 2, a half note will get one beat. Any number that is representative of a kind of note can be used to equal one beat, as shown in figure 16.5.

Figure 16.5. Time Signatures

(A) Four beats in a measure with a quarter note getting one beat
(B) The letter C in place of a fraction is a shorthand symbol for the 4/4 time signature
(C) Three beats in a measure with a quarter note getting one beat
(D) Two beats in a measure with a quarter note getting one beat
(E) The letter C with a vertical line through it is shorthand for 2/4 time
(F) Six beats in a measure with an eighth note getting one beat
(G) Nine beats in a measure with an eighth note getting one beat

Dotted Notes and Ties—A dot added to the right side of a note increases its value by one-half. Therefore, in 4/4 time where a half note will get two beats, a dotted half note will get three beats. The formula applies to all notes with a dot added to its right side.

Two dots added to the right side of a note will increase its value by three-quarters. The first dot increases the value by one-half, and the second dot increases the note by half of the half, or one quarter. The result is a double-dotted half note that will equal three and a half beats, two beats for the half note, one beat for half of the half note, and a half beat for half of the one-beat increase. Figure 16.6 shows some examples of notes tied together to equal the equivalent of the dotted notes. See the next paragraph for an explanation of ties.

Figure 16.6. Dotted Notes and Ties

(A) A dotted whole note in 4/4 time is equal to six beats
(B) A dotted half note in 4/4 time is equal to three beats
(C) A dotted eighth note in 4/4 time is equal to ¾ of a beat
(D) A double dotted half note would be equal to 3½ beats

Ties are curved lines that combine the value of the notes tied together. Figure 16.6 illustrates the value of dotted notes by using a tie to combine two notes, which become equal in value to the dotted note.

If a half note valued at two beats is tied to a quarter note valued at one beat, the total value of the tied notes becomes three beats, two for the half note and one for the quarter note. Ties are used if the composer wishes to extend a note beyond the length of a measure. An example would be an eight beat-long note in 4/4 time. A whole note placed in two consecutive measures and tied together would equal an uninterrupted sound for eight beats.

Beamed Notes—Notes in series can be written individually, or grouped to facilitate reading them. If a selection requires a series of sixteen sixteenth notes, they can be written individually or bundled in groupings of four (figure 16.7) so the reader can visualize them more easily than seeing sixteen individual notes. These notes are called beamed notes.

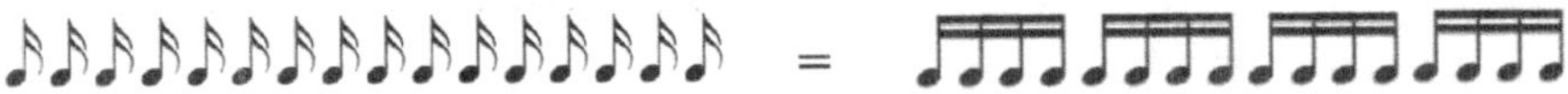

Figure 16.7. Beamed Notes

Stems—The stems of notes can appear in two different directions depending on the location of the note on the staff. Notes written below the middle (third) line have their stems in the up position. Notes written above the third line have their stems in the down position. Notes written on the third line can have their stems in either direction depending on the position of the notes immediately adjacent to the subject note. If the adjacent notes are below the third line, the stem of the third line note will join them. The reverse is the same.

Intervals—In music, interval refers to the distance between two notes. If the notes are adjacent to each other and played separately, they may be termed horizontal, linear, or melodic. If the notes are sounded together, they may be called vertical or harmonic.

Intervals are measured in half steps. A half step is the closest distance between two notes in Western music. On a keyboard instrument, from any one key to the very next one in either direction is a half step. Progressing from any key to the next possible key while skipping a key in between is a whole step. More on this to follow.

Accidentals—An accidental is a symbol that modifies a note by either raising or lowering it. The symbol ♯ (sharp) preceding a note raises it a half step. The symbol ♭ (flat) preceding a note lowers it a half step. The symbol ♮ (natural) cancels any preceding accidental so that the subject note reverts to its natural pitch.

Double Sharps and Flats—These symbols indicate an adjustment to the subject note by a full step. A double sharp (✕) will raise a note a whole step (two half steps). A double flat (♭♭) will lower a note a whole step.

Enharmonic Notes—This is a term applied to notes that sound the same but can be called by different names. The note D-sharp on a keyboard is the same as E-flat; therefore, D-sharp and E-flat bear different names but will sound the same when played on a keyboard instrument. The reader will note in the paragraph below on chromatic scales that, when notes are used in an ascending series, they will be labeled using sharps, but when descending, flats will be used.

SCALES

A scale is a series of notes progressing in whole and half steps in ascending or descending order usually within the span of eight notes called an octave. There are different kinds of scales.

Major Scale—A major scale ascending consists of a pattern of whole and half steps as follows: W (whole), W, H (half), W, W, W, H.

On a keyboard, a diatonic scale consists of all the white keys between any note C and the next note C up or down. This occurs because a half step exists between the third and fourth, and seventh and eighth notes in that series. The pattern of half and whole steps falls into place with no adjustments needed.

If one were to start a major scale on any other note on the keyboard, it would be necessary to include both black and white keys to produce the pattern of two whole steps, one half step, three whole steps, and one half step. It is at this point that accidentals (sharps, flats, and naturals) come into play. If one begins a scale on the note D and follows the prescribed pattern for a diatonic scale, it will be necessary to use F-sharp instead of F and C-sharp instead of C in order to keep the pattern of whole and half steps (figure 16.8).

Figure 16.8.   Scale Degree Names

Scale Degree Names—Each degree (step) of a scale is named as follows: 1 = tonic, 2 = super tonic, 3 = mediant, 4 = subdominant, 5 = dominant, 6 = submediant, 7 = leading tone, 8 = tonic (octave).

Minor Scales—In addition to the major scales there are three minor scales. These are called the natural minor, harmonic minor, and melodic minor; they are derivatives of ancient modes, which will be discussed later.

The **natural minor** scale ascending pattern consists of W, H, W, W, H, W, W, as compared to W, W, H, W, W, W, H of the major scale. The natural minor scale is also called the relative minor because it has a directly related major scale. If one were to begin an ascending scale on the sixth degree of any major scale and ascend using the same notes from the major scale, the pattern of a natural minor scale, which is W, H, W, W, W, H, W, would occur without any need to modify a note.

The **harmonic minor** scale is a slightly modified natural minor scale. The pattern for a harmonic minor scale is W, H, W, W, H, W+H, H. The distance between the sixth and seventh degree of the scale is a step and a half.

In the **melodic minor** scale the sixth and seventh degrees are raised a half step ascending, but are natural descending. The result is ascending W, H, W, W, W, W, H, and, descending with the sixth and seventh degrees natural, the intervals descending are W, W, H, W, W, H, W.

Chromatic Scale—This scale is made up of twelve notes that are all half steps apart. Starting on any note on a keyboard, simply play all the white and black keys in succession within an octave in either direction. When written, an ascending chromatic scale uses all sharps as accidentals, whereas a descending chromatic scale uses all flats.

Whole Tone Scale—Unlike other scales that are composed of a combination of whole and half steps, a whole tone scale is comprised of only whole steps. When this scale is used as a basis for a composition, the tonality becomes somewhat hazy because of the absence of an audio perceived point of resolution that occurs in music based on a diatonic scale. In a diatonic scale, the seventh degree of the scale is called a leading tone because in sound, it leads the listener to the tonic, or eighth, final degree. If one sings a scale using the syllables *do, re, mi, fa, sol, la, ti,* and stops there, the audio sensation will be incomplete. The note *ti* is called a leading tone because in sound it leads to the final note *do* which will give the listener a sense of resolution. Whole tone scales do not have any leading tones, and therefore a vague sense prevails throughout a piece based on a whole tone scale.

Pentatonic Scale—A pentatonic scale consists of five notes within an octave. The effect is one of a diatonic major scale with something missing. The simplest way to construct a pentatonic scale is to play an ascending scale on the black keys only of the piano, starting with C-sharp. The notes would be C-sharp, D-sharp, F-sharp, G-sharp, and A-sharp. Another approach is to create a diatonic major scale, omitting the fourth and seventh degrees of that scale. Starting on C, the pentatonic scale would be C, D, E, G, and A.

Two terms used to label pentatonic scales are hemitonic and anhemitonic. A hemitonic scale contains at least one half step. An anhemitonic scale is constructed of all whole steps. Pentatonic scales can be major or minor.

A major pentatonic scale consists of the notes 1, 2, 3, 5, and 6 of any major scale. Notes 4 and 7 are omitted. An example would be C, D, E, G, and A.

A minor pentatonic scale consists of notes 1, 3, 4, 5, and 7 of any natural minor scale. Notes 2 and 6 are omitted. An example starting on the note A is A, C, D, E, and G.

Modes—This topic is discussed from an historical perspective in Chapter 18. Modes are a series of eight-note scales that can easily be played on all the white keys of the piano. Starting from the note D and playing an ascending series of all white keys and ending on D an octave higher will produce a scale called the Dorian Mode. An all-white key scale from E to E is a Phrygian mode; F to F, Lydian; G to G, Mixolydian; A to A, Aeolian; B to B, Locrian; and C to C, Ionian. These modes were used as a basis on which one wrote chant (see chapter 18). In each of these modes, the note on which the chant ends is the same as the first note of the mode and is called the finalis, the equivalent of the tonic in the diatonic scale explained above.

Another series of modes based on those above are called plagal modes. These start on the fifth degree of the primary mode, ascend an octave on the white keys of the piano, but maintain the finalis of its parent mode. As an example, a chant written in the plagal mode to the Dorian mode, which starts on D, will instead start on the fifth degree of the Dorian mode which is A, and then end on D, which is the finalis of the Dorian mode.

These modes retain the same names as their parents, with the addition of the prefix hypo. The names thus become Hypodorian, A to A; Hypophrygian, B to B; Hypolydian, C to C; Hypomixolydian, D to D; Hypoaeolian, E to E; Hypolocrian, F to F; and Hypoionian, G to G.

Intervals—As stated above, the distance in pitch between two notes is called an interval. Intervals can be expressed in generic or specific terms.

A **generic interval** is the distance between two notes on a staff. When two notes are on the same line or space they are called a perfect unison. Progressing upward alphabetically using C as the prime, the next note up would be D. C to D is called a second; C to E, a third; C to F, a fourth; C to G, a fifth; C to A, a sixth; C to B, a seventh; and C to C, an octave. These are generic labels in that they do not account for any possible alterations using accidentals.

A **specific interval** is one whose label is modified to account for any adjustment made by an accidental. A sharp, flat, or natural can be added to one or both notes in an interval, thereby altering it. As an example, the generic name for the interval from C to A is a sixth; however, one can use a sharp or flat to alter the A. Doing so will alter the interval and change its sound; thus, the need for a more specific nomenclature. Five more terms must be added to the generic nomenclature to accurately account for all of the possible altered intervals. These terms are major, minor, augmented, diminished, and perfect.

Seconds, thirds, sixths, and sevenths can be major or minor. The number of half steps in these intervals is as follows:

A major second = two half steps
A minor second = one half step
A major third = four half steps
A minor third = three half steps
A major sixth = nine half steps
A minor sixth = eight half steps
A major seventh = eleven half steps
A minor seventh = ten half steps

Fourths, fifths, and octaves can be perfect, augmented, or diminished. The number of half steps in perfect, augmented, or diminished intervals is as follows:

A perfect fourth = five half steps
An augmented fourth = six half steps
A diminished fourth = four half steps
A perfect fifth = seven half steps
An augmented fifth = eight half steps
A diminished fifth = six half steps
A perfect octave = twelve half steps
An augmented octave = thirteen half steps
A diminished octave = eleven half steps

CHORDS

A chord consists of three or more notes to be played simultaneously.

Triad—A triad is the simplest form of basic chord upon which more elaborate chords can be built by adding notes.

Major Triad—Three notes beginning with a note on which a major third (up four half steps) and perfect fifth (up seven half steps) are added. C, E, and G together make a major triad.

Minor Triad—A minor triad is a major triad with the third flatted. This is formed when a minor third (three steps up) and a perfect fifth (seven steps up) are added to any note. C, E-flat, and G together make a minor triad.

Augmented Triad—An augmented triad is a major triad with the fifth sharped. This is formed when a major third (four half steps up) and an augmented fifth (eight steps up) are added to any note. C, E, and G-sharp together make an augmented triad.

Diminished Triad—A diminished triad is a major triad with the third and fifth flatted. This is formed when a minor third (three half steps up) and a diminished fifth (six half steps) are added to any note. C, E-flat, and G-flat together make a diminished triad.

Seventh Chord—A seventh chord is a triad with the seventh degree of the scale added. There are different kinds of seventh chords.

A **dominant seventh chord** is a triad with a diminished seventh added. The notes would be C, E, G, and B-flat.

A **major seventh chord** is a triad with a major seventh added. The notes would be C, E, G, and B.

A **minor seventh chord** is a minor triad with a minor seventh added. The notes would be C, E-flat, G, and B-flat.

A **diminished seventh chord** is a diminished triad with a diminished seventh added. The notes would be C, E-flat, G-flat, and B-double-flat (actually A).

A **half diminished seventh chord** is a diminished triad with a diminished seventh added. The notes would be C, E-flat, G-flat, and B-flat.

A **minor major seventh chord** is a minor triad with a major seventh added. The notes would be C, E-flat, G, and B.

An **augmented major seventh chord** is an augmented triad with a major seventh added. The notes would be C, E, G-sharp, and B.

An **augmented seventh chord** is an augmented triad with a minor seventh added. The notes would be C, E, G-sharp, and B-flat.

Neapolitan Sixth Chord—A major triad built on the flatted second degree of a scale. In the key of C, the notes in a Neapolitan chord would be D-flat, F, and A-flat. This chord is called a Neapolitan sixth because it is frequently used in the first inversion, resulting in a minor sixth between F and D-flat.

Inversions—When the notes in any chords are rearranged from their original triad configuration, the new arrangement is called an inversion. The C triad written as C, E, G is called root position because the bottom note of the chord is its name. When the chord is written as E, G, C, it is in its first inversion. If the chord is written as G, C, E, it is in its second inversion. When a seventh chord has the seventh in the lowest (root) position, it is in its third inversion.

When intervals are inverted, their names become the opposite of their original interval.

A **major interval inverted** (turned upside down) becomes a minor interval. C to E is a major third, whereas E to C is a minor sixth.

A **minor interval inverted** becomes a major interval. E to G is a minor third, whereas G to E is a major sixth.

A **perfect interval** remains a perfect interval. "Perfect" indicates that the interval is neither augmented nor diminished. C to G is a perfect fifth, whereas G to C, which is a fourth, is still a perfect interval. Fifths and fourths are both perfect intervals.

Augmented and **Diminished Intervals** inverted become their opposite. C to G-sharp is an augmented fifth, whereas G-sharp to C is a diminished fourth.

Review—In their inversions, minor becomes major, major becomes minor, augmented becomes diminished, diminished becomes augmented, and perfect remains perfect.

KEY SIGNATURES

Sharp, flat, and natural signs are called accidentals. These are used to adjust notes as needed to create a particular tonality or musical center of gravity. Music is usually written based on scales such as those described above. This is called writing in a key. If one were to write a piece based on the scale of E, the piece would be in the key of E.

The E scale has four sharps in its formula. These sharps are F-sharp, C-sharp, G-sharp, and D-sharp. In order to write in that key, it would be necessary to place a sharp before every F, C, G, and D every time one of those notes appears. The result would be a score replete with symbols. To accommodate for that and simplify writing and reading a score, key signatures are used.

A key signature is a collection of appropriate accidentals (sharps and flats) written at the beginning of a piece after a clef and before a time signature. The accidentals in the key signature apply to all of the indicated notes in the piece unless the accidental is nullified with a natural sign or modified in some other manner. If there is a sharp symbol on the F line in a key signature, all F notes in the piece are automatically played as F-sharp unless otherwise modified. Figure 16.9 shows the key signatures for all major keys and their relative minor key signatures. Note on the chart that the relative minor of any key is three half steps below the major key name.

The following mnemonics help determine what key a signature represents:

In keys with sharps in their signature, the name of the key is the note one half step above the last sharp. The key of A major has F-sharp, C-sharp, and G-sharp as its key signature. The last sharp is G-sharp. One half step above G-sharp is A.

In keys with flats in their signature, the flat before the last is the name of the key. The key of E-flat major has B-flat, E-flat, and A-flat as a key signature. E-flat is the flat before the last.

Exceptions are the key of C, which has no key signature, and the key of F, which has only one flat.

Another common mnemonic is the progression of fifths. Beginning with the key of C, which has no sharps or flats in its key signature, one can progress in intervals

Figure 16.9. Major and Relative Minor Key Signatures

of five notes to determine the key signature for any key with sharps in its signature. Five notes up from C is G, which has one sharp. Five up from G is D, two sharps; five up from D is A, three sharps; and so on.

When the key of F-sharp, which has six sharps, is reached in the progression, the enharmonic change (same note with a different name) of the six sharps is made to six flats, which is the key of G-flat. From that point on the progression continues in reverse with the flat keys. The key of G-flat has six flats; D-flat, five flats; A-flat, four flats; and so on. Study figure 16.9.

Summary—The preceding has been an introduction to the basic information required to read music notation and to understand the fundamental structures and formulae used in creating music. One must realize that each topic was presented at a preliminary level to provide the reader with a fundamental knowledge to serve as a first step to more advanced study. The amount of material that exists on these topics is unimaginable, as is the level of complexity and erudition that can be reached by serious advanced study. The ball is in your court.

17

Ensembles

The term *ensemble* refers to any number of individual units that, when assembled, become a cohesive unit or a whole. This concept can apply to an assembly of musical instruments, musicians, vocalists, dancers, or actors, as well as to inanimate objects such as clothing or furniture. The individual parts of an ensemble forfeit some degree of their individuality for the benefit of the whole.

Performers can be grouped in any number from two on. The terms used to identify these groups, starting with a group of two, are duo, trio, quartet, quintet, sextet, septet, and octet. This nomenclature covers groups from two to eight. From this point on the terminology becomes a bit less familiar. For a group of nine the term is nonet; for ten, dectet, decimette, or tentet have been used; and for a group of eleven, hendectet or undectet. These latter terms are less popular, and mostly unknown to the general public.

In instrumental music, ensembles can be formed using a string, woodwind, brass, or percussion choir. A string ensemble would include violins for the soprano range, violas for the alto, cellos for the tenor and bass range, or the addition of a double bass for the bass range. A string trio usually consists of a violin, viola, and cello. For a string quartet, add a second violin to the trio. It is also possible to add a double bass to a string quartet and it becomes a string quintet. If one were to add a piano to a string quartet, the label then becomes a piano quintet.

For woodwinds, a flute, clarinet, oboe, and bassoon would comfortably cover the range and produce a pleasingly homogeneous sound. If an instrument family has sufficient members to cover the range required for a particular piece, an ensemble can be formed of those instruments. An example would be a saxophone quartet, which would consist of a soprano, alto, tenor, and baritone or bass saxophone. The same could be accomplished with a grouping of clarinets with sopranino, soprano, alto, and bass clarinets. These two models can also follow the format of the string quartet by having two alto saxes, one tenor, and a baritone; for the clarinet quartet, two soprano clarinets, one alto, and one bass clarinet.

Brass instruments have an excellent assortment of instruments in each range. In descending order starting with the upper range, there is the trumpet, cornet, French horn, mellophone, flugelhorn, trombone, euphonium, baritone horn, bass trombone, and tuba. In selecting brass instruments for an ensemble of any size, the objective would be to use instruments that were compatible in timbre and that will cover the range required for the subject piece.

A small ensemble can consist of any number of performers up to about a dozen. The members sacrifice their individuality for the good of the ensemble. The group may consist of any combination of performers that have musical compatibility and will fulfill the intentions of the composer.

Larger instrumental ensembles can be named by their size, the type of music they play, or their instrumentation. The following are some examples:

Chamber Orchestra—About twenty members, primarily made up of strings, with a small section of woodwinds and/or brass as needed for the music.

String Orchestra—Usually small to medium in size, this orchestra has violins, violas, cellos, and double basses as its members.

Sinfonietta—An orchestra of a size between a chamber orchestra and symphony orchestra. Often, but not always, a sinfonietta is made up entirely of strings.

Symphony Orchestra—A symphony orchestra can range in size from about thirty-five to whatever number is required for the music. There can be as many as one hundred or more players consisting of string, woodwind, brass, and percussion sections. If the performance is a concerto, the solo instruments are then added to the ensemble. The instrumentation for each section can vary in number and variety depending on the requirements of the program.

A string section will consist of first and second violins, violas, cellos, and double basses in numbers prescribed by the music.

The woodwind section includes flutes, a piccolo if needed, a section of clarinets which can include soprano, alto, and bass, with occasional sopranino and contra-bass clarinets as needed. Oboes, English horns, bassoons, and possibly a contrabassoon as needed, complete the woodwind section.

Brass sections will have trumpets, trombones, French horns, and one or more tubas. This section can also be expanded to include a piccolo trumpet that plays in a higher register than the traditional B-flat trumpet, a flugelhorn that plays in a lower register, and possibly a mid-range baritone, alto, or euphonium horn if needed. These last three are more frequently members of the concert band, to be discussed later.

A basic percussion section will include a snare drum, bass drum, several timpani, cymbals as required, and any number of the myriad percussion instruments as required by the music score.

Pops Orchestra—This orchestra can include as much or as little of the instrumentation of the symphony orchestra or symphonic band as needed, depending on the music to be performed. Pops orchestras perform popular, light classical, jazz, and show music. It is not uncommon to add electronic instruments such as guitars and keyboards, depending on the requirements of the music.

Concert or Symphonic Band—This organization is composed of woodwind, brass, and percussion sections similar to those of the symphony orchestra but expanded in both size and instrumentation. There is no string section, although occasionally a double bass section is added to enhance the timbre of the lower register instruments.

The saxophone section, which is not found in the symphony orchestra, is included in the symphonic band. This section usually includes alto, tenor, and baritone saxophones, but can also be expanded by adding a soprano and a bass saxophone.

The brass section will include B-flat trumpets with the possible addition of D or piccolo trumpets, French horns, tenor and bass trombones, a euphonium or baritone horn, and tubas.

The percussion section will include a snare and bass drum, crash cymbals, timpani in the quantity and range prescribed by the score, at times a trap set if needed, and then any assortment of other percussion instruments as required.

Jazz Band—As the name implies, a jazz band is equipped to play jazz. Its instrumentation and number of players are determined by the type of jazz and where the performance will take place. The basic instruments will be a percussion section with some additional melody instruments. The percussion section usually centers about an elaborate trap set (see chapter 14). In addition there are woodwind and brass instruments, a keyboard, and/or guitars of various kinds. The size of the jazz band can vary from as few as three pieces to any size suitable for the music to be performed. Larger bands will have multiple players on certain instruments and a greater range of instruments within each choir. Two alto saxophones, one tenor, and a baritone are a common instrumentation used in a big jazz band.

Dance Band—A dance band can share all the elements of a jazz band in both size and instrumentation. The difference between the two is in the music being played. A dance band will perform music that is suitable for dancing. That can vary by the audience and type of dancing the music is intended to serve. These can include the more traditional dance styles but can also gear up to rock, disco, and anything else the audience desires.

Rock Band—Intended to play rock-and-roll style music, these bands usually focus on electronic instruments such as the electric guitar and bass guitar, supported by an elaborate set of percussion instruments. It is not uncommon for one of the guitar players to be a lead singer and others to join him or her as "backup." The instrumentation varies in number and type by the kind of rock music to be performed. At this writing there are more than two hundred different labels for categories of rock music. I will pass on that research.

Vocal Ensembles—Voices are classified by the range in which they perform. The four basic classifications from the highest to the lowest are soprano, alto, tenor, and bass (SATB). In order to cover the total range of notes with a balanced harmonic structure, a vocal ensemble with members in all four categories (SATB) would be best. This does not preclude the other options of having as few as just two singers for a duet up to an entire chorus of one hundred or more.

The basic vocal ensemble groupings are the same as those stated in the beginning of this chapter, namely, duo, trio, quartet, quintet, sextet, septet, and octet, nonet, dectet, decimette, and hendectet, or undectet. Groups larger than these then begin to fall into the category of choir, choral, or chorus. These three terms are used interchangeably, because there is no prescribed vocal distribution or number of members required to qualify using any of the labels. The choice is more a case of which title best suits the situation for which the ensemble is intended. In an opera, a group may be called the chorus, whereas the same group in a church could be called a choir.

Summary—Music ensembles can be comprised of just about any assembly of instrumentalists, vocalists, or both that are required to produce the sounds prescribed by the composer. Over the years, labels for the various groups have evolved with a reasonable degree of definition. However, one must allow some latitude when considering the structure of a performing group on the basis of its label. The label should just be considered an indication of the kind of performing group in terms of its size and instrumentation, a product of the music to be performed, and the venue in which the performance is to take place.

18

Anatomy of an Opera

Opera can be defined in the simplest terms as theater set to music. However, that simple definition, although valid, does not do justice to the scope and complexity of this art form. Opera has developed to the point where now a production can be so grand as to warrant the label Grand Opera. This is not to say that all opera is grand. Opera exists at all levels of showmanship and musicality.

A comprehensive definition of opera would require an introduction to a multitude of interrelated art forms required for a performance. For an opera to reach the stage, the different areas of expertise needed include a composer, librettist, choreographer, conductor, instrumentalists, soloists, dancers, a chorus, choral director, set designer, artists, carpenters, sculptors, painters, electricians, special effects designers, one or more staging directors, costume designers, tailors, seamstresses, makeup artists, hairdressers, wig makers, publicity agents, theater personnel, janitors, investors, printers, an administrative staff, and others. Of those twenty-some-odd categories, only a few such as the composer, librettist, and conductor are usually but not always individuals. The orchestra can number one hundred, the chorus fifty, stage hands twenty, and on and on. It is not uncommon to have about three hundred or more participants involved in the process of preparing a performance.

THE BEGINNING

As stated in chapter 1, the earliest work considered by some to be the first opera was composed at the end of the sixteenth century by Jacopo Peri. A sufficient amount of the score of his *Dafne* has survived to qualify it to be considered so. However, the complete score of the opera *L'Orfeo*, written by Claudio Monteverdi in 1607, did survive, thereby fully justifying its consideration as the first opera. Monteverdi's *L'Orfeo* can be heard at https://www.youtube.com/watch?v=5JQ-tdULkGE.

It was during the Baroque period from 1600 to the mid-1700s that opera began to develop into a primary form of entertainment for the elite and royalty. This did not remain the case for too long, as the works of George Frideric Handel, Antonio Vivaldi, and Jean-Baptiste Lully gained popularity not only with the cognoscenti but throughout all of the general population. These beginnings took place in Italy. Review chapter 1 to recall how opera in its early stages was composed in two genres: opera seria or serious opera and opera buffa, comic opera.

Many major opera houses, such as the Metropolitan Opera in New York and the Sydney Opera House in Australia, offer backstage tours where one can see much of the logistical machinations involved in preparing and performing an opera.

The orchestra used for an opera consists of the same elements as those of a symphony orchestra. Opera orchestras are made up of the four instrumental choirs, those being strings, woodwinds, brass, and percussion. Depending on the particular opera, there will be variations in the orchestra's size and instrumentation. Different operas may require special effects and simpler or more elaborate orchestration depending on the intent of the composer.

The conductor of the orchestra also conducts the singers on stage during the performance (see chapter 19). In an opera the conductor's role is particularly significant. It is his or her job to combine the orchestra's performance with that of the singers so that each maintains its position as prescribed by the composer. There may be times when one or the other is to be predominant, but ultimately, the efforts of each should maintain a balance that will enhance the work of the other.

OPERA SINGING

The singers are the stars of the show. Usually in the costume of the period of the opera being performed, the artist's job is to transmit the plot to the audience by singing the libretto. In some opera formats, the composer will intersperse singing with spoken words; however, the usual form consists of two performance styles, called aria and recitativo.

An aria is a song-like presentation that is lyrical, usually performed by an individual who is accompanied by some instruments or the entire orchestra. Recitativo (recitative in English) is sung speech. The dialog is structured in the cadence of the spoken phrases combined with some repeated musical tones.

Recitativo can take two forms, called recitativo secco (dry recitative) and recitativo stromentato (with instruments). The rhythmic structure of recitativo secco is predicated on the accent patterns of the text and centers around a few notes. This form of recitative is usually rhythmically somewhat unrestricted, the rhythm determined by that of the dialogue. Originally, this form of recitativo was accompanied by a single instrument, often a keyboard. That practice eventually developed to the point where the accompaniment, while still simple, can be an instrument or combination of instruments.

Recitativo stromento has a more formalized rhythm supported by a fuller instrumentation, often the full orchestra. This form of recitative has a melodic character, affording the performer an opportunity to portray a more dramatic situation.

To hear an excellent assortment of arias from some of the most popular operas, google "YouTube opera aria." You will have an opportunity to listen to numerous arias performed by some of the world's greatest singers. These performances are often preceded by commercials telling the listener how and where to buy the recordings. Perhaps not a bad thing.

The technique used in operatic singing differs from that used in singing popular music. Opera singers do not use electronic amplification, whereas singers of popular music modify their sounds almost entirely through the use of electronic systems. This equipment permits the singer of popular music to add vibrato or echo effects and to create different moods ranging from tenderness or romantic intimacy to powerful house-rocking dynamism.

Singing in an operatic voice is entirely dependent on one's ability to project excellent quality sound to whatever degree necessary to satisfy the requirements of the music. This is done without the aid of a microphone. An opera singer cannot raise or lower the volume or modify the timber by turning a knob. It is, therefore, necessary for the opera singer to develop his or her physical capacity to amplify, modify, and project the sound through the use of the parts of the human body that are associated with achieving those ends.

Producing vocal sound is the product of a synergism that begins with the respiratory system, namely the lungs and diaphragm, as the supply of energy to activate the next partner in the system, the vocal cords. The sounds produced by the vocal cords travel to the cranial sinus cavities and concurrently to those cavities of the upper chest. When combined, these spaces provide amplification similar to that which occurs when sounds from a violin string reach the violin's body (see chapters 4, 5, and 6). The sound that travels within the body of the instrument increases in volume and is modified in timber by the particular attributes of those cavities. A good violin with a good set of strings will produce a good sound. A good physiology with a good set of vocal cords will do likewise.

Bel Canto—Bel canto had its origin in Italy in the mid-seventeenth century. Literally translated, it means "beautiful singing." The term "bel canto" originally had a general inference that included all facets of a performance. It was the amalgamation of staging with the content and textual fluidity of the libretto, the melody to which it was attached, and, of course, the quality of the voice performing. All aspects of the performance were to be considered in the bel canto. However, over time its meaning metamorphosed into an assortment of vocal music–related definitions. The term came to refer to a smooth, somewhat liquid (the musical term is legato) style of performance with the singer able to manifest that quality throughout his or her entire range. The listener was not to discern the singer's transitioning throughout the vocal registers. The singer was to smoothly and fully engage his or her physical amplification system described above. To be included in this liquescence was the singer's ability to articulate coloratura (the ornamentation of a melody) and all vocal ornamental maneuvers such as trills and other embellishments, especially those in the performer's upper register.

Range—All ensembles in music are designed to encompass the range of notes needed to produce the sounds desired by composers. Using the violin family covered in chapters 3, 4, and 5 as an example of range, the violin, viola, cello, and double bass combined are capable of producing pitches that range from the very highest desirable notes to almost the lowest. Every grouping of instruments, regardless of size, is able to produce a similar range of high to low pitches, making it possible for those ensembles to perform melody and harmony as prescribed by the music at hand. Operatic voices also enjoy that attribute. When combined, female and male voices with varying ranges cover the spectrum. These differing voice ranges are given labels.

Women's voices are named starting from the highest: coloratura soprano, lyric soprano (sometimes called dramatic soprano), mezzo soprano, and contralto. The names given to male voices starting from the highest are counter tenor, tenor, baritone, bass baritone, and bass or basso profundo. These titles are arrived at by the range of pitches one can produce musically. The range in which an individual can comfortably perform a set of sounds is referred to as his or her tessitura. This is also true of instruments.

Using the alphanumeric system discussed in chapter 16 for identifying pitches, in which the note middle C is named C4, the C below that is C3, and the one above C4 is called C5, the following are the generally accepted tessitura for the above-named female and male voices. Of course there are always exceptions.

Note: The following classifications and delineations are general in nature. Each definition can be modified and varied to the extent commensurate with the uniqueness of the human voice.

Lyric Coloratura Soprano—Range from C4 to F6. The term *coloratura* denotes the ability of the singer to perform intricate embellishments to a fundamental theme. A lyric coloratura denotes one whose voice is delicate and supple enough to perform rapid coloratura (embellishments).

Coloratura Soprano—Range from B3 to F6. One with the ability to perform coloratura within the noted range with a bit stronger timbre than that of a lyric coloratura.

Lyric Soprano—Sometimes called dramatic soprano; range from C4 to D6. This voice produces a mellower, more engaging tone quality than that of the above listed sopranos.

Mezzo Soprano—Range from A3 to A5 (mezzo means "half"). The mezzo soprano range and voice quality straddles (is halfway between) the range and tone quality of the soprano and contralto. The tone quality of this voice is less brilliant than that of the upper sopranos.

Contralto—Range from F3 to F5. This is the lowest of the female voices. It bridges that gap between the female sopranos and the male countertenor, the contralto being the lowest female voice and the countertenor the highest male voice.

Countertenor—Range from G3 to D5. As stated above, the highest male voice equivalent in range to that of the contralto but with an identifiable male timbre in the tone production.

Tenor—Range from C3 to C5. Although a bit lower in range than the countertenor, the tenor is the highest male voice most commonly used in vocal music. Certain musical circumstances may give a tenor the opportunity to increase his range up a bit to that of the countertenor or down to enter the baritone range.

Baritone—Range from G2 to G4. The next step down in the progression of men's voice ranges. This is where most men's voices, good or bad, will fall.

Bass Baritone—Range from F2 to F-sharp4. This voice has a tessitura that can perform comfortably in the baritone range, with the additional ability to drop down into the upper bass range. Such a voice range is needed in several of the Wagnerian operas.

The bass baritone label can be further refined into two more distinctive categories. There is a lyric bass baritone, which has a lighter tone quality with a tessitura that tends toward the upper range of the spectrum. Contrasting with that is the dramatic bass baritone, which has a darker tone quality and a tessitura favoring the lower notes of the range, with a more robust resonance.

Bass—With a range from E2 to E4, this is the lowest category of male voice. It enjoys an assortment of additional labels to identify the variants of this range. Among these are the basso profundo and oktavist.

Basso Profundo—Range from C2 to C4. Translated, the profound bass is one who can produce tones in the lowest range (C2 or below) with great volume while retaining a desirable sonority and a fortissimo volume. Qualifying for this label is more a case of the breadth and intensity of the sound being produced than a matter of extended range.

Oktavist—Range from G1 to C4. This voice produces notes approximately an octave below the normal bass range, hence the name oktavist or at the octave. The skill of these performers is not necessarily their ability to sing such low notes, but that they can do so without amplification and with a resonance and timbre that is compatible with a vocal ensemble.

The classification of voices and their ranges is not an exact science. The fact is, the range of an individual can always be extended up or down by a few notes but often at the risk of tone quality and pitch accuracy. In order to more closely identify these differences, in the late nineteenth century the German opera cognoscenti created a system of categorizing each type of voice. The intention was to facilitate the audition process and simplify casting. Called the Fach System, singers were classified by the characteristics of their voices. The singers then studied those roles appropriate for them and then were cast when those particular roles became available. The criteria for placement included depth of tone quality, projection, tessitura, timbre, physiological control of sound within the body's resonating chambers, vocal register and range, speech articulation, and the individual's physical size, age, and experience. This system is still in use primarily in Europe and utilizes twenty-five different classifications of voices, which account for every identifiable subtle difference related to vocal performance.

Summary—The preceding merely touches the surface of the many components of opera. As is the case with most topics in music, the amount of information on opera is enormous. From deciding which opera was the first one, to a definition of bel canto or determining the range of a countertenor, the number and variety of opinions are immense. Musicologists and performers dedicate their entire professional lives to studying and partaking professionally in the field of opera. This brief introduction should be considered just that.

GLOSSARY OF TERMS RELATED TO THE OPERA

This glossary will help the reader define terms that are related to opera. See the descriptions above for more in-depth information on these items.

A capella Vocal music without instrumental accompaniment.

Act The major segments of an opera delineating the progress of the plot.

Apron The portion of the stage from the front edge (audience side) up to the point where the closed curtain reaches the stage.

Aria A song-like presentation that is lyrical, usually performed by an individual with instrumental accompaniment.

Baritone A male voice with a range from A2 to A4, between that of a bass and tenor.

Baroque The period from 1600 to the mid-1700s when opera began to develop into a primary form of entertainment for the elite and royalty.

Bass A male voice with a range from E2 to E4; this is the lowest category of male voice.

Basso profundo Translated, the profound bass is one who can produce tones in the lowest range (C2 or below) with great volume while retaining a desirable sonority and a fortissimo volume.

Bel canto "Beautiful singing." The term referred to a smooth, somewhat liquid (the musical term is legato) style of performance with the singer able to manifest that quality throughout his or her entire range.

Blocking Positioning performers on the stage.

Brava Feminine Italian for "well done." Bravo is masculine, Bravi is plural for both tenses.

Cadenza A passage with little restriction by the composer, intended to demonstrate the performer's versatility.

Camerata A group of academics, philosophers, artists, and musicians assembled in the mid-sixteenth century with the intent to marry the Greek arts with music and the stage, ultimately leading to the first opera.

Cantabile In a smooth singing style. Canta in Italian means "sing."

Cantata A narrative arranged for vocal solo and ensemble with orchestral accompaniment.

Canzone Italian word for song.

Canzonetta Italian for the diminutive of canzone, meaning a small song.

Chorus A group of vocalists singing.

Classical Traditional, as being derived from the archetypal works from the past. In music it is the period from 1750–1830.

Coda An episode of any length added to the end of a major piece or movement as an extension of the final ending passage.

Coloratura A female voice with a range from C4 to F6. The term denotes the ability of the singer to perform intricate embellishments to a fundamental theme.

Composer One who writes music.

Comprimario Second performer to the primary role.

Continuo A system of music composition common during the Baroque period, in which a bass line called a figured bass was transcribed with numbers to indicate the harmony that should be used to accompany each note. The bass line could be played by one of the lower non-fretted string instruments, with a keyboard instrument improvising the upper parts.

Contralto Range from F3 to F5. This is the lowest of the female voices. It bridges that gap between the female sopranos and the male countertenor.

Countertenor Range from G3 to D5. The highest male voice, equivalent in range to that of the contralto, but with an identifiable male timbre in the tone production.

Diva A female opera singer of note.

Duet A musical composition performed by two musicians.

Encore Italian for "again."

Entr'acte An interval between acts of a major work that serves as an intermission or during which music is performed.

Falsetto A method used to limit the activity of the vocal cords to increase the upper range of a male voice.

Finale The end of a performance.

Fioritura Italian for "flowery." In opera this refers to coloratura (see above), that being the ability to perform intricate embellishments to a fundamental theme.

Grand opera As the name implies, opera on the grandest scale, usually with an intense libretto and all the trappings to present an epic of great scope.

Heldentenor A tenor voice with a tessitura in the middle to lower range, manifesting a darker, bolder resonance while still able to perform in the traditional upper tenor range.

Intermezzo A short selection performed between two longer selections or as an interruption in a longer piece.

Legato A flowing smooth technique in vocal or instrumental performance.

Leitmotif A melodic or rhythmic theme associated with a particular individual, idea, or action.

Libretto The story or text on which an opera is based.

Lied German for "song."

Maestro A musician of great distinction, often referring to the conductor.

Marking A technique singers use during lengthy rehearsals, where the voice is spared by singing lightly or in a less strenuous register.

Mezza voce Italian for "half voice"; sing softly.

Mezzo soprano Range from A3 to A5. Mezzo means "half"; halfway between the range and tone quality of the soprano and contralto.

Opera buffa Comic opera.

Operetta Light opera (see chapter 1).

Oratorio A composition based on a religious storyline performed by solo voice, chorus, and instruments in a concert setting.

Orchestra An assembly of instrumentalists consisting of string, woodwind, brass, and percussion choirs.

Orchestra pit A section below stage and audience level, between the stage apron and the first row of audience seats. It is where the orchestra is seated.

Ornamentation Notes added to decorate a melody line.

Overture Instrumental introductory music containing themes from a major work to follow.

Pitch A given frequency. The highness or lowness of tone.

Portamento A smooth transition (slide) from one note to another.

Prelude A short instrumental piece as an introduction to a longer piece or act.

Prima donna The first lady in an opera company.

Prompter An individual situated in a small pit forward of the stage apron to prompt the singers with text and entrances as needed.

Prop A small ancillary object such as a glass or bottle relevant to the action on stage.

Range– The span of notes a singer or instrument can perform.

Recitativo Sung speech. The dialogue is structured in the cadence of the spoken phrases combined with some repeated musical tones.

Recitativo secco "Dry recitative." Sung speech with a few notes and a rhythmic structure determined by the accent patterns of the dialog.

Recitativo stromento A more formalized rhythm and melody supported by a fuller instrumentation, often the full orchestra.

Romanticism A state of being in which a participant's philosophy and creativity are focused on the preeminence of the individual. Effective in the arts during the late nineteenth through early twentieth century.

Set A structural representation of the narrative, period, and location in which an opera is taking place.

Singspiel A German performance technique that combines the spoken word with music.

Soprano A term for the various categories of women's voices in the highest range. Women's voices are named, starting from the highest, coloratura soprano, lyric soprano (sometimes called dramatic soprano), mezzo soprano, and contralto.

Sotto voce Performing in a stage whisper of hushed volume.

Staccato Notes to be detached from each other.

Stage right or left From the point of view of the audience, the terms are reversed. Stage right is to the audience's left and conversely, left is right.

Supernumerary A member of a performing group on stage who does not have a speaking or singing part, such as a server or guard.

Tempo The speed at which a musical selection is performed.

Tenor The term used to categorize male voices in the highest range. A countertenor has the highest range followed by the tenor.

Tessitura The comfortable and most effective range of a singer or instrument.

Upstage and downstage Upstage is the rear of the stage and downstage is the front.

Verismo Meaning "truth," this label was given to a type of opera in the period at the end of the nineteenth century where the libretti began to deal with the life issues of the common people.

Vibrato The deliberate, slight, moderately timed variation in pitch by a singer or instrumentalist, resulting in a more resonant tone quality.

19

The Role of the Conductor

Singers spend their lives refining their art. They sing one word at a time with one note at a time in one key at a time—a tough job indeed. Even doing it badly requires talent and much work. When a performer does it magnificently or even just moderately well, he or she deserves tremendous credit. With a few exceptions, instrumentalists enjoy the same protocol without the added factor of words. They usually play one note at a time in one key at a time. The exceptions are keyboard instruments, strummed string instruments such as the guitar, non-fretted string instruments such as the violin, viola, cello, and double bass on which one can play more than one note at a time (double stops), and certain mallet percussion instruments such as the marimba. This is all easy to understand by simply observing those musicians in action.

In addition to vocalists and instrumentalists performing, one will often see a conductor directing large groups. From an observer's point of view, a conductor stands in front of a group and beats time by waving a stick. And that in fact is true. But that is not all he or she does. The task of conducting any group of musicians is actually multidimensional. It involves one's musicality, intellect, esthetic sense, physical prowess, artistic sensibility, leadership ability, interpretive insight, communication skills, and general knowledge of the totality of music. No easy task!

To begin with, the act of waving a stick in itself can be a fatiguing exercise. The average classical music performance usually consists of two to three hours of music. Try standing and mindlessly waving a stick in the air for a period of two to three hours. Not an easy thing to do. Add to that the list of activities that are taking place while that stick is being waved and one will be surprised and impressed with the job that conductor is doing.

As stated above, vocalists and instrumentalists generally perform one note at a time, in one key, and have it fit in with the other performers in the group. For a member of a chorus, it is the same drill. The conductor has a totally different job. In an opera, it is to shape all solo and choral voices, all libretti, and all instrumentalists of the orchestra in all keys into a performance that will represent the artistic intention of the composer. For an instrumental work such as a symphony, the process is a bit simpler since there is only an orchestra to deal with. To conduct an opera, one must first learn all the parts of all the singers and players. These performers only learn their own part and its relationship to the total performance. Then at rehearsals, the conductor uses words, examples, a baton, and anything else that will help prepare the group to perform the music successfully. At the final performance all he or she has to use as an instrument to control, cue, shape, direct, set tempo, and totally direct the entire ensemble, which can number in the hundreds, is that stick . . . the one you couldn't mindlessly swing back and forth for several hours.

The orchestra that is accompanying the singers on stage can be made up of as many as one hundred players. These are divided into four sections, those being the strings, woodwinds, brass, and percussion. Each of these sections is divided into numerous subsections such as first and second violins, first and second trumpets, and so on. Each section plays different notes and in many cases the notes that the players are reading on the page are not necessarily the same notes that are being heard. That may sound bizarre but it is, in fact, the way of the instrumental world. It is called transposition. Simply put, in order for a trumpet to sound the same C that a violin sounds, the trumpet must play a D. So, when the conductor looks at his score, he sees a C for the violins, a D for the trumpets, a G for the French horns and so on (see the chapters on definitions of instruments). Additionally, these instruments play in several different clefs (see chapter 16 on clefs) so a note on the first line of the music could be an E, G, or an F. They all look the same on the page but can sound different depending on the clef that introduces that line of music.

Remember, the singers and the instrumentalists all perform one note at a time in one key—a mere bagatelle compared to the conductor's job.

Finally, if one looks at the sheet of music for any singer or instrumentalist, one will see again single notes in a single key. The conductor's score shows everyone's part concurrently, so that what is one measure to an individual could easily be fifteen or more measures to the conductor. He is reading fifteen or more lines simultaneously while everyone else is reading one measure on one line. Look up at the preceding fifteen lines and try to read all lines at once across the page. That's what a conductor does with the score. See figure 19.1 as an example of a conductor's score.

Summary—It is safe to say that conducting is the most difficult job in music performance. The conductor is responsible for everything that happens from the first rehearsal to the final performance. The bigger the ensemble, the bigger the task. The conductor must determine how a selection should be interpreted, what the composer's intentions were, what the nature of performance was in the era in which the music was composed, the quality and balance of the sound to be produced by the performers, the special acoustical requirements of the venue in which the performance is taking place, along with assuring that everything else relevant to making that performance successful is identified and accounted for.

Figure 19.1. Eight Measures of a Conductor's Score

GLOSSARY OF TERMS USED BY COMPOSERS IN CONDUCTOR'S SCORES

The following terms are used to describe the tempo, style, and general character of a musical selection. These terms are used by composers to indicate to the conductor and performers how to perform the music symbols on a page. Most terms are Italian, which is the universal language of music.

Adagio Slow tempo.
Alla In the style of . . .; like . . .
Allegro Fast-spirited tempo but three levels below presto (defined below).
Andante Moderately slow.
Assai Very.

Brio Energetic, lively, animated.

Cantabile Song-like, melodic style. Canta is Italian for "sing."

Crescendo Gradually increase the volume. The symbol < will appear in the score, indicating the music should gradually become louder.

Da capo Back to the beginning; Italian for "to the head."

Decrescendo Gradually diminish the volume. The symbol > will appear in the score indicating a gradual decrease in volume.

Diminuendo Decreasing in volume and general tonal character.

Forte Loud. The symbol f will appear in the score indicating that the music should be played loudly.

Forte-piano Loud-soft. The symbol fp will appear in the score indicating that the music should be attacked with force followed by an immediate diminution in volume.

Fortissimo Very loud. The symbol ff will appear in the score indicating that the music should be played very loudly.

Fortississimo Extremely loud. The symbol fff will appear in the score indicating that the music is to be played extremely loudly.

Giocoso Lighthearted, lively.

Giusto Accurate, exact.

Grave Somber, slow.

Grazioso Gracefully, stylishly.

L'istesso tempo At the same tempo (speed).

Largo Slow, expansive execution of the subject music.

Larghetto A lesser form of largo.

Legato Flowing, unbroken.

Leggiero Light, graceful.

Lento Slow.

Maestoso Majestically, in a grand manner.

Meno Less.

Mesta Solemn, melancholy.

Mezzo piano Half soft. The symbol mp will appear in the score indicating that the music is to be played half soft, or half the volume of piano.

Mezzo forte Half loud. The symbol mf will appear in the score indicating that the music is to be played half loud, or half as loud as forte.

Moderato Moderate.

Molto Much.

Mosso Motion. Can be used with adjective meno (less) as in meno mosso, less motion or piu (more) as in piu mosso, more motion.

Piano Soft. The symbol p in the score will indicate that the music is to be played softly.

Pianissimo Very soft. The symbol pp in the score will indicate that the music is to be played very softly.

Pianississimo Very, very soft. The symbol ppp will appear in the score to indicate that the music is to be played extremely softly.

Piu More, as in more fast or faster.

Poco Little. Used with a noun, such as poco presto, referring to the diminutive of the noun: a little fast or slightly fast.

Presto Fast.

Rallentando Gradually slowing.

Ritardando Slowing.

Ritenuto Immediate slowing.

Ritornello Refers to a recurring section that can vary to some degree.

Rubato To steal time. In an effort to be more expressive, the performer flexes the beat by stealing a bit of time from one place and then replacing it at another.

Scherzo The literal translation is "joke." In music it has come to mean a lighthearted movement of a major work such as in a symphony.

Score A complete transcript of a musical selection, including all sections, movements, voices, and instrumentation.

Sempre Always.

Senza Without.

Sforzando A sudden, intense accent on a note or chord. The symbol *sfz* will appear in the score indicating that a particular note or chord should be heavily accented.

Slur A curved line over a group of notes to denote those notes should be performed smoothly.

Sostenuto Sustained.

Sotto Voce Below the normal amplitude being used at the time. Sotto = under, voce – voice.

Staccato Notes to be played short and detached.

Tempo The speed at which the music is to be played.

Timbre The distinctive character or quality of a sound that results from the intensity of its overtones.

Time signature The symbol in the form of a fraction at the beginning of a selection indicating the number of beats in a measure and the kind of note that gets one beat.

Tonic The fundamental first note of a scale or key.

Treble The name of the clef, also known as the G clef, used to indicate the higher notes on a music staff.

Tuning The act of adjusting the pitch of an instrument.

Tutti Italian for "everything" or "everyone."

Unison All performers playing the same note.

Vivace Play in a rapid, crisp style.

Conclusion

Music is a subject that, when viewed in its entirety, is indeed monumental in scope. The preceding pages provided an introduction to some of the topics basic to the study. However, there are numerous additional areas both directly and tangentially integral to an all-embracing study of music. If one were to google the question, "How many books on music?" the answer is 895,000,000. Quite a reading assignment.

The Basic Elements of Music is a starting point from which one can proceed to more advanced study in an area or areas of particular interest. The topics presented have introduced the reader to the world of music that is in most cases outside one's limited experience, a new exposure that can serve as a redirection in music study, or as an augmentation of one's existing knowledge. A chapter of particular interest can be used as a point from which to pursue further study, a source of material for a teacher planning a lesson, or as a resource from which to gather information to expand the scope of a music lesson. This is a start. The extent to which the reader will approach additional study is a decision that can be based on one's personal interests, professional obligations, or both.

Additional information is plentiful and very available both on library shelves, in bookstores, and on the Internet. The fact is, information on all phases of music study exists in such large quantities as to possibly intimidate one interested in advancing study. Where to start? Entering "the history of music" (the topic of chapter 1 in this book) on a Google search yielded 1,710,000,000 results. "Sound production on musical instruments" (chapter 2) produced a mere 10,500,000 results. The pattern continues with all the topics covered in this book. It is for that very reason *The Basic Elements of Music* was written with carefully selected information that provides a comfortable yet erudite introduction to the many facets of music study. Further inquiry now becomes a matter of how to approach this mountain of words in a manner that will yield succinct, relevant results without having to plod through tons of irrelevant prattle.

BOOKS

When searching through library books using the Dewey Decimal System (DDS), the numbers 780 through 789 are used to categorize books on music. Each number covers a subset of topics and represents the location of books on the topic associated with that number. Below is a list of the chapters in this book followed by the DDS classification numbers for books related to each chapter. To gather additional information from a library source, simply seek the appropriate number on the library shelf.

1. An Overview of the History of Music—780.8, .9; 781.4; 782.8; 783.2, .5, .9; 784.1, .3; 785.7, .8
2. Sound Production—781.1
3. Non-fretted String Instruments Defined—787.1, .2, .3, .4
4. The History of Non-fretted String Instruments—787. 4
5. How Non-fretted Instruments Work—787.1, .2, .3, .4
6. Brass Instruments Defined—788.2, .3, .41, .48
7. The History of Brass Instruments—788.2, .3, .41, .48
8. How Brass Instruments Work—788.2, .41, .48
9. Woodwind Instruments Defined—788.43, .5, .6, .7, .8
10. The History of Woodwind Instruments—788.43, .5, .6, .7, .8
11. How Woodwind Instrument Work—788.43, .5, .6, .7, .8
12. Percussion Instruments Defined—789.1, .5, .9
13. The History of Percussion Instruments—789.1, .5, .9
14. How Percussion Instruments Work—789.1, .5, .9
15. Form in Music—781.4, .5; 783.4; 785.1, .2, .3, .4, .5, .6, .7, .73, .74. .75, .76, .77, .78
16. Music Theory—781.2, .3, .5
17. Ensembles—784.86
18. Anatomy of an Opera—782.1, .2, .3, .4, .5, .6, .7, .8; 783.8; 784.2
19. The Role of the Conductor—no DDS number

Bookstores usually separate their wares by topic so one can easily find a section on music. The problem with bookstores is that of variety and quantity. Given the statistics stated above, it is not very likely that the average local bookstore will have sufficient titles to begin to cover such a vast subject. Perhaps a university bookstore with a high-functioning music department would be a better source for a comprehensive inventory.

The following is a list of additional books on relevant topics.

Anthony Baines, *The Oxford Companion to Musical Instruments* (Oxford: Oxford University Press, 1992).
Philip Bohlman, *World Music: A Very Short Introduction* (Oxford: Oxford University Press, 2002).

Martin Clayton, Trevor Herbert, and Richard Middleton, *The Cultural Study of Music: A Critical Introduction* (New York: Routledge, 2003).

Nicholas Cook, *A Guide to Musical Analysis* (Oxford: Oxford University Press, 1994).

Nicholas Cook, *Music: A Very Short Introduction* (Oxford: Oxford University Press, 2000).

Richard Crawford, *An Introduction to America's Music* (New York: W.W. Norton & Co., 2001).

Charles Hiroshi Garrett, *The Grove Dictionary of American Music*, 2nd ed. (Oxford: Oxford University Press, 2013).

Geoffrey Hindley, *Larousse Encyclopedia of Music* (New York: Excalibur Books, 1981).

Michael Kennedy and Joyce Bourne, *The Oxford Dictionary of Music*, 2nd ed. (Oxford: Oxford University Press, 2006).

Barry Kernfeld, *The New Grove Dictionary of Jazz*, 2nd ed. (Oxford: Oxford University Press, 2002).

Alison Latham, *The Oxford Companion to Music* (Oxford: Oxford University Press, 2011).

Laurence Libin, *The Grove Dictionary of Musical Instruments*, 2nd ed. (Oxford: Oxford University Press, 2014).

Michael J. Pagliaro, *Everything You Should Know about Musical Instruments* (San Rafael, CA: Columbia Pacific Press, 1992).

Michael J. Pagliaro, *The Flute: How It Works* (Scarsdale, NY: Ardsley Press, 2003).

Michael J. Pagliaro, *The Instrumental Music Director's Guide to Comprehensive Program Development* (Lanham, MD: Rowman and Littlefield, 2014).

Michael J. Pagliaro, *The Musical Instrument Desk Reference* (Lanham, MD: Scarecrow Press, 2012).

Michael J. Pagliaro, *The String Instrument Owner's Handbook* (Lanham, MD: Rowman and Littlefield, 2015).

Michael J. Pagliaro, *The Violin: How It Works* (Scarsdale, NY: Ardsley Press, 2002).

Michael J. Pagliaro, *The Violin Workbook* (Scarsdale, NY: Ardsley Press, 2004).

Stanley Sadie, *The New Grove Dictionary of Opera* (Oxford: Oxford University Press, 2015).

Stanley Sadie and Laura Macy, *The Grove Book of Operas* (Oxford: Oxford University Press, 2009).

Stanley Sadie and John Tyrrell, *The New Grove Dictionary of Music and Musicians*, 2nd ed. (Oxford: Oxford University Press, 2001).

Carl E. Seashore, *Psychology of Music* (New York: Dover Publications, 1938).

Nicholas Slonimsky, *Baker's Biographical Dictionary of Musicians* (New York: G. Schirmer, 1965).

Richard Taruskin, *A History of Western Music* (Oxford: Oxford University Press, 2004).

Oscar Thompson, Nicholas Slonimsky, and Robert Sabin, *The International Encyclopedia of Music and Musicians* (New York: Dodd, Mead, & Co., 1964).

ONLINE RESOURCES

Bookstores and libraries are no match for the almighty Internet where it is possible to find almost anything. That brings us to the website http://www.bydewey.com/780-799.html#780, titled *A Research Guide for Students* by I. Lee. This site provides a "Virtual library of useful URLs arranged by the Dewey Decimal Classifications." Highly recommended! Some other relevant websites are listed below by the appropriate chapter number from this book.

Chapter 1
 www.ipl.org/div/mushist/
 http://www.historyworld.net/wrldhis/listhistories1.asp?gtrack=mtop1

Chapter 2
 https://artsedge.kennedy-center.org/students/features/connections/science-and
  -music
 http://www.livescience.com/14395-science-music-ria.html
 http://www.mus.cam.ac.uk/directory/research-themes/music-and-science

Chapters 3–5
 http://www.beginband.com/strings.shtml

Chapters 6–8
 http://www.annabrake.com/instrument-repair-blog
 https://talkingtrumpet.wordpress.com/2015/04/29/master-trumpet-maker-dom
  inick-calicchio-born-1901/
 http://orgs.usd.edu/nmm/UtleyPages/Utleyfaq/brassfaq.html#rims
 http://www.monette.net/newsite/

Chapter 9
 http://hyperphysics.phy-astr.gsu.edu/hbase/hframe.html
 http://www.orsymphony.org/edu/instruments/woodwinds.aspx

Chapter 10
 http://mkwhistles.com/mkshop/history-of-wind-instruments

Chapter 11
 http://newt.phys.unsw.edu.au/jw/woodwind.html

Chapter12
 https://en.wikipedia.org/wiki/List_of_percussion_instruments

Chapter 13
   http://historyofdrumsandpercussion.weebly.com/timeline-of-drums.html

Chapter 14
   http://www.cafemuse.com/soundgarden/makingmusic/percussion.htm

Chapter 15
   http://learn.midsouthcc.edu/learningObjects/music/MusicalForm/Musical
   _Form.html

Chapter 16
   http://musictheoryblog.blogspot.com/
   http://www.8notes.com/theory/
   http://www.dolmetsch.com/musictheory12.htm

Chapter 17
   http://musiced.about.com/od/musicinstruments/a/ensembles.htm

Chapter 18
   http://www.vam.ac.uk/content/articles/t/early-opera/

Chapter 19
   http://www.npr.org/sections/deceptivecadence/2012/11/27/165677915/do-or
   chestras-really-need-conductors

These recommendations are but a snowflake on the tip of an iceberg. Do not be intimidated. Pick a topic, start to read, open your mind, see what strikes your fancy and, like the seventh degree of the scale, the leading tone described in chapter 16, you will be drawn toward that phase of music study that will enchant you for your remaining years.

Index

About the Author

Michael J. Pagliaro is certified by the New York State Department of Education as a Teacher of Music (grades K–12), Supervisor of Secondary Education, Secondary School Principal, and by the New York City Board of Education as Teacher of Orchestral Music. He holds the degrees of BS in music, MA in music education, MS in school administration and supervision, and ScD in musical instrument technology. He has dedicated over six decades to teaching music, music education, and the technology and science of acoustic orchestral and band instruments to teachers, students, technicians, supervisors, and professionals in the field of music.

Throughout his professional career, Pagliaro has held the positions of professor of music in two colleges, military band master, church choir director, founder of two musical instrument companies still in operation, and inventor and patent holder of four music-related products sold worldwide. His publications include twenty articles on musical instruments and music in general in various periodicals and professional house publications. His previous published books include *Everything You Should Know about Musical Instruments* (1992), *The Violin: How It Works* (2002), *The Flute: How It Works* (2003), *The Violin Workbook* (2004), *The Musical Instrument Desk Reference: A Guide to How Band and Orchestral Instruments Work* (2012), *The Instrumental Music Director's Guide to Comprehensive Program Development* (2014), and *The String Instrument Owner's Handbook* (2015).